Archibald Wilberforce

Spain and her colonies

Archibald Wilberforce

Spain and her colonies

ISBN/EAN: 9783337150679

Printed in Europe, USA, Canada, Australia, Japan

Cover: Foto ©ninafisch / pixelio.de

More available books at **www.hansebooks.com**

THE KING OF SPAIN AND THE QUEEN REGENT

Spain, Frontispiece.

SPAIN

AND

HER COLONIES

COMPILED FROM THE BEST AUTHORITIES

BY

ARCHIBALD WILBERFORCE

ILLUSTRATED

NEW YORK
PETER FENELON COLLIER
MDCCCXCVIII

CONTENTS

CHAPTER I
Spain in Antiquity.. 5

CHAPTER II
The Caliphate of Cordova.. 14

CHAPTER III
Medieval Spain.. 28

CHAPTER IV
Moorish Spain... 58

CHAPTER V
The Inquisition... 80

CHAPTER VI
Their Catholic Majesties... 96

CHAPTER VII
United Spain... 135

CHAPTER VIII
Modern Spain... 156

CHAPTER IX
Colonial Spain... 199

CHAPTER X
The Fall of an Empire.. 218

CHAPTER XI
The Philippines.. 244

CHAPTER XII
The Hispano-American War... 313

CHAPTER XIII
Spanish Art, Literature, and Sport... 328
    I. Painting and Architecture.. 328
    II. Spanish Literature.. 341
    III. Sport... 347
Appendix... 356

LIST OF ILLUSTRATIONS

SPAIN

Frontispiece—The King of Spain and the Queen Regent .
View of Cadiz
Alicanti
War Ministry Department .

HISTORY OF SPAIN

CHAPTER I

SPAIN IN ANTIQUITY

THE FIRST LAWS AND THE FIRST INVADERS — GREEKS, PHŒNICIANS, ROMANS AND GOTHS

HISPANIA was the name by which the Romans called the peninsula which is made up of Spain and Portugal. The origin of the name is disputed. To the Greeks the country was known as Hesperia—the Land of the Setting Sun. According to Mariana,* Spain is called after its founder, Hispanus, a son or grandson of Hercules. But, for reasons hereinafter related, better authorities derive it from the Phœnician *Span*.

There is a legend which Mariana recites, to the effect that the primal laws of Spain were written in verse, and framed six thousand years before the beginning of Time. To medieval makers of chronicles, Tubal, fifth son of Japhet, was the first to set foot on its shore. But earlier historians, ignorant of Noah's descendant, and, it may be, better informed, hold that after the episodes connected with the Golden Fleece, the Argonauts, guided by Her-

---

* "Historia general de España," by Juan de Mariana. 9 vols., Valencia, 1783-96.

cules, sailed the seas and loitered a while in Spain, where they were joined by refugees escaping from the totter and fall of Troy. Black was their national color. It has been retained in the mantillas of to-day. After the Greek adventurers came the Phœnicians. The latter, a peaceful people, born traders, as are all of Semitic origin, founded a colony at Gaddir (Cadiz). In a remoter era they had established themselves at Canaan, where they built Bylos, Sidon and Tyre. From Tyre emigrants moved to Africa. Their headquarters was Kartha-Hadath, literally Newtown, that Carthage in whose ruins Marius was to weep. The Phœnicians, as has been noted, were a peaceful people. Under a burning sun their younger brothers developed into tigers. They had the storm for ally. They ravaged the coast like whirlwinds. They took Sicily, then Sardinia. Presently there was a quarrel at Gaddir. It was only natural that the Phœnicians should ask aid of their relatives. The Carthaginians responded, and, finding the country to their taste, took possession of it on their own account. To the Romans, with whom already they had crossed swords, they said nothing of this new possession. It seemed wiser to leave it unmentioned than to guard it with protecting, yet disclosive, treaties. More than once they scuttled their triremes—suspicious sails were following them to its shore. From this vigilance the name of Spain is derived. In Punic, *Span* signifies hidden.

The hiding of Spain was possible when the Romans were still in the nursery. But when the Romans grew up, when they had conquered Greece, and all of Italy was theirs, their enterprises developed. Up to this time the two nations had been almost allies. At once they were open rivals. It was a question between them as to whom the world should belong.

The arguments on this subject, known as the Punic Wars, were three in number. The first resulted in a loss of Sicily and Sardinia. In the second, Spain went. In the third, Carthage was razed to the ground.

It was with the conquest of Sagentum—a conquest not achieved until the surviving inhabitants of that beleaguered city had committed suicide—that annexation began. Then, slowly, at one time advancing, at another retreating, now defeated, now defeating, the Romans promenaded their eagles down the coast. Scipio came and watched the self-destruction of the Numantians, as Hannibal had watched the Sagentums fall. Pompey, boasting that he had made the Republic mistress of a thousand towns, came too; and after him Cæsar, who, long before, as simple quæstor, had wept at Cadiz because of Alexander, who at his age had conquered the world—Cæsar, his face blanched with tireless debauches, came back and gave the land its *coup de grace.* In this fashion, with an unhealed wound in every province, Spain crawled down to Augustus's feet. A toga was thrown over her. When it was withdrawn the wounds had healed. She was a Roman province, the most flourishing, perhaps, and surely the most fair.

The fusion of the two peoples was immediate. The native soldiery were sent off to bleed in the four corners of the globe, to that Ultima Thule where the Britons lived and which it took years to reach, or nearer home in Gaul, or else far to the north among the Teuton States; and, in the absence of an element which might have turned ugly, the Romans found it easy work to open school. They had always been partial to Greek learning, and they inculcated it on the slightest pretext. They imported their borrowed Pantheon, their local Hercules, all the metamorphosed and irritable gods, and with becoming liberality added to them those divinities whom their adopted children most revered. It was in this way that the fusion of the two races came about. When Augustus assumed the purple, throughout the entire peninsula Latin was generally in use. It was not of the purest, to be sure. It had been beaten in with the sword, the accent was rough and the construction bristled with barbarisms; but still it was Latin, and needed only a generation of sandpaper to become polished and refined. But perhaps the least recognized factor in the fusion of the two peoples was a growing and common taste for polite literature. Such as the Romans possessed was, like their architecture, their science, philosophy and religion, borrowed outright from the Greeks. They were hungry for new ideas. These the Spaniards undertook to provide. They had descended from a race whose fabulous laws were written in verse, and something of that legendary inspiration must have accompanied them through ages of preceding strife, for suddenly Boetica was peopled with poets. In connection with this it may be noted that, apart from the crop of Augustan rhymsters and essayists, almost everything in the way of literature which Rome subsequently produced is the work of Spaniards. Lucan and the Senecas were Boeticans—Martial, Florus, Quintillian, Pomponius Mila were all of that race. J'en passe et des meilleurs. The Romans, trained by the Greeks, were, it is true, the teachers. Under their heavy hand the young Andalusians lost their way among the clouds of Aristophanes, just as we have done ourselves; they spouted the *Tityre tu*, and the *arma virum*, they followed the Odyssey and learned that in ages as remote to them as they are to us, Ulysses had visited their coast. Indeed the Romans did what they could, and if their pupils surpassed them it was owing to the lack-luster of their own imaginations. But the education of backward Spain was not limited to Greek poets and Augustan bores. Lessons in drawing were given, not as an extra, but as part of the ordinary curriculum. The sciences, too, were taught, the blackboard was brought into use, and Euclid—another Greek—was expounded on the very soil that under newer conquerors was to produce the charms and seductions of Algebra. Added to this, industry was not neglected. The Romans got from them not poets alone, but woolens, calicoes, and barbers too, emperors even. Trajan was an Andalou, so was Hadrian, and so also was that sceptered misanthrope Marcus Aurelius. As for arms, it is written in blood that the Romans would have no others than those which came from Spain. The plebs dressed themselves there. Strabo says that all the ready-made clothing came from Tarragona. From Malaga, which in a fair wind was but six days' sail from the Tiber's mouth, came potted herring, fat, black grapes that stained the chin, and wax yellow as amber. From Cadiz came the rarest purple, wine headier than Falernian, honey sweeter than that of Hymettus, and jars of pale, transparent oil. To Iviça the Romans sent their togas; there was a baphia there, a dyeing establishment, which, to be simply charming, needed but the signboard *Morituri te salutamus*. And from the banks of the Betis there came for the lupanars girls with the Orient in their eyes, and lips that said "Drink me." In this pleasant fashion Rome, after conquering Spain, sat down to banquet on her products. The Imperial City then was not unlike a professional pugilist who is unable to find a worthy opponent; possible rivals had been slugged into subjection. Perhaps she was weary, too. However great the future of a combatant may be, there comes an hour when contention palls and peace has charms. In any event, Rome at that time was more occupied in assimilating her dominions than in extending the wonders of her sway. And it was during this caprice that Spain found her fifty races fused in one. On the distant throne was a procession of despots, terribly tyrannical, yet doing what good they could. In return for flowers, fruits and pretty girls, they gave roads, aqueducts, arenas, games and vice. Claud introduced new fashions; Nero, the saturnalia. Each of the emperors did what he was able, even to Hadrian, who increased the number of Jews. It was during his reign that were felt the first tremors of that cataclysm in which antiquity was to disappear. Rome was so thoroughly mistress of the world that to master her Nature had to produce new races. The parturitions, as we know, were successful. Already the blue victorious eyes of Vandal and of Goth were peering down at Rome; already they had whispered together, and over the hydromel had drunk to her fall.

The Goths were a wonderful people. When they first appear in history their hair was tossed and tangled by the salt winds of the Baltic. Later, when in tattered furs they issued from the fens of the Danube, they startled the hardiest warriors of the world, the descendants of that nursling of the gaunt she-wolf. Little by little from vagabond herders they consolidated first into tribes, then into a nation, finally into an army that beat at the gates of Rome. There they loitered a moment, a century at most. When they receded again with plunder and with slaves they left an emperor behind. Soon they were more turbulent than ever. They swept over antiquity like a tide, their waves subsiding only to rise anew. And just as the earth was oscillating beneath their weight, from the steppes of Tartary issued cyclones of Huns. Where they passed, the plains remained forever bare. In the shock of their onslaught the empire of the Goths was sundered. Some of them, the Ostrogoths, went back to their cattle, others, the Visigoths, went down to have another word with Rome. It was then that their cousins the Vandals got their fingers on her throat and frightened the world with her cries. In the strain of incessant shrieks the Imperial City fell. From out the ruins a mitered prelate dragged a throne. Paganism had been strangled; antiquity was dead; new creeds and new races were refurbishing the world. Among the latter the Goths still prowled. In the advance through the centuries, in the journey from the Baltic to the Mediterranean, in the friction with the Attic refinement which the Romans had acquired, the Goths left some of their barbarism on the road —not much, however. Historians have it that when they took possession of Spain they manifested a love of art, a desire for culture, and that they affected the manners and usages of polite society. But historians are privileged liars. The majority of those who have treated the subject admired the Goths because they fancied them Christians, and in the admiration they placed them in flattering contrast to their predecessors who were pagans, and to their successors who were Muhammadans. As a matter of fact—one that is amply attested in local chronicles—they were coarse, illiterate and stupid as carps; moreover, they were not Christians, they were Arians, and they were Arians precisely as they were Goths—they were born so. To the dogma of the Trinity and the consubstantiability or non-consubstantiability of Jesus the Christ they were as ignorant as of the formation of the earth. Throughout Europe at that time not a thread of light was discernible. The dark ages had begun. In the general obscurity the Goths were not a bit more brilliant than their neighbors. Under their hand civilization disappeared; in return they gave the Spanish nothing but gutturals and a taste for chicanery. In ninety and nine cases, the specimens of architecture which cheap-trippers admire as due to them are of Saracen workmanship. The monuments which they did erect are not disproportioned perhaps; yet, whatever the casuist may affirm, there is still a margin between the commonplace and the beautiful. In brief, to the Visigoths the world owes less than nothing. They let Andalusia retrograde for three hundred years, and delayed the discovery and development of America. Previous to their coming Cadiz had been a famous seaport. The Romans called it The Ship of Stone. Its sons had been immemorial explorers. The presentment of another land across the sea was theirs by intuition. They were constantly extending their expeditions. They were in love with the sunset, they sailed as near it as they could, returned for more provisions, and sailed again; nearer, and ever nearer that way. To the Church the theory of the antipodes was an abominable heresy. It was taught that the earth was a flat parallelogram, its extremities walled by mountains that supported the skies. Lactance was particularly vehement on this point, so too was St. Jerome. Vergilius in asserting the contrary threw Christendom into indignant convulsions. It may be remembered that the most serious obstacle which Columbus subsequently encountered lay in the decisions of the Fathers. Now Cadiz had been more or less converted before the advent of the Visigoths, but it had not for that reason put aside its habits and customs. It continued to be essentially maritime, but when the Visigoths came, navigation languished, the Ship of Stone no longer turned to the west, it foundered in a sea of ignorance which was then undyked, and the possible discovery of America was indefinitely postponed. By way of compensation, the Visigoths framed a code of laws the spirit of which still survives, and which is serviceable in showing that the framers possessed two distinct traits, a love of agriculture and a hatred of Jews. Traits which are significant when it is understood that it was through agriculture they were supported and through the Jews they were overthrown. It was the Jews that beckoned the Berbers and their masters the Arabs—the Moors, as those Arabs were called who had deserted the deserts for the African Riviera.

CHAPTER II

THE CALIPHATE OF CORDOVA

THE CRESCENT AND THE CROSS—CORDOVA IN THE MIDDLE AGES—THE GLORIES OF AZ ZAHRA—THE RISE OF ALMANZOR

It was in 712 that Spain, after remaining for nearly three centuries in the possession of the Visigoths, fell under the yoke of the Saracens. For some time past, from a palace at Tandjah (Tangiers), a Mussulman emir had been eying the strip of blue water which alone separated him from that Andalusia which, like the other parts of this world and all of the next, had been promised to the followers of Muhammad. The invasion that ensued was singularly pacific. The enthusiasm which distinguished the youthful period of Muhammadism might account for the conquest which followed, even if we could not assign additional causes—the factions into which the Goths had become divided, the resentment of disappointed pretenders to the throne, the provocations of one Count Julian, whose daughter, seduced by Roderic, the last of the Gothic kings, caused him, it is said, to urge the Moors to come over. It is more surprising that a remnant of this ancient monarchy should not only have preserved its national liberty and name in the northern mountains, but waged for some centuries a successful, and generally an offensive, warfare against the conquerors, till the balance was completely turned in its favor and the Moors were compelled to maintain almost as obstinate and protracted a contest for a small portion of the peninsula. But the Arabian monarchs of Cordova found in their success and imagined security a pretext for indolence; even in the cultivation of science and contemplation of the magnificent architecture of their mosques and palaces they forgot their poor but daring enemies in the Asturias; while, according to the nature of despotism, the fruits of wisdom or bravery in one generation were lost in the follies and effeminacy of the next. Their kingdom was dismembered by successful rebels, who formed the states of Toledo, Huesca, Saragossa, and others less eminent; and these, in their own mutual contests, not only relaxed their natural enmity toward the Christian princes, but sometimes sought their alliance.

Be that as it may, of all who had entered Spain, whether Greek, Phœnician, Vandal or Goth, the Moors were the most tolerant. The worship of God was undisturbed. The temples were not only preserved, new ones were built. In every town they entered, presto! a mosque and a school, and mosques and schools that were entrancing as song. On the banks of the Betis, renamed the Great River, Al-Ouad-al-Kebyr (Guadalquivir), twelve hundred villages bloomed like roses in June. From three hundred thousand filigreed pulpits the glory of Allah, and of Muhammad his prophet, was daily proclaimed.

They were superb fellows, these Moors. In earlier ages the restless Bedouins, their ancestors, were rather fierce, and when the degenerate Sabaism they professed was put aside for the lessons of Muhammad, they were not only fierce, they were fanatic as well. A drop of blood shed for Allah, equaled, they were taught, whole months of fasting and of prayer. Thereafter, they preached with the scimiter. But in time, that great emollient, they grew less dogmatic. In the ninth century the court of Haroûn al Raschid, was a free academy in which all the arts were cultivated and enjoyed. Under the Moors, Cordova surpassed Bagdad.

In the tenth century it was the most beautiful and most civilized city of Europe. Concerning it Burke, in his "History of Spain"—a work to which we are much indebted—writes as follows:

There was the Caliph's Palace of Flowers, his Palace of Contentment, his Palace of Lovers, and, most beautiful of all, the Palace of Damascus. Rich and poor met in the Mezquita, the noblest place of worship then standing in Europe, with its twelve hundred marble columns, and its twenty brazen doors; the vast interior resplendent with porphyry and jasper and many colored precious stones, the walls glittering with harmonious mosaics, the air perfumed with incense, the courtyards leafy with groves of orange trees—showing apples of gold in pictures of silver. Throughout the city, there were fountains, basins, baths, with cold water brought from the neighboring mountains, already carried in the leaden pipes that are the highest triumph of the modern plumber.

But more wonderful even than Cordova itself was the suburb and palace of Az Zahra. For five-and-twenty years the Caliph Abdur Rahman devoted to the building of this royal fancy one-third of the revenues of the State;

and the work, on his death, was piously continued by his son, who devoted the first fifteen years of his reign to its completion. For forty years ten thousand workmen are said to have toiled day by day, and the record of the refinement as well as the magnificence of the structure, as it approached completion, almost passes belief. It is said that in a moment of exaltation the Caliph gave orders for the removal of the great mountain at whose foot the fairy city was built, as the dark shade of the forests that covered its sides overshadowed the gilded palace of his creation.

Convinced of the impossibility of his enterprise, An Nasir was content that all the oaks and beech trees that grew on the mountain side should be rooted up; and that fig trees, and almonds, and pomegranates should be planted in their place; and thus the very hills and forests of Az Zahra were decked with blossom and beauty.

Travelers from distant lands, men of all ranks and professions, princes, embassadors, merchants, pilgrims, theologians and poets, all agreed that they had never seen in the course of their travels anything that could be compared with Az Zahra, and that no imagination, however fertile, could have formed an idea of its beauties. Of this marvelous creation of Art and Fancy not one stone remains upon another—not a vestige to mark the spot on which it stood; and it is hard to reconstruct from the dry records of Arab historians the fairy edifice of which we are told no words could paint the magnificence. According to these authors the inclosing wall of the palace was four thousand feet in length from east to west, and two thousand two hundred feet from north to south. The greater part of this space was occupied by gardens, with their marble fountains, kiosks and ornaments of various kinds, not inferior in beauty to the more strictly architectural parts of the building.

Four thousand three hundred columns of the rarest and most precious marbles supported the roof of the palace; of these some were brought from Africa, some from Rome, and many were presented by the Emperor at Constantinople to Abdur Rahman. The halls were paved with marble, disposed in a thousand varied patterns. The walls were of the same material, and ornamented with friezes of the most brilliant colors. The ceilings, constructed of cedar, were enriched with gilding on an azure ground, with damasked work and interlacing designs. Everything, in short, that the wealth and resources of the Caliph could command was lavished on this favorite retreat, and all that the art of Constantinople and Bagdad could contribute to aid the taste and executive skill of the Spanish Arabs was enlisted to make it the most perfect work of its age. Did this palace of Zahra now remain to us, says Mr. Fergusson, we could afford to despise the Alhambra and all the other works of the declining ages of Moorish art.

It was here that Abdur Rahman an Nasir received Sancho the Fat, and Theuda, queen of Navarre, the envoys from Charles the Simple of France, and the embassadors from the Emperor Constantine at Constantinople. The reception of these imperial visitors is said to have been one of the most magnificent ceremonies of that magnificent court. The orator who had been at first intrusted with the speech of ceremonial greeting, was actually struck dumb by the grandeur of the scene, and his place was taken by a less impressionable rhetorician.

Nor was it only material splendor that was to be found at Cordova. At a time when Christian Europe was steeped in ignorance and barbarism, in superstition and prejudice, every branch of science was studied under the favor and protection of the Ommeyad Caliphs. Medicine, surgery, botany, chemistry, poetry, the arts, philosophy, literature, all flourished at the court and city of Cordova. Agriculture was cultivated with a perfection, both theoretical and practical, which is apparent from the works of contemporary Arab writers. The Silo, so lately introduced into England as a valuable agricultural novelty, is not only the invention of the Arabs, but the very name is Arabic, as is that of the Azequia and of the Noria of modern Spain. Both the second and the third Abdur Rahman were passionately fond of gardening and tree-planting; and seeds, roots and cuttings were brought from all parts of the world and acclimatized in the gardens at Cordova. A pomegranate of peculiar excellence, the Safari, which was introduced by the second Abdur Rahman from Damascus, still maintains its superiority, and is known in Spain to the present day as the Granada Zafari.

Thus, in small things as in great, the Arabs of Cordova stood immeasurably above every other people or any other government in Europe. Yet their influence unhappily was but small. They surpassed, but they did not lead. The very greatness of their superiority rendered their example fruitless. Medieval chivalry, indeed, was largely the result of their influence in Spain. But chivalry as an institution had itself decayed long before a new-born Europe had attained to the material and moral perfection of the great Emirs of Cordova. Their political organization was unadapted to the needs or the aspirations of Western Europe, and contained within itself the elements, not of development, but of decay. Their civilization perished, and left no heirs behind it—and its place knows it no more.

The reign of Hakam II., the son and successor of the great Caliph, was tranquil, prosperous and honorable, the golden age of Arab literature in Spain. The king was above all things a student, living the life almost of a recluse in his splendid retreat at Az Zahra, and concerning himself rather with the collection of books for his celebrated library at Cordova than with the cares of State and the excitements of war. He sent agents to every city in the East to buy rare manuscripts and bring them back to Cordova. When he could not acquire originals he procured copies, and every book was carefully catalogued and worthily lodged. Hakam not only built libraries, but, unlike many modern collectors, he is said to have read and even to have annotated the books that they contained; but as their number exceeded four hundred thousand, he must have been a remarkably rapid student.

The peaceful disposition of the new Caliph emboldened his Christian neighbors and tributaries to disregard the old treaties and to assert their independence of Cordova. But the armies of Hakam were able to make his rights respected, and the treaties were reaffirmed and observed. Many were the embassies that were received at Cordova from rival Christian chiefs; and Sancho of Leon, Fernan Gonzalez of Castile, Garcia of Navarre, Rodrigo Velasquez of Gallicia, and finally Ordoño the Bad, Pretender to the crown of Leon, were all represented at the court of Az Zahra.

The reign of this royal scholar was peaceful and prosperous; but kingly power tends to decline in libraries, and when Hakam ceased to build and to annotate, and his kingdom devolved upon his son, the royal authority passed not into the hands of the young Hisham, who was only nine years of age at the time of his father's death, but into those of the Sultana Sobeyra and of her favorite, Ibn-abu-amir, who is known to later generations by the proud title of Almanzor.*

Ibn-abu-amir began his career as a poor student at the University of Cordova. Of respectable birth and parentage, filled with noble ambition, born for empire and command, the youth became a court scribe, and, attracting the attention of the all-powerful Sobeyra by the charm of his manner and his nobility of bearing, he soon rose to power and distinction in the palace; and as Master of the Mint, and afterward as Commander of the City Guard, he found means to render himself indispensable, as he had always been agreeable, to the harem. Nor was the young courtier less acceptable to the Caliph. Intrusted by him on a critical occasion with the supremely difficult mission of comptrolling the expenditure of the army in Africa, where the general-in-chief had proved over-prodigal or over-rapacious, Ibn-abu-amir acquitted himself with such extraordinary skill and tact that he won the respect and admiration, not only of the Caliph whose treasury he protected, but of the general

---

* *Al Manzor al Allah:* "The Victor of God; or, Victorious by the Grace of God."

whose extravagance he checked, and even of the common soldiers of the army, who are not usually drawn to a civilian superintendent, or to a reforming treasury official from headquarters. The expenses were curtailed; but the campaign was successful, and the victorious general and the yet more victorious Cadi shared on equal terms the honor of a triumphal entry into the capital.

On the death of Hakam, in September, 976, Ibn-abu-amir showed no less than his usual tact and vigor in suppressing a palace intrigue, and placing the young Hisham on the throne of his father. The Caliph was but twelve years of age, and his powerful guardian, supported by the harem, beloved by the people, and feared by the vanquished conspirators, took upon himself the entire administration of the kingdom, repealed some obnoxious taxes, reformed the organization of the army, and sought to confirm and establish his power by a war against his neighbors in the north. The peace which had so long prevailed between Moor and Christian was thus rudely broken, and the Moslem once more carried his arms across the northern frontier. The campaign was eminently successful. Ibn-abu-amir, who contrived not only to vanquish his enemies but to please his friends, became at once the master of the palace and of the army. The inevitable critic was found to say that the victor was a diplomatist and a lawyer rather than a great general; but he was certainly a great leader of men, and if he was at any time unskilled in the conduct of a battle, he owned from the first that higher skill of knowing whom to trust with command. Nor was he less remarkable for his true military virtue of constant clemency to the vanquished.

In two years after the death of Hakam, Almanzor had

attained the position of the greatest of the *maires du palais* of early France, and he ruled all Mohammedan Spain in the name of young Hisham, whose throne he forbore to occupy and whose person was safe in his custody. But if Almanzor was not a dilettante like Abdur Rahman II., nor a collector of MSS. like Hakam, he was no vulgar fighter like the early kings of Leon or of Navarre. A library of books accompanied him in all his campaigns; literature, science, and the arts were munificently patronized at court; a university or high school was established at Cordova, where the great mosque was enlarged for the accommodation of an increasing number of worshipers. Yet in one thing did he show his weakness. He could afford to have no enemies. The idol of the army, the lover of the queen, the prefect of the city, the guardian of the person of the Caliph, Almanzor yet found it necessary to conciliate the theologians; and the theologians were only conciliated by the delivery of the great library of Hakam into the hands of the Ulema. The shelves were ransacked for works on astrology and magic, on natural philosophy, and the forbidden sciences, and after an inquisition as formal and as thorough and probably no more intelligent than that which was conducted by the curate and the barber in the house of Don Quixote, tens of thousands of priceless volumes were publicly committed to the flames.

Nor did Almanzor neglect the more practical or more direct means of maintaining his power. The army was filled with bold recruits from Africa, and renegades from the Christian provinces of the north. The organization and equipment of the regiments was constantly improved; and the troops were ever loyal to their civilian benefactor.

Ghalib, the commander-in-chief, having sought to overthrow the supreme administrator of the kingdom, was vanquished and slain in battle (981). The Caliph was practically a prisoner in his own palace, and was encouraged by his guardian and his friends, both in the harem and in the mosque, to devote himself entirely to a religious life, and abandon the administration of his kingdom to the Hájib, who now, feeling himself entirely secure at home, turned his arms once more against the Christians on the northern frontiers; and it was on his return to Cordova, after his victories at Simancas and Zamora in 981, that he was greeted with the well-known title of Almanzor.

In 984 he compelled Bermudo II. of Leon to become his tributary. In 985 he turned his attention to Catalonia, and after a brief but brilliant campaign he made himself master of Barcelona. Two years later (987), Bermudo having dismissed his Moslem guards and thrown off his allegiance to Cordova, Almanzor marched into the northwest, and after sacking Coimbra, overran Leon, entirely destroyed the capital city, and compelled the Christian king to take refuge in the wild fastnesses of the Asturias.

Meanwhile, at Cordova, the power of Almanzor became year by year more complete. Victorious in Africa as well as in Spain, this heaven-born general was as skillful in the council chamber as he was in the field. The iron hand was ever clad in a silken glove. His ambition was content with the substance of power, and with the gradual assumption of any external show of supreme authority in the State. In 991 he abandoned the office and title of Hajib to his son, Abdul Malik. In 992 his seal took the place of that of the monarch on all documents of State. In 993 he assumed the royal cognomen of Mowayad. Two years later he arrogated to himself alone the title of Said; and in 996 he ventured a step further, and assumed the title of Malik Karim, or king.

But in 996 Almanzor was at length confronted by a rival. Sobeyra, the Navarrese Sultana, once his mistress, was now his deadly enemy, and she had determined that the queen, and not the minister, should reign supreme in the palace. Almanzor was to be destroyed. Hakam, a feeble and effeminate youth, was easily won over by the harem, who urged him to show the strength that he was so far from possessing, by espousing the cause of his mother against his guardian. The queen was assured of victory. The treasury was at the disposal of the conspirators. A military rival was secretly summoned from Africa. The minister was banished from the royal presence. The palace was already jubilant.

But the palace reckoned without Almanzor. Making his way into Hakam's chamber, more charming, more persuasive, more resolute than ever, Almanzor prevailed upon the Caliph not only to restore him to his confidence, but to empower him, by a solemn instrument under the royal sign-manual, to assume the government of the kingdom. Sobeyra, defeated but unharmed by her victorious and generous rival, retired to a cloister; and Almanzor, contemptuously leaving to one of his lieutenants the task of vanquishing his subsidized rival in Africa, set forth upon the most memorable of all his many expeditions against Christian Spain (July 3, 997).

Making his way, at the head of an army, through Lusitania into far away Gallicia, he took Corunna, and destroyed the great Christian church and city of Santiago de Compostella, the most sacred spot in all Spain, and sent the famous bells which had called so many Christian pilgrims to prayer and praise to be converted into lamps to illuminate the Moslem worshipers in the mosque at Cordova.

Five years later, in 1002, after an uncertain battle, Almanzor died in harness, if not actually in the ranks, bowed down by mortal disease, unhurt by the arm of 'the enemy. The relief of the Christians at his death was unspeakable; and is well expressed, says Mr. Poole, in the simple comment of the Monkish annalist, "In 1002 died Almanzor, and was buried in Hell."

In force of character, in power of persuasion, in tact, in vigor, in that capacity for command that is only found in noble natures, Almanzor has no rival among the Regents of Spain. His rise is a romance; his power a marvel; his justice a proverb. He was a brilliant financier; a successful favorite; a liberal patron; a stern disciplinarian; a heaven-born courtier; an accomplished general; and no one of the great commanders of Spain, not Gonsalvo de Aguilar himself, was more uniformly successful in the field than this lawyer's clerk of Cordova.

Hisham, in confinement at Az Zahra, was still the titular Caliph of the West, but Almanzor was succeeded as commander-in-chief and virtual ruler of the country by his favorite son, his companion-in-arms, and the hero of an African campaign, Abdul Malik Almudaffar, the Hajib of 991. But the glory of Cordova had departed. Abdul Malik indeed ruled in his father's place for six years. But on his death, in 1008, he was succeeded by his half-brother, Abdur Rahman, who, as the son of a

Christian princess, was mistrusted both by the palace and by the people; and the country became a prey to anarchy.

Cordova was sacked. The Caliph was imprisoned; rebellions, poisonings, crucifixions, civil war, bigotry and skepticism, the insolence of wealth, the insolence of power, a Mahdi and a Wahdi, Christian alliance, Berber domination, Slav mutineers, African interference, puppet princes, all these things vexed the Spanish Moslems for thirty disastrous years; while a number of weak but independent sovereignties arose on the ruins of the great Caliphate of the West.

The confused annals of the last thirty years of the rule of the Ommeyades are mere records of blood and of shame, a pitiful story of departed greatness.

On the death of Hisham II., the Romulus Augustulus of Imperial Cordova, Moslem Spain was divided into a number of petty kingdoms, Malaga, Algeciras, Cordova, Seville, Toledo, Badajoz, Saragossa, the Balearic Islands, Valencia, Murcia, Almeria, and Granada. And each of these cities and kingdoms made unceasing war one upon another.

From the death of Hisham, if not from the death of Almanzor, the center of interest in the history of Spain is shifted from Cordova to Castile.

CHAPTER III

MEDIEVAL SPAIN

THE FOUNDERS OF MODERN SPAIN — THE KINGDOMS OF THE ASTURIAS AND OF LEON — THE DEFEAT AT RONCESVALLES — THE CID CAMPEADOR

THE Crescent had conquered, but the Cross endured. The refuge of the latter was in the Asturias. There — eight or ten years after the death of the last of the Gothic kings — Pelayo, one of the early heroes of Spanish history, was reigning over refugees from Moslem rule. It was these refugees who laid the foundation of modern Spain, and it is related that in their fastness at Covadongo, thirty of them, with Pelayo at their head, actually routed, if they did not destroy, an entire army of four hundred thousand Moslem besiegers.

The story is of course mythological, but the good fortune of Pelayo did much to kindle the national spirit by which ultimately Spain was conquered for the Spaniards, and thus the story, if critically false, becomes metaphorically true.

Nor [says Burke] do the Arabs seem to have made any attempt to retrieve or avenge the fortunes of the day. Well satisfied, no doubt, with their unopposed dominion over the rich plains of the genial south country, they were willing to abandon the bleak and inhospitable mountains to their wild inhabitants and the emboldened refugees whom they sheltered. Be the reason what it may, Pelayo seems to have had peace all the days of his life after his victory at Covadonga in 718. Prudently confining his attention to the development of his little kingdom, he reigned, it is said, for nineteen years at Cangas, and, dying in 737, he was peacefully succeeded by his son Favila.

Pelayo, no doubt, was but a robber chieftain, a petty mountain prince, and the legends of his royal descent are of later date, and of obviously spurious manufacture; but Pelayo needs no tinsel to adorn his crown. He was the founder of the Spanish monarchy.

Meanwhile, in the recesses of the Pyrenees, a second Christian kingdom, that of Navarre, had been founded by Garcias Iniguez, which, together with Catalonia and Aragon, Charlemagne a little later (778) entered and subdued. In repassing the Pyrenees, however, the Navarrese, led by Fortun Garcias, fell upon the Frankish troops and cut to pieces the rear guard, and even, it is said, the main body of the army.

How far the Spanish Christians were aided, as it has been stated they were, by the Moors, it is impossible to discover. The fact of such an alliance, in itself sufficiently improbable, is quite unnecessary to explain the ever-famous defeat at Roncesvalles.

Nor can we speak with much greater confidence of the prowess or even of the existence of the equally famous Roland, in the ranks of the invading or evading army: or of that of the no less celebrated Bernardo del Carpio in the ranks of the pursuers.

Taillefer, who sang the song of Roland upon the battlefield of Hastings, and Terouldes, whose thirteenth century epic suggested the poems of Pulci, of Boiardo, and of greatest Ariosto, all these have made Roland one of the favorite heroes of the Middle Ages. But in the story, as it is told in the Spanish ballads, it is Bernardo del Carpio, the nephew of the chaste but pusillanimous Alfonso, who is the true hero of Roncesvalles, and who not only repulsed the host of Charlemagne, but caught up the invulnerable Roland in his arms, and squeezed him to death before his army. No carpet knight nor courtier was Bernardo, but a true Cantabrian mountaineer.

In 790 Alfonso II., the great-grandson of the great Pelayo, then king of Oviedo, repulsed the Mussulman army with great slaughter, and abolished the ignominious tribute of one hundred virgins, an annual tribute paid to the Mohammedan ruler, fifty virgins being of noble and fifty of base or ignoble birth. From this circumstance is derived, by some historians, his surname of the Chaste; attributed by others to his having made a solemn vow of virginity, and observed it, even in marriage. This vow, and the austere temper in which it probably originated, had considerable influence over Alfonso's life. He so deeply resented his sister Ximena's private marriage with a subject, the Count of Saldanha, that he shut her up in a convent; and putting out her husband's eyes, sentenced him to perpetual imprisonment.

The royal line of Navarre or Sobrarve was at this time extinct, Ximenes Garcias, the grandson of Fortun Garcias, having died without children. The nobles availed themselves of the opportunity to establish the famous code entitled "Los Fueros de Sobrarve"—the laws of Sobrarve—which subsequently became the ground-work of the liberties of Aragon. Navarre was soon afterward recovered by the Moors, and Sobrarve included in the Spanish March.

Alfonso ruled upward of fifty years. Incessant wars now followed between the followers of the Cross and the Crescent, and a frenzy for martyrdom on the part of the Christians had to be repressed by a Christian archbishop at the solemn request of the Cadis.

Garcia of Oviedo died without children shortly after his accession; when his brother Ordoño II. reunited the whole of his father's dominions, 900-957. He transferred the seat of government to Leon, and altered the title of King of Oviedo into that of King of Leon.

This Ordoño abandoned the peaceful policy of his greater father, and undertook many expeditions with varying and uncertain success against the Arabs. He plundered Merida in 917, and routed the Berbers in Southern Spain in 918. Yet three years later, at Val de Junqueras (921), near Pamplona, the Christians suffered disastrous defeat. The usual rebellion at home was appeased by the treacherous execution or murder of no less than four counts of Castile in 922, and was followed by the king's death in 923.

Of Fruela II. (923-925), Alfonso IV. (925-930), and Ramiro II. (930-950), little need be said, but that they lived and reigned as kings of Leon.

To Ramiro, however, is due, at least, the honor of an authentic victory over the Moslem forces of the great Caliph, Abdur Rahman an Nasir (939), at Simancas, and afterward in the same year at Alhandega.

Ramiro, after the usual rebellion, abdicated, in 950,

in favor of his son Ordoño—who had married Urraca, daughter of the principal rebel of the day, Fernan Gonzalez, count of Castile—and who succeeded his father as Ordoño III.

But decapitation was a far more certain way of suppressing rebellion than matrimony; and Fernan Gonzalez lived to intrigue against his daughter and her royal husband in favor of Sancho, a younger brother of the king. Ordoño, however, held his own against his brother, and revenged himself on his father-in-law, by repudiating his wife; who, with her personal and family grievances, was promptly *acquired* by Sancho, who succeeded, on his brother's death, to the crown of which he had failed to possess himself by force. But even as a legitimate sovereign, Sancho, surnamed the Fat, was not allowed to reign in peace. He was driven from his kingdom by that most versatile rebel, Count Fernan Gonzalez, and sought refuge at the court of his uncle Garcia of Navarre at Pamplona. Thence, in company with Garcia, and his mother Theuda, he journeyed to the court of the Caliph at Cordova, where the distinguished visitors were received with great show of welcome by Abdur Rahman at Az Zahra; and where Hasdai, the Jew, the most celebrated physician of the day, succeeded in completely curing Sancho of the distressing malady—a morbid and painful corpulency—which incapacitated him from the active discharge of his royal duties.

The study and practice of medicine were alike disregarded by the rude dwellers in Leon; but the Cordovan doctor, surpassing in his success, if not in his skill, the most celebrated physicians of the present day, contrived to reduce the king's overgrown bulk to normal proportions, and restored him to his former activity and vigor, both of body and mind. Nor was the skill of Hasdai confined to the practice of medicine. An accomplished diplomatist, he negotiated a treaty with his Christian patient, by which Sancho bound himself to give up ten frontier fortresses to the Caliph, on his restoration to the crown of Leon, while Don Garcia and Dona Theuda undertook to invade Castile in order to divert the attention of the common foe, the ever ready Fernan Gonzalez.

In due time Sancho, no longer the fat, but the hale, returned to Leon at the head of a Moslem army, placed at his disposal by his noble host at Cordova, drove out the usurper, Ordoño the Bad, and reigned in peace in his Christian dominions. The visit of this dispossessed Ordoño to the court of the Caliph Hakam at Cordova, in 962, is an interesting specimen of the international politics or policy of his age and country.

As Sancho had recovered his throne by the aid of Abdur Rahman, so Ordoño sought to dethrone him and make good his own pretensions by the aid of Hakam. The Caliph, already harassed by Fernan Gonzalez, and doubting the honesty of King Sancho, was not ill-pleased to have another pretender in hand, and Ordoño was invited to Cordova, and received by Hakam in the palace at Az Zahra with the utmost pomp and display. The Leonese prince craved in humble language the assistance of the Moslem, and professed himself his devoted friend, ally, and vassal; and he was permitted to remain at the Court of Hakam, to await the issue of events in the North. Some few days afterward a treaty was solemnly signed between the Caliph and the Pretender, and once more the glories of Az Zahra were displayed to the eyes of the astonished barbarian from Leon.

Nor did the fame of these splendid ceremonies fail to reach Sancho in the northwest; and his spirit of independence was considerably cooled by the prospect of a Moslem army, headed by his cousin Ordoño, making its appearance before his ill-defended frontiers. The maneuver was sufficiently familiar; and the reigning monarch lost no time in disassociating himself from the hostile proceedings of Fernan Gonzalez; and sending an important embassy to Hakam at Cordova, to assure him of his unwavering loyalty, he hastened to announce his readiness to carry out to the letter all the provisions of his recent treaty with the Caliph. Hakam was satisfied. Ordoño languished disregarded at Cordova, despised alike by Moslem and Christian, but unharmed and in safety as the guest of the Arab. Sancho reigned in peace until 967, when he was poisoned by the rebel count of the day, Sanchez of Gallicia. His son, who was known as Ramiro III., an unwise and incapable monarch, reigned at Leon from 967 to 982, without extending the possessions or the influence of the Christians in Spain; and Bermudo II., who usurped the throne, was no match for the fiery Almanzor, who ravaged his kingdom, took possession of his capital, and compelled the Christian Court to take refuge in the wild mountains of the Asturias, and once more to pay tribute to the Moslem at Cordova.

Bermudo died in 999; and on the death of Almanzor, three years later, the Christian fortunes under the young Alfonso V., who had succeeded his father Bermudo, at the age of only five, began to mend. Cordova was given up to anarchy. The Moslem troops retired from Northern Spain. Leon became once more the abode of the king and his court, and though Alfonso gave his sister in marriage to Mohammed, an Emir or Vali of Toledo, he extended his Christian dominion in more than one foray against the declining power of the Moslem.

Alfonso V., who is known in Spanish history as the Restorer of Leon, sought to consolidate his own power, as he certainly exalted that of his clergy, by the summoning of a Council, after the manner of the Visigothic Councils of Toledo. The Council met at the city of Leon on the 1st of August, 1020, in the Cathedral Church of St. Mary. The king and his queen Elvira presided, and all the bishops and the principal abbots and nobles of the kingdom took their seats in the assembly. And if there was no Leander, nor Isidore, nor Julian to impose his will upon king or council, the interests of the Church were not entirely overlooked. Of the fifty-eight decrees and canons of this Council, the first seventeen relate exclusively to matters ecclesiastical, the next twenty are laws for the government of the kingdom, the remaining thirty-one are municipal ordinances for the city of Leon.

But Alfonso V. was not exempted from the usual rebellions, and marriages, and assassinations, and executions, which constituted the politics of the day. Garcia, the last Count of Castile, was treacherously slain in 1026; and Alfonso was himself more honorably killed in an attack upon a Moslem town in Lusitania in 1027.

The life of Fernan Gonzalez, the Warwick of medieval Spain, is almost as much overlaid with romantic legends as that of Roderic or Roland. The lives and deeds of his ancestors, and the origin of his ever-celebrated County of Castile, are involved in the utmost confusion and obscurity; but Fernan Gonzalez himself is at least a historical personage. He married Sancha, daughter of Sancho Abarca of Navarre, and their son, Garcia Fernandez, succeeded him as hereditary Count of Castile.

As early as the year 905, Sancho, a Christian chief of whose ancestors and predecessors much has been written, much surmised, and nothing is certainly known, was king or ruler of the little border state of Navarre. A prudent, as well as a warlike sovereign, he fortified his capital city of Pamplona, and when his son, in alliance with Ordoño II. of Leon, was defeated by the Moslems at Val de Junquera, the Navarrese not only made good their retreat to that celebrated fortress, but succeeded in course of a short time in driving the Moslems out of their country. The grandson of this successful general was Sancho El Mayor—or the Great—the most powerful of the Christian princes in Spain (970–1035). Besides Navarre and Sobrarve he held the lordship of Aragon; in 1026, in right of his wife, Muña Elvira, he became king or count of Castile; while his successful interference in the affairs of Leon made him virtual master of all Christian Spain outside the limits of the quasi Frankish county of Catalonia.

Sancho the Great died in 1035, when his territories were divided, according to his will, among his four sons; and from this time forth the history of Navarre, so far as it is not included in the history of Aragon, of Castile, and of France, is a confused and dreary record of family quarrels, of plots and assassinations, of uncertain alliances, of broken treaties. The marriage of the Princess Berengaria with Richard I. of England, in 1191, failed to secure for Sancho V. the influence that he had hoped to secure: and with Sancho VI., who died in 1234, the male line of the house of Sancho Iñiguez or Inigo, the founder of Navarre, was extinct. A French prince was chosen by the Navarrese to rule over them. And from the death of Sancho VI., in 1234, to the death of Charles the Bad, in 1387—one hundred and fifty years—the history of Navarre is that of France.

Bermudo III., who succeeded, on the death of his father, Alfonso V., in 1027, as king of Leon, was at once attacked by his powerful neighbors, and the little States were distracted by family quarrels and civil war until the death of Bermudo in battle, in 1037, when the male line of the house of Leon became extinct.

On the death of Bermudo III. in 1037, Ferdinand I., king of Castile, the second son of Sancho the Great, succeeded to the kingdom of Leon, and became, after over twenty years of civil war (1058), the most powerful monarch in all Spain. The Moslems offered but an uncertain and half-hearted resistance to his arms. For while the Christians were growing strong, the Moslem empire was already declining to its fall. And the decay of the Caliphate of Cordova, and the internal dissensions of the Arabs, enabled Ferdinand not only to recover all the territory that had been conquered by Almanzor, but to pursue the disheartened Moslem as far as Valencia, Toledo, and Coimbra. Ferdinand confirmed the Fueros of Alfonso V., and summoned a council at Coyanza (Valencia de Don Juan), over which, with his Queen Sancha, he presided in 1050. All the bishops and abbots, together with a certain number of lay nobles thus assembled *ad restaurationem nostræ Christianitatis*, proceeded to make decrees or canons, after the manner of the Councils of Toledo, of which the first seven were devoted to matters ecclesiastical, and the remainder connected with the civil government of the country. With territories thus recovered and augmented, with cities restored and fortified, Ferdinand determined to excel all his Christian predecessors, and to emulate the noble example of the Arab, by enriching his dominion, not with treasures of art or literature, with schools, with palaces, with manuscripts—but with the bones of as many martyrs as he could collect.

An army was raised for this sacred purpose, and the country of the Moors was once more invaded and harried by the Christian arms. Ibn Obeid of Seville, learning the objects of the invasion, offered Ferdinand every facility for research in his city; and a solemn commission of bishops and nobles were admitted within the walls to seek the body of Justus, one of the martyrs of Diocletian. But in spite of all the diligence of the Christians, and all the good will of the Arabs, the sacred remains could nowhere be found. At length the spirit of Saint Isidore removed the difficulty by appearing miraculously before the Commission, and offering his own bones in the place of those of Justus, which were destined, said he, to remain untouched at Seville. The Commission was satisfied. And the body of the great Metropolitan, "fragrant with balsamic odors," was immediately removed to the Church of St. John the Baptist at Leon — to the great satisfaction of both Christians and Moors, in 1063.

It was on the occasion of the return of these blessed relics to the Christian capital that Ferdinand proclaimed the future division of his kingdom. For after all the success that had attended the Union of the dominions of Leon and Castile under the sole authority of Ferdinand, who rather perhaps for his sanctity than for his wisdom had earned the title of the Great, the king made the same grievous mistake that his father had done before him, in dividing his united territories at his death (1065) among his sons and daughters. To Sancho, the eldest son, he left the kingdom of Castile; to Alfonso, Leon and the Asturias; to Garcia, Gallicia; to his younger daughter, Elvira, the town and district of Toro, and to her elder sister Urraca the famous border city of Zamora, the most debatable land in all Spain, and a strange heritage for a young lady. Thus Castile and Leon were once more separated; and the usual civil wars and family intrigues naturally followed. Alfonso, though not at first the most successful, survived all his rivals, and was at length proclaimed king of Leon and Castile.

But the successes and glories of Alfonso VI., such as they were, are overshadowed by the prowess of a Castilian hero, whose exploits form one of the most favorite chapters in the national history of Spain—the Christian knight with the Moslem title—Ruy Diaz, THE CID.

Two years before William of Normandy landed at Hastings, a Castilian knight, a youth who had already won for himself the proud title of The Challenger, from his reckless bravery and his success in single combat, is found leading the royal armies of Sancho of Castile against the enemy. The knight was Ruy Diaz de Bivar. The enemy was Alfonso VI. of Leon, the brother of Sancho, who was endeavoring to reunite the inheritance divided by his father, in the good old medieval fashion in Spain.

Of noble birth and parentage, a Castilian of the Castilians, Roderic or Ruy Diaz was born at Bivar, near Burgos, about the year 1040. His position in the army of Sancho was that of Alferez, in title the Standard-bearer, in effect the major-general or second in command, if not commander-in-chief of the king's army.

For seven years Alfonso of Leon and Sancho of Castile had been at war, each seeking to destroy the other; and at length at Golpejara, near Carrion, on the eve of what promised to be a decisive battle, a solemn engagement was entered into by the brothers that whichever of the two were worsted in the encounter should resign his kingdom to the other without further bloodshed. The Castilians, in spite of Sancho and his famous Champion, were defeated at Golpejara; and Alfonso of Leon, foolishly trusting his brother's word, took no heed to improve his victory, and his unsuspecting army was overwhelmed the next day by the Castilian troops under Ruy Diaz de Bivar, the author of this exceedingly characteristic, if not entirely authentic, piece of treachery.

It is scarcely surprising that the Cid was not trusted by Alfonso of Leon, when he, in his turn, succeeded to the crown of Castile. But for the moment Alfonso was not only deprived of his throne and of his liberty by his more successful brother, but he was compelled to purchase his life by a promise to enter the monastery of Sahagun. Disregarding this vow, and making good his escape to Toledo, the royal refugee was received with the usual hospitality of the Arab by El Mamun, the Moslem ruler of the city, who sheltered and entertained him, as he himself admitted, "like a son."

Sancho meanwhile had turned his arms against his brother Garcia, whom he dispossessed of his territories; against his sister Elvira, who met with a similar fate, and, lastly, against his sister Urraca, who withstood him boldly in her city of Zamora. And not only did this time-honored fortress resist the attack of Sancho and his wily major-general, but the king was slain outside the walls of the city by one of his sister's knights. Alfonso thus not only recovered his own kingdom of Leon, but, swearing perpetual friendship with El Mamun of Toledo, he was elected king of Castile by the Commons assembled at Burgos; and the defeated refugee of 1071 found himself, in less than two years, the greatest prince in Christian Spain; Alfonso the Sixth of Leon and of Castile.

Yet the legend runs that Alfonso was compelled to undergo the indignity of a public examination, and a triple oath before the knights and nobles assembled at Burgos, to the effect that he had had no share in the murder of King Sancho; and the oath was administered by Ruy Diaz of Bivar, the companion in arms of the Castilian king, sometime the faithless enemy of Carrion, but now the acknowledged leader of the Castilian nobility.

Alfonso of Leon may have forgiven the treachery in the field, but he never forgot the insult in the Council. He restrained his indignation, however, and was even induced by reasons of State to grant to the bold Castilian lord the hand of his cousin Ximena in marriage, and to intrust him with the command of an expedition into Andalusia. But the royal favor was of brief duration; and in 1081 we find that Roderic, partly owing to the intrigues of Garcia Ordonez, and partly to the enduring enmity of the king, was banished from the Christian dominions.

Of all the petty sovereignties that came into existence on the breaking up of the Ommeyad Caliphate of Cordova, that of Moctadir, the chief of the Ben-i-hud of Saragossa, was the most powerful in Northern or Central Spain; and at the Moslem court of Saragossa, Ruy Diaz, with his fame and his followers, was warmly welcomed (1081) by Moctadir as a Said or Cid—a lord or leader of the Arabs. He had been driven out of Castile by Alfonso. He found a home and honorable command at Saragossa. So long as he could make war upon his neighbors, all countries were alike to Roderic of Bivar. Nor was it long before his prowess brought honor and profit to Moctadir, or, rather, to his son and successor, Motamin.

Ramon Berenguer III., count of Barcelona, was engaged, like other Christian princes of his time, in chronic warfare with his Moslem neighbors; and Motamin, with his Castilian Cid, marching against the Catalans, defeated the Christians with great slaughter at Almenara, near Lerida, and brought Ramon Berenguer a prisoner to Saragossa (1081), where the victorious Cid was loaded with presents by the grateful Motamin, and invested with an authority in the kingdom subordinate only to that of the king himself. Two years later (1083) an expedition was undertaken by the Moslems, under Roderic, against their Christian neighbors in Aragon. King Sancho Ramirez was completely defeated by the Castilian champion, who returned once more to Saragossa loaded with booty and renown. In 1084 the Cid seems to have paid a friendly visit to the court of Alfonso VI. But although he was apparently well received, he suspected treachery, and, returning to the court of the Moslem, once more took service under the delighted Motamin. His next campaign, undertaken in the following year, was not against any Christian power, but against the hostile Moslems of northern Valencia, and was crowned with the usual success. Motamin died in 1085, but the Cid remained in the service of his son and successor, Mostain, fighting against Christian and Moslem as occasion offered, partly for the King of Saragossa, but chiefly for the personal advantage of Ruy Diaz of Bivar. A stranger national hero it is hard to imagine! Nor were his subsequent proceedings in any degree less strange.

Al Mamun, the host and protector of Alfonso VI., had died in 1075, leaving his grandson, Cadir, to succeed him as sovereign of Toledo. Abdulaziz, the viceroy of the subject city of Valencia, took advantage of the weakness of the young prince to declare himself independent, and placing himself under the protection of the Christians, undertook to pay a large subsidy to Alfonso VI. in return for his recognition and support. The subsidy was punctually paid, and, in spite of a present of no less than a hundred thousand pieces of gold handed over by Moctadir of Saragossa to Alfonso as the price of Valencia, Abdulaziz retained his hold of the city until his death in 1085. On this, numerous pretenders to the government immediately arose, including Moctadir of Saragossa, a purchaser for value, and the two sons of Abdulaziz; while Alfonso took advantage of the confusion that ensued to persuade Cadir to surrender Toledo, much coveted by the Christian king, and to accept, or, more exactly, to retain, for himself the sovereignty of Valencia, under the humiliating protection of Castile. Alfonso cared nothing that Toledo was the inheritance of his youthful ally, the home of his old protector, when he himself was a hunted refugee. He cared nothing that the Valencians were hostile to Cadir, and that powerful neighbors were prepared to dispute his possession. He cared nothing that Moctadir, who had actually purchased the city from Alfonso himself, was on the way to make good his claim. A treaty was forced upon Cadir by which Toledo was surrendered to Alfonso VI. (1085), and the Christian king was bound to place and maintain the unhappy prince in possession of his own subordinate city of Valencia.

Toledo thus became the capital of Christian Spain; and the evicted sovereign, escorted by a large force of Castilian troops under Alvar Fanez, made his sad and solemn entry into Valencia, despised at once by the citizens of Toledo, whom he had abandoned to the Christian sovereign, and by the citizens of Valencia, where his power was maintained by Christian lances. And costly indeed was this Christian maintenance. Six hundred pieces of gold is said to have been the daily allowance of the army of Castilian Mercenaries; and the taxes that were necessitated by their presence only added to the unpopularity of the government. many of Cadir's Moslem subjects fled from the city; and their place was taken by his Christian supporters or pensioners, whose rapacity was, if possible, exceeded by their cruelty. But the coming of the Almoravides gave a new turn to the fortunes of the city. Alvar Fanez and his knights were recalled by Alfonso, and after the defeat of the Christians at Zalaca, in October, 1086, Cadir found himself threatened with immediate expulsion by his own citizens, supported by Mondhir of Lerida, the uncle of Mostain of Saragossa. In this difficulty he once more sought the protection of Christian lances, and applied for aid to the Cid, who immediately advanced on Valencia.

An intriguer at all times and places, Roderic promised his support to Cadir in return for admission within the walls. He entered into a formal treaty with Mostain that the city should be his, if all the booty were handed over to the Campeador; and he sent envoys to Alfonso to assure him that in all these forays and alliances he thought only of the advantage of Christendom and the honor of Castile. Mondhir, overawed by the appearance of the allied army from Saragossa, hastily retired from before Valencia, where Mostain and his Christian Said were welcomed as deliverers by Cadir.

But although the Cid imposed a tribute upon the unhappy Valencians, he failed to give over the city to Mostain, and assuring Cadir of his constant support, as long as a monthly allowance of ten thousand golden dinars was punctually paid, he withdrew himself from the remonstrances of the disappointed Mostain—to whom he continued to protest his continued devotion—on the plea of a necessary visit to his Christian sovereign in Castile, to explain or excuse his position, and to engage some Castilian troops for his army. Mostain, during his absence, perceiving that he could not count upon so versatile and so ambitious a Said in the matter of the handing over of Valencia, entered into an alliance with his old enemy, Ramon

Berenguer, of Barcelona; and the Catalans had actually laid siege to the city when the return of the Cid induced them to abandon their trenches and retire to Barcelona.

If the Cid was a hero of romance, he did not wield his sword without the most magnificent remuneration. At this period of his career (1089–92), in addition to the eighty thousand golden pieces received from Ramon Berenguer, he is said to have drawn fifty thousand from the son of Mondhir, one hundred and twenty thousand from Cadir of Valencia, ten thousand from Albarracin, ten thousand from Alpuente, six thousand from Murviedro, six thousand from Segorbe, four thousand from Jerica, and three thousand from Almenara.

With such an amount of personal tribute, the Cid cannot, says Lafuente, have been greatly inconvenienced by the action of Alfonso VI. in despoiling him of his estates. Supporting his army of seven thousand chosen followers on the rich booty acquired in his daily forays upon Eastern Spain, from Saragossa to Alicante; regardless of Christian rights, but the special scourge of the Moslems; no longer a Saragossan general, but a private adventurer, the Cid could afford to quarrel at once with Mostain and with Alfonso, and to defy the combined forces of Mondhir and Ramon Berenguer.

The rivalry between the Cid and the Catalan was ever fierce in Eastern Spain. The opposing armies met at Tebar del Pinar in 1090, and although the Cid was wounded in the battle, his army was completely successful. Mondhir fled from the field; and Ramon Berenguer was once more a prisoner in the hands of Roderic. Nor was the Christian count released from a confinement more harsh than was generous or necessary until he had given good security for the payment of the enormous ransom of eighty thousand marks of gold.

It is not easy, nor would it be fruitful to follow the various movements of the Cid at this period of his career. His quarrels and his intrigues with Alfonso of Castile, with Cadir of Valencia, with the various parties at the court of Saragossa, with Ramon Berenguer at Barcelona, and even with the Genoese and Pisans, are neither easy nor interesting to follow. But his principal objective was the rich city of Valencia. Alfonso of Leon, ever jealous of his great and most independent subject, resolved to thwart him in his design; and having secured the co-operation of the Pisans and Genoese, who had arrived with a fleet of four hundred vessels to assist the Cid, the king took advantage of the absence of his rival on some foray to the north of Saragossa to advance upon Valencia, and to push forward his operations to the very walls of the city. Ruy Diaz riposted after his fashion.

Leaving the Valencians to make good the defense of their own city, he carried fire and sword into Alfonso's peaceful dominions of Najera and Calahorra, destroying all the towns, burning all the crops, slaughtering the Christian inhabitants; and razing the important city of Logrono to the ground. This savagery was completely successful, and met with no reproach. The Cid is one of those fortunate heroes to whom all things are permitted. His excesses are forgotten; his independence admired; his boldness and his success are alone remembered. Alfonso, thus rudely summoned to the north of the Peninsula, abruptly raised the siege of Valencia.

Nor was the king's action at Valencia without a favorable influence upon the fortunes of the Cid. Far from wresting the city from the grasp of Roderic, Alfonso had rather precipitated the crisis which was ultimately to lead to his triumphal entry as the independent ruler of the city. Cadir was murdered by a hostile faction within the walls: and the Cid, advancing with his usual prudence, spent some time in possessing himself of the suburbs and the approaches to the city, before the siege was commenced in good earnest, in July, 1093.

The operations were carried on in the most ferocious fashion by the attacking force. Roderic burned his prisoners alive from day to day within the sight of the walls, or caused them to be torn in pieces by his dogs under the very eyes of their fellow-townsmen.

The blockaded city was soon a prey to the utmost horrors of famine. Negotiation was fruitless. Succor came not. Neither Christian nor Moslem, neither Alfonso the Castilian, nor Yusuf the Almoravide, nor Mostain of Saragossa, appearing to defend or to relieve the city, Valencia capitulated on the 15th of June, 1094.

The Moslem commander, Ibn Jahaf, was burned alive. The Moslem inhabitants were treated with scant consideration, and the Cid, as might have been supposed, proclaimed himself sovereign of Valencia, independent of either Christain Alfonso or Moorish Mostain; and at Valencia he lived and reigned until the day of his death, but five years afterward, in 1099. His rule was often threatened by the Almoravides; but as long as the champion lived they could effect no entry within the walls of his city.

For full three years after his death, moreover, his widow

Ximena, and his cousin Alvar Fanez, maintained a precarious sovereignty at Valencia. At length, unsupported by Alfonso of Leon, and unable to stand alone in the midst of the Moslems, they retired to Burgos, carrying with them the body of the Cid embalmed in precious spices, borne, as of old, on his faithful steed Babieca, to its last resting place in Castile. Valencia was immediately occupied by the Almoravides, and became once more a Moslem stronghold; nor did it finally pass into Christian hands until it was taken by James the First of Aragon in 1238. The Cid was buried in the Monastery of Cardena, near Burgos; and the body of his heroic wife, Doña Ximena, who died in 1104, was laid by his side in the tomb.

The legend of the marriage of the Cid's daughters with the Infantes of Carrion, of their desertion, and of the vengeance of the Cid upon their unworthy husbands, is undoubtedly an invention of the Castilian minstrels.

The legend of the death of the Cid's son at the battle of Consuegra is certainly fallacious. There is no evidence that a son was ever born to him at all. But he had undoubtedly two daughters, one of whom, Christina, married Ramiro, Infante of Navarre, and the other, Maria, became the countess of Ramon Berenguer III. of Barcelona. The issue of Ramon Berenguer III. was a daughter who died childless, but a granddaughter of Ramiro of Navarre married Sancho III. of Castile, whose son, Alfonso VIII., was the grandfather both of St. Ferdinand and of St. Louis. And thus in a double stream, through the royal houses of Spain and of France, the blood of the Cid is found to flow in the veins of his Majesty Alfonso XIII., the reigning king of Spain.

To understand or appreciate the position that is occupied by the Cid in Spanish history is at the present day supremely difficult. A medieval condottiere in the service of the Moslem, when he was not fighting to fill his own coffers with perfect impartiality against Moor or Christian: banished as a traitor by his Castilian sovereign, and constantly leading the forces of the Infidel against Aragon, against Catalonia, and even against Castile, he has become the national hero of Spain. Warring against the Moslem of Valencia, whom he pitilessly despoiled, with the aid of the Moslem of Saragossa, whose cause he cynically betrayed, while he yet owned a nominal allegiance to Alfonso of Castile, whose territories he was pitilessly ravaging; retaining conquered Valencia for his personal and private advantage, in despite of Moslem or Christian kings, he has become the type of Christian loyalty and Christian chivalry in Europe. Avaricious, faithless, cruel and bold, a true soldier of fortune, the Cid still maintains a reputation which is one of the enigmas of history.

The three favorites of medieval Spanish romance, says Senor Lafuente, Bernardo del Carpio, Fernan Gonzalez, and the Cid, have this at least in common, that they were all at war with their lawful sovereigns, and fought their battles independently of the crown. Hence their popularity in Spain. The Castilians of the Middle Ages were so devoted to their independence, so proud of their Fueros, such admirers of personal prowess, that they were disposed to welcome with national admiration those heroes who sprang from the people, who defied and were ill-treated by their kings.

The theory is both ingenious and just, yet it by no

means solves the difficulty. Ruy Diaz of Bivar, who was one of the proudest nobles of Castile, can scarcely be said to have sprung from the people, nor do we clearly perceive why his long service under Moslem kings, even though he was a rebel against his own sovereign, should have endeared him to the Christian Spaniards, however independent or however democratic. Yet we may learn at least from the character of the hero, ideal though it be, that the medieval Castilians were no bigots, and that they were slaves neither to their kings nor to their clergy.

The people of Aragon no doubt held their king in a more distinctly constitutional subjection. No Castilian chief-justice was found to call the sovereign to order: no Privilege of Union legalized a popular war in defense of popular liberties. But Roderic took the place of the justiciary in legend, if not in history, when he administered the oath to Alfonso at Burgos; and he invested himself with the privilege of warring against an aggressive king, when he routed Alfonso's forces, and burned his cities, to requite him for his attack upon Valencia.

It is this rebellious boldness which contributed no doubt very largely to endear the Cid to his contemporaries. It is one of the most constant characteristics of his career; one of the features that is portrayed with equal clearness by the chroniclers and the ballad makers of Spain. For the Cid is essentially a popular hero. His legendary presentment is a kind of poetic protest against arbitrary regal power. The Cid ballads are a pæan of triumphant democracy. The ideal Cid no doubt was evolved in the course of the twelfth century; and by the end of the fifteenth century, when the rule of kings and priests had become harder and heavier in Spain, an enslaved people looked back with an envious national pride to the Castilian hero who personified the freedom of bygone days.

The Cid is the only knight-errant that has survived the polished satire of Cervantes. For his fame was neither literary nor aristocratic; but, like the early Spanish proverbs, in which it is said he took so great a delight, it was embedded deep in the hearts of the people.* And although the memory of his religious indifference may not have added to his popularity in the sixteenth century in Spain, it is a part of his character which must be taken into account in gauging the public opinion of earlier days.

From the close of the eighth century to the close of the fifteenth, the Spanish people, Castilians and Aragonese, were, if anything, less bigoted than the rest of Europe. The influence of their neighbors the Moors, and of their Arab toleration, could not be without its effect upon a people naturally free, independent, and self-reliant, and the Cid, who was certainly troubled with no religious scruples in the course of his varied career, and who, according to a popular legend affronted and threatened the Pope on his throne in St. Peter's, on account of some fancied slight,†

---

* *Mas Moros mas ganancia*, "The more the Moors, the greater the booty," was one of his sayings, and it has passed into a well-known national proverb.

† Having kicked to pieces the splendid furniture and beaten the Papal chamberlain, he proceeded to threaten to caparison his horse with the rich hangings of the chapel, if the Pope refused him instant Absolution!

>Si no me absolveis, el Papa,
>Seriaos mal contado
>Que de vuestras ricas ropas
>Cubriré yo mi caballo!
>—Wolf and Hofmann, "Cid Ballads."

could never have been the hero of a nation of bigots. The degenerate Visigoths from the time of Reccared the Catholic to the time of Roderic the Vanquished could never have produced a Cid. Yet, even in the dark days of Erwig and Egica, there was found a Julian, who boldly maintained the national independence against the pretensions of the Pope of Rome. For a thousand years after the landing of St. Paul—if, indeed, he ever landed upon the coast—the Spanish Church was, perhaps, the most independent in Europe. The royal submission to the Papal authority, first by Sancho I. of Aragon, in 1071, and afterward by Alfonso VI. of Leon, in 1085, in the matter of the Romish Ritual, was distinctly unpopular. Peter II. found no lack of recruits for the army that he led against the Papal troops in Languedoc, and King James I., the most popular of the kings of Aragon, cut out the tongue of a meddlesome bishop who had presumed to interfere in his private affairs (1246). It was not until the Inquisition was forced upon United Spain by Isabella the Catholic, and the national lust for the plunder of strangers was aroused by the destruction of Granada, that the Spaniard became a destroyer of heretics. It was not until the spoliation and the banishment of Jews and Moriscos, and the opening of a new world of heathen treasure on the discovery of America, that the Castilian, who had always been independent himself, became intolerant of the independence of others. Then, indeed, he added the cruelty of the priest to the cruelty of the soldier, and wrapping himself in the cloak of a proud and uncompromising national orthodoxy, became the most ferocious bigot in two unhappy worlds.

But in the beginning it was not so. And if the Cid

could possibly have been annoyed by Torquemada, his knights would have hanged up the Inquisitor on the nearest tree. No priests' man, in good sooth, was Roderic of Bivar, nor, save in that he was a brave and determined soldier, had the great Castilian Free Lance anything in common with the more conventional heroes of United Spain.

If history affords no reasonable explanation of his unrivaled renown beyond that which has already been suggested, we find but little in the early poetry to assist us. The Cid ballads impress us "more by their number than their light." They are neither very interesting in themselves, nor are they even very suggestive. Only thirty-seven ballads are considered by Huber to be older than the sixteenth century. "La plupart de ces romances," says M. Dozy, "accusent leur origine moderne;" and according to Mr. Ormsby they do but little toward the illustration of the Cid, either as a picturesque hero of romance or as a characteristic feature of medieval history.

The great French dramatist scarcely touches the true history of his hero. The scene of the play is laid at Seville, where no Christian king set his foot for a hundred and fifty years after the death of Roderic. The title which he accepted from his employer, Mostian of Saragossa, is said to have been granted by Alfonso of Leon, after the capture of two imaginary Moorish kings, unknown to history, in an impossible battle on the banks of the Guadalquivir, which was never seen by the Cid. The whole action of the play turns upon the moral and psychological difficulties arising from the purely legendary incident of the killing of Chimene's father by her lover, avenging an insult offered to his own sire, and of the somewhat artificial indignation of the lady, until she is appeased by a slaughter of Moors. Corneille's drama abounds in noble sentiments expressed in most admirable verse; but it does not assist us to understand the character of the Cid, nor the reasons of his popularity in his own or in any other country. But certain at least it is that from the earliest times the story of his life and his career took a strong hold upon the popular imagination in Spain, and his virtues and his vices, little as they may seem to us to warrant the popular admiration, were understood and appreciated in the age in which he lived, an age of force and fraud, of domestic treason and foreign treachery, when religion preached little but battle and murder, and patriotism was but a pretext for plunder and rapine. Admired thus, even in his lifetime, as a gallant soldier, an independent chieftain, and an ever successful general, fearless, dexterous, and strong, his free career became a favorite theme with the jongleurs and troubadours of the next generation; and from the Cid of history was evolved a Cid of legendary song.

It is most difficult at the present day to know exactly where serious history ends and where poetry and legend begin. Yet the Cid as represented to us by M. Dozy, one of the most acute of modern investigators of historic truth, is not so very different from the Cid represented by Southey, or even by earlier and less critical poets, but that we may form a reasonable estimate, from what is common to both history and tradition, of what manner of man he was. The Cid of the twelfth century legends, indeed, though he may be more marvelous, is by no means more moral than the Cid of history. It was reserved for the superior refinement of succeeding generations, and more especially for the anonymous author of the poem of the thirteenth century to evolve a hero of a gentler and nobler mold; a creature conforming to a higher ideal of knightly perfection. From this time forward we have a glorified Cid, whose adventures are no more historically false, perhaps, than those of the unscrupulous and magnificent Paladin of the legends and romances of the twelfth century, but whose character possesses all the dignity and all the glory with which he could be invested by a generous medieval imagination. And it is this refined and idealized hero; idealized, yet most real; refined, yet eminently human, that has been worshiped by nineteen generations of Spaniards as the national hero of Spain.

Ruy Diaz—as he lived and died—was probably no worse a man than any of his neighbors. Far better than many of them he was, and undoubtedly bolder and stronger, more capable, more adroit, and more successful.

Seven of the Christian princes of Spain at this period fell in battle warring against their own near relations, or were murdered by their hands in cold blood. Garcia of Castile was slain by the sword of the Velas. Bermudo III. of Leon and Garcia Sanchez of Navarre died fighting against their brother, Ferdinand of Castile. Sancho II. of Castile was assassinated by order of his sister Urraca, besieged by him in her city of Zamora. Among the Christian kings of the century immediately before him, Garcia of Gallicia was strangled in prison by the hands of his brothers, Sancho and Alfonso; Sancho Garcia of Navarre was assassinated by his brother Ramon, at Peñalva; Ramon Berenguer II. of Barcelona died by the dagger of his brother Berenguer Ramon; Sancho the Fat, in 967, was poisoned at a friendly repast by Gonzalo

Sanchez; Ruy Velasquez of Castile, in 986, murdered his seven nephews, the unfortunate Infantes de Lara; Sancho of Castile, in 1010, poisoned his mother, who had endeavored to poison him. At the wedding festivities at Leon, in 1026, Garcia, Count of Castile, was assassinated at the church door, and the murderers were promptly burned alive by his friends; Garcia of Navarre, in 1030, as an incident in a family dispute about a horse, accused his mother of adultery. Such was the standard of the eleventh century in the north of the Peninsula.

To judge the Cid, even as we now know him, according to any code of modern ethics, is supremely unreasonable. To be sure, even now, that we know him as he was, is supremely presumptuous. But that Ruy Diaz was a great man, and a great leader of men, a knight who would have shocked modern poets, and a free lance who would have laughed at modern heroes, we can have no manner of doubt. That he satisfied his contemporaries and himself; that he slew Moors and Christians as occasion required, with equal vigor and absolute impartiality; that he bearded the King of Leon in his Christian council, and that he cozened the King of Saragossa at the head of his Moslem army; that he rode the best horse and brandished the best blade in Spain; that his armies never wanted for valiant soldiers, nor his coffers for gold pieces; that he lived my Lord the Challenger, the terror of every foe, and that he died rich and respected in the noble city that had fallen to his knightly spear—of all this at least we are certain; and, if the tale is displeasing to our nineteenth century refinement, we must be content to believe that it satisfied the aspirations of medieval Spain.

CHAPTER IV

MOORISH SPAIN

THE LAST OF THE CALIPHS—THE RISE AND FALL OF GRANADA—FERDINAND AND ISABELLA—THE GREAT CAPTAIN

Moslem rule in Spain may be conveniently summarized as consisting, first, in the Caliphs of Cordova; second, in the dynasty of the Almoravides; third, in that of the Almohades; and, finally, the kings of Granada.

Concerning the first it may be noted that in the long reign of the last Abdur Rahman were the seeds of its dissolution. Brooking no rival during his lifetime, at his death he found no successor. Then upon the ruins of the great Caliphate twenty independent and hostile dynasties surged. Meanwhile Alfonso was eying them from his citadel. At the gates of Valencia was the Cid. For common safety the Moslem rivals looked for a common defender. In Africa that defender was found in Yusuf, the Berber chief of a tribe of religious soldiers known as the Almoravides.

Invited to Spain he crossed over, and, meeting Alfonso at Zalaca, near Bajadoz, on the 23d of October, 1086, he routed him with great and historic slaughter.

Yusuf [says Burke] had come as a Moslem defender, but he remained as a Moslem master. And once more in Spanish history, the over-powerful ally turned his victorious arms against those who had welcomed him to their shores. Yet Yusuf was no vulgar traitor. He had sworn to the envoys of the Spanish Moslems that he would return to Africa, in the event of victory, without the annexation to his African empire of a field or a city to the north of the Straits. And his vow was religiously kept. Retiring empty-handed to Mauritania, after the great battle at Zalaca, he returned once more to Spain, unfettered on this new expedition by any vow, and set to work with his usual vigor to make himself master of the Peninsula. Tarifa fell in December. The next year saw the capture of Seville, and of all of the principal cities of Andalusia. An army sent by Alfonso VI., under his famous captain, Alvar Fanez, was completely defeated, and all Southern Spain lay at the feet of the Berber, save only Valencia, which remained impregnable so long as the Cid lived to direct the defense. In 1102, after the hero's death, Valencia succumbed, and all Spain to the south of the Tagus became a province of the great African empire of the Almoravides.

The rule of these hardy bigots was entirely unlike that of the Ommeyad Caliphs of the West. Moslem Spain had no longer even an independent existence. The sovereign resided not at Cordova, but at Morocco. The poets and musicians were banished from court. The beauties of Az Zahra were forgotten. Jews and Christians were alike persecuted. The kingdom was governed with an iron hand. But if the rule of the stranger was not generous, it was just, and for the moment it possessed the crowning merit that it was efficient. The laws were once more respected. The people once more dreamed of wealth and happiness. But it was little more than a dream.

On the death of Yusuf in 1107 the scepter passed into the hands of his son Ali, a more sympathetic but a far less powerful ruler.. In 1118 the great city of Saragossa, the last bulwark of Islam in the north of the Peninsula, was taken by Alfonso I. of Aragon, who carried his victorious arms into Southern Spain, and fulfilled a rash vow by eating a dinner of fresh fish on the coast of Granada.

Yet it was by no Christian hand that the empire of the Almoravides was to be overthrown.

Mohammed Ibn Abdullah, a lamplighter in the Mosque at Cordova, had made his way to remote Bagdad to study at the feet of Abu Hamid Algazali, a celebrated doctor of Moslem law. The strange adventures, so characteristic of his age and nation, by which the lowly student became a religious reformer—a Mahdi—and a conqueror in Africa, and at length overthrew the Almoravides, both to the north and the south of the Straits of Gibraltar, forms a most curious chapter in the history of Islam; but in a brief sketch of the fortunes of medieval Spain, it must suffice to say that having established his religious and military power among the Berber tribes of Africa, Ibn Abdullah, the Mahdi, landed at Algeciras in 1145, and possessed himself in less than four years of Malaga, Seville, Granada, and Cordova. The empire of the Almoravides was completely destroyed; and, before the close of the year 1149, all Moslem Spain acknowledged the supremacy of the Almohades.

These more sturdy fanatics were still African rather than Spanish sovereigns. Moslem Spain was administered by a Vali deputed from Morocco; and Cordova, shorn of much of its former splendor, was the occasional abode of a royal visitor from Barbary. For seventy years the Almohades retained their position in Spain. But their rule was not of glory but of decay. One high feat of arms indeed shed a dying luster on the name of the Berber prince who reigned for fifteen years (1184-99) under the auspicious title of Almanzor, and his great Moslem victory over Alfonso II. at Alarcon in 1195 revived for the time the drooping fortunes of the Almohades. But their empire was already doomed, decaying, disintegrated, wasting away. And at length the terrible defeat of the Moslem forces by the united armies of the three Christian kings at the Navas de Tolosa in 1212, at once the most crushing and the most authentic of all the Christian victories of medieval Spain, gave a final and deadly blow to the Moslem dominion of the Peninsula. Within a few years of that celebrated battle, Granada alone was subject to the rule of Islam.

It was in the year 1228 that a descendant of the old Moorish kings of Saragossa rebelled against the Almohades and succeeded in making himself master not merely of Granada, but of Cordova, Seville, Algeciras, and even of Ceuta, and, obtaining a confirmation of his rights from Bagdad, assumed the title of Amir ul Moslemin—Commander of the Moslems—and Al Mutawakal—the Protected of God.

But a rival was not slow to appear. Mohammed Al Ahmar, the Fair or the Ruddy, defeated, dethroned, and slew Al Mutawakal, and reigned in his stead in Andalusia. Despoiled in his turn of most of his possessions by St. Ferdinand of Castile, Al Ahmar was fain at length to content himself with the rich districts in the extreme south of the Peninsula, which are known to fame, wherever the Spanish or the English language is spoken, as the Kingdom of Granada. And thus it came to pass that the city on the banks of the Darro, the home of the proud and highly cultivated Syrians of Damascus, the flower of the early Arab invaders of Spain, became also the abiding place of the later Arab civilization, overmastered year after year, and destroyed, by the Christian armies ever pressing on to the southern sea. Yet, in the middle of the thirteenth century, the flood tide of reconquest had for the moment fairly spent itself. The Christians were not strong enough to conquer, and above all they were not numerous enough to occupy, the districts that were still peopled by the Moor; and for once a wise and highly cultivated Christian shared the supreme power in the Peninsula with a generous and honorable Moslem. Alfonso X. sought not to extend his frontiers, but to educate his people, not to slaughter his neighbors, but to give laws to his subjects, not to plunder frontier cities, but to make Castile into a kingdom, with a history, a civilization, and a language of her own. If the reputation of Alfonso is by no means commensurate with his true greatness, the statesmanship of Mohammed Al Ahmar, the founder of the ever famous Kingdom of Granada, is overshadowed by his undying fame as an architect. Yet is Al Ahmar worthy of remembrance as a king and the parent of kings in Spain. The loyal friend and ally of his Christian neighbor, the prudent administrator of his own dominions, he collected at his Arab court a great part of the wealth, the science, and the intelligence of Spain. His empire has long ago been broken up; the Moslem has been driven out; there is no king nor kingdom of Granada. But their memory lives in the great palace fortress whose red towers still rise over the sparkling Darro, and whose fairy chambers are still to be seen in what is, perhaps, the most celebrated of the wonder works of the master builders of the world.

After his long and glorious reign of forty-two years, Mohammed the Fair was killed by a fall from his horse near Granada, and was succeeded by his son, Mohammed II., in the last days of the year 1272. Al Ahmar had ever remained at peace with Alfonso X., but his son, taking advantage of the king's absence in quest of an empire in Germany, sought the assistance of Yusuf, the sovereign or emperor of Morocco, and invaded the Christian frontiers.

Victory was for some time on the side of the Moors. The Castilians were defeated at Ecija in 1275, and their leader, the Viceroy Don Nunez de Lara, was killed in battle, as was also Don Sancho, Infante of Aragon and Archbishop of Toledo, after the rout of his army at Martos, near Jaen, on the 21st of October, 1275; and the victorious Yusuf ravaged Christian Spain to the very gates of Seville.

In the next year, 1276, the Castilian armies were again twice defeated, in February at Alcoy and in the following July at Lucena. To add to their troubles, King James of Aragon died at Valencia in 1276. Sancho of Castile sought to depose his father Alfonso, at Valladolid. All was in confusion among the Christians; and had it not been for the defection of Yusuf of Morocco, the tide of fortune might have turned in favor of Islam. As it was, the African monarch not only abandoned his cousin of Granada, but he was actually persuaded to send one hundred thousand ducats to his Christian rival at Seville in 1280.

The value of this assistance was soon felt. Tarifa was taken in 1292, and the progress of the Moor was checked forever in Southern Spain. Mohammed II. died in 1302, and was succeeded by his son, Mohammed III., who was usually considered by the Moslem historians to have been the ablest monarch of his house. But he reigned for only seven years, and he was unable to defend Gibraltar from the assaults of his Christian rivals.

From this time the court of Granada became a sort of city of refuge for the disaffected lords and princes of Castile, who sometimes, but rarely, prevailed upon their Moslem hosts to assist them in expeditions into Christian Spain, but who were always welcomed with true Arab hospitality at the Moslem capital. To record their various intrigues would be a vain and unpleasing task. The general course of history was hardly affected by passing alliances. The Christian pressed on—with ever increasing territory behind him —on his road to the southern sea.

In 1319, Abdul Walid or Ismail I. of Granada defeated and slew Don Pedro and Don Juan, Infantes of Castile, at a place near Granada, still known as the Sierra de los Infantes. But no important consequences followed the victory.

In the reign of Yusuf (1333-54) was fought the great battle of the Salado (1340), when the Christians, under Alfonso XI., were completely successful; and the capitulation of Algeciras three years later deprived the Moslems of an important harbor and seaport. Day by day—almost hour by hour —the Christians encroached upon Granada, even while cultivating the political friendship and accepting the private hospitality of the Moslem. Their treacherous intervention reached its climax in 1362, when Peter the Cruel decoyed the King Abu Said, under his royal safe-conduct, to the palace at Seville, and slew him with his own hand.

With Mohammed or Maulai al Aisar, or the Left-handed, the affairs of Granada became more intimately connected with the serious history of Spain. Al Hayzari, proclaimed king in 1423, and dethroned soon after by his cousin, another Mohammed, in 1427, sought and found refuge at the court of John II., by whose instrumentality he was restored to his throne at the Alhambra in 1429. Yet within four years a rival sovereign, Yusuf, had secured the support of the fickle Christian; and Muley the Left-handed was forced a second time to fly from his capital. Once again, by the sudden death of the new usurper, he returned to reign at Granada, and once again for the third time he was supplanted by a more fortunate rival, who reigned as Mohammed IX. for nearly ten years (1445-54). At the end of this period, however, another pretender was dispatched from the Christian court, and after much fighting and intrigue, Mohammed ibn Ismail, a nephew of Maulai or Muley the Left-handed, drove out the reigning sovereign and succeeded him as Mohammed X.

Yet were the dominions of this Christian ally unceasingly ravaged by his Christian neighbors. Gibraltar, Archidona, and much surrounding territory were taken by the forces of Henry IV. and his nobles; and a treaty was at length concluded in 1464, in which it was agreed that Mohammed of Granada should hold his kingdom under the protection of Castile, and should pay an annual subsidy or tribute of twelve thousand gold ducats. It was thus, on the death, in 1466, of this Mohammed Ismail of Granada, that a vexed and harassed throne was inherited by his son Muley Abul Hassan, ever famous in history and romance as "The old king"—the last independent sovereign of Granada.

Meanwhile, Henry's only daughter Joanna being regarded as the fruit of the queen's adultery, he was deposed, but restored after acknowledging as his heiress his sister Isabella, who subsequently, through her marriage with Ferdinand of Aragon, joined the two most powerful of Spanish kingdoms into one yet more powerful State.

To return now to Muley Abul Hassan.* For many years after his accession he observed with his Christian neighbors the treaties that had been made, nor did he take advantage of the civil war which arose by reason of Joanna's pretensions to add to the difficulties already existing, and in the spring of 1476 sought a formal renewal of the old Treaty of Peace.

Ferdinand, however, made his acceptance of the king's proposal contingent upon the grant of an annual tribute; and he sent an envoy to the Moslem court to negotiate the terms of payment. But the reply of Abul Hassan was decisive. "Steel," said he, "not gold, was what Ferdinand should have from Granada!" Disappointed of their subsidy, and unprepared for war, the Christian sovereigns were content to renew the treaty, with a mental reservation that as soon as a favorable opportunity should present itself they would drive every Moslem not only out of Granada, but out of Spain.

---

* Muley is an Arabic word meaning "my lord."

For five years there was peace between Abul Hassan and the Catholic sovereigns. The commencement of hostilities was the capture of Zahara by the Moslems at the close of the year 1481; which was followed early in next year, 1482, by the conquest of the far more important Moorish stronghold of Alhama, not by the troops of Ferdinand and Isabella, but by the followers of Ponce de Leon, the celebrated Marquis of Cadiz. Alhama was not merely a fortress. It was a treasure-house and a magazine; and it was but five or six leagues from Granada. The town was sacked with the usual horrors. The Marquis of Cadiz, having made good his position within the walls, defied all the attacks of Abul Hassan, and at the same time sent messengers to every Christian lord in Andalusia to come to his assistance—to all save one, his hereditary enemy, the Duke of Medina Sidonia, chief of the great family of the Guzmans. Yet it was this generous rival, who, assembling all his chivalry and retainers, was the first to appear before the walls of Alhama, and relieve the Christians from the threatened assault of the Moslem. The days of civil discord had passed away in Castile; and against united Christendom, Islam could not long exist in Spain.

Meanwhile, Ferdinand, seeing that war had finally broken out, started from Medina del Campo, and marched with all speed to Cordova, where he was joined by Isabella early in April, 1482. The Inquisition had now been for over a year in full blast at Seville. The fires of persecution had been fairly lighted. The reign of bigotry had begun, and the king and queen were encouraged to proceed from the plunder of the Jews or New Christians to the plunder of the Moslems. Ferdinand accordingly repaired in person to Alhama, with a large train of prelates and ecclesiastics of lower degree. The city was solemnly purified. Three mosques were consecrated by the Cardinal of Spain for Christian worship. Bells, crosses, plate, altar cloths were furnished without stint; and Alhama having been thus restored to civilization, Ferdinand descended upon the fruitful valley or Vega of Granada, destroyed the crops, cut down the fruit trees, uprooted the vines, and, without having encountered a single armed enemy in the course of his crusade, returned in triumph to Cordova. A more arduous enterprise in the following July was not attended with the same success, when Ferdinand attacked the important town of Loja, and was repulsed with great loss of Christian life. An expedition against Malaga, later in the year, undertaken by Alfonso de Cardenas, Grand Master of Santiago, and the Marquis of Cadiz, was even more disastrous, for a small body of Moors in the mountain defiles of the Axarquia fell upon the Christian marauders, and no less than four hundred "persons of quality" are said to have perished in the retreat, including thirty commanders of the great military order of Santiago. The Grand Master, the Marquis of Cadiz, and Don Alfonso de Aguilar escaped as by a miracle, and the survivors straggled into Loja and Antequera and Malaga, leaving Abul Hassan and his brother Al Zagal, or the Valiant, with all the honors of war.

But the successes of the Moor in the field was more than counterbalanced by treason in the palace. By Zoraya, a lady of Christian ancestry, Muley Abul Hassan had a son, Abu Abdallah, who has earned a sad notoriety under the more familiar name of Boabdil. Jealous of some rival, or ambitious of greater power, the Sultana and her son intrigued against their sovereign, and having escaped from the State prison, in which they were at first prudently confined, raised the standard of revolt, and compelled Abul Hassan, who was thenceforth more usually spoken of as the Old King, to seek refuge on the seacoast at Malaga.

Boabdil, jealous of the success of his father and his uncle at Loja and in the Axarquia, and anxious to confirm his power by some striking victory over the Christians, took the field and confronted the forces of the Count of Cabra, near Lucena. The battle was hotly contested, but victory remained with the Christians. Ali Atar, the bravest of the Moorish generals, was slain by the hand of Alfonso de Aguilar, and Boabdil himself was taken prisoner by a common soldier, Hurtado by name, and fell into the hands of the victorious Count of Cabra. The captivity of Boabdil, the Little King, el Rey Chico, as he was called by the Castilians, was the turning point in the history of the Moorish dominion in Spain. Released on payment of a magnificent ransom provided by his mother Zoraya, and bound to his Christian captors by a humiliating treaty, he returned to Granada, disgraced and dishonored, as the ally of the enemies of his country. Driven out of the capital by the forces of his father, who had returned to occupy the great palace-fortress of Alhambra, Boabdil and his mother retired to Almeria, the second city in the kingdom; and the whole country was distracted by civil war.

Yet for four years the Castilians refrained from any important expedition against Granada. Their tactics were rather those of Scipio at Numantia. For Delay was all in favor of Disintegration.

Yet the merciless devastation of fields and crops was carried on with systematic and dreadful completeness. Thirty thousand destroyers of peaceful homesteads, granaries, farmhouses, and mills, were constantly at work, and ere long there was scarce a vineyard or an oliveyard, scarce an orchard or an orange-grove existing within reach of the Christian borders. Under cover of the treaty with Boabdil, this devilish enginery of destruction was steadily pushed forward, while the old king and his more vigorous brother El Zagal were prevented by domestic treason from making any effectual defense of their fatherland. Some of the border towns, moreover, fell into the hands of the Christians, and many forays were undertaken which produced rich booty for the marauders. Ferdinand in the meantime occupied himself rather with the affairs of the Inquisition and of foreign policy, while Isabella was personally superintending the enormous preparations for a final attack on Granada. Artillery was cast in large quantities, and artificers imported from France and Italy; large stores of ammunition were procured from Flanders. Nothing was hurried; nothing was spared; nothing was forgotten by Isabella. A camp hospital, the first, it is said, in the history of warfare, was instituted by the queen, whose energy was indefatigable, whose powers of organization were boundless, and whose determination was inflexible. To represent her as a tender and timid princess is to turn her true greatness into ridicule. But her vigor, her prudence, and her perseverance are beyond the vulgar praise of history.

Meanwhile, Granada was gradually withering away. The "pomegranate," as Ferdinand had foreseen and foretold, was losing one by one the seeds of which the rich and lovely fruit had once been all compact. The old king, defeated but not disgraced, blind, infirm, and unfortunate, was succeeded too late by his more capable brother, El Zagal, a gallant warrior, a skillful commander, and a resolute ruler. But if "the valiant one" might hardly have held his own against the enormous resources of the Christians in Europe, he was powerless against the combination of foreign vigor and domestic treachery. The true conqueror of Granada is Boabdil, the rebel and the traitor, who has been euphemistically surnamed the Unlucky (El Zogoibi). Innocent, perchance, of the massacre of the brave Abencerrages, he is guilty of the blood of his country.

The capture of Velez Malaga by Ferdinand, already well supplied with a powerful train of artillery, in April, 1487—while El Zagal was fighting for his life against Boabdil in Granada—was soon followed by the reduction, after a most heroic defense, of the far more important city of Malaga in August, 1487. But the heroism of the Moslem woke no generous echo in the hearts of either Ferdinand or Isabella. The entire population of the captured city, men, women, and children—some fifteen thousand souls—were reduced to slavery, and distributed not only over Spain, but over Europe.

A hundred choice warriors were sent as a gift to the Pope. Fifty of the most beautiful girls were presented to the Queen of Naples, thirty more to the Queen of Portugal, others to the ladies of her court, and the residue of both sexes were portioned off among the nobles, the knights, and the common soldiers of the army, according to their rank and influence.

For the Jews and renegades a more dreadful doom was reserved; and the flames in which they perished were, in the words of a contemporary ecclesiastic, "the illuminations most grateful to the Catholic piety of Ferdinand and Isabella." The town was repeopled by Christian immigrants, to whom the lands and houses of the Moslem owners were granted with royal liberality by the victors. The fall of Malaga, the second seaport and the third city of the kingdom of Granada, was a grievous loss to the Moors; and the Christian blockade was drawn closer both by land and by sea. Yet an invasion of the eastern provinces, undertaken by Ferdinand himself in 1488, was repulsed by El Zagal; and the Christian army was disbanded as usual at the close of the year, without having extended the Christian dominions.

But in the spring of 1489 greater efforts were made. The Castilians sat down before the town of Baza, not far from Jaen, and after a siege which lasted until the following December, the city surrendered, not, as in the case of Malaga, without conditions, but upon honorable terms of capitulation, which the assailants, who had only been prevented by the arrival of Isabella from raising the siege, were heartily glad to accept. The fall of Baza was of more than passing importance, for it was followed by the capitulation of Almeria, the second city in the kingdom, and by the submission of El Zagal, who renounced as hopeless the double task of fighting against his nephew at the Alhambra, and resisting the Christian sovereigns who had already overrun his borders. The fallen monarch passed over to Africa, where he died in indigence and misery, the last of the great Moslem rulers of Spain.

In the spring of 1490, Ferdinand, already master of the greater part of the Moorish kingdom, sent a formal summons to his bondsman, Boabdil, to surrender to him the city of Granada; and that wretched and most foolish traitor, who had refrained from action when action might have saved his country, now defied the victorious Christians, when his defiance could only lead to further suffering and greater disaster.

Throughout the summer of 1490, Ferdinand, in person, devoted himself to the odious task of the devastation of the entire Vega of Granada, and the depopulation of the town of Guadix. But in the spring of the next year, Isabella, who was ever the life and soul of the war, took up her position within six miles of the city, and pitched her camp at Ojos de Huescar at the very gate of Granada.

And here was found assembled, not only all the best blood of Castile, but volunteers and mercenary troops from various countries in Europe. France, England, Italy, and even Germany, each provided their contingent; and a body of Swiss soldiers of fortune showed the gallant cavaliers of the Christian army the power and the value of a well disciplined infantry. Among the foreigners who had come over to Spain in 1486 was an English lord, the Earl of Rivers, known by the Spaniards as El Conde de Escalas, from his family name of Scales, whose magnificence attracted the admiration of all, even at the magnificent court of Isabella.

But the destruction of Granada was not brought about by these gilded strangers, nor even by the brilliant knights and nobles of Spain. It was not due to skillful engineers nor to irresistible commanders. The gates were opened by no victory. The walls were scaled by no assault. The Christian success was due to the patient determination of Isabella, to the decay and disintegration of the Moorish Commonwealth, and, to some extent, to the skillful negotiation and diplomatic astuteness of a young soldier whose early influence upon the fortunes of Spain have been overshadowed by the greatness of his later achievements.

For among all the splendid knights and nobles who assembled in the camp of Isabella, the chroniclers wellnigh overlooked a gay cavalier of modest fortune, the younger brother of Alfonso de Aguilar, distinguished rather as a fop than a warrior—Gonsalvo Hernandez of Cordova, whose fame was destined to eclipse that of all his companions in arms, and who has earned an undying reputation in the history of three countries as "The Great Captain."

The life of Gonsalvo de Cordova is interesting as being the history of a brave soldier and an accomplished general, who flourished at a very important period of the history of Europe. But it is further and much more interesting as being the history of a man who united in himself many of the characteristics of ancient and of modern times. His bravery was the bravery of an old Castilian knight, and although he had many splendid rivals, he was pronounced by common consent to be their superior. Yet his individual courage was the least remarkable of his qualities. He was a general, such as the Western world had not known for a thousand years, and he was the first diplomatist of modern Europe. In personal valor, in knightly courtesy, in brave display, he was of his own time. In astute generalship, and in still more astute diplomacy, he may be said to have inaugurated a new era; and although greater commanders have existed after him, as well as before him, he will always be known as "The Great Captain."

The conquest of Granada marks an epoch, not only in the history of Spain, but in the history of Europe; and Gonsalvo was the hero of Granada. The expedition of Charles VIII. into Italy is a subject of almost romantic interest, very nearly preferred by Gibbon to his own immortal theme; and Gonsalvo in Italy was the admired of all French and Italian admirers. The succeeding expedition of Louis XII. was scarcely less interesting, and the part played by Gonsalvo was even more remarkable. At his birth artillery was almost unknown. At his death it had become the most formidable arm of offense; it had revolutionized the rules and manner of warfare; and it was employed by The Great Captain in both his Italian campaigns with marked skill and success.

Gonsalvo Hernandez was born at Montilla, near Cordova, in 1453, of the noble and ancient family of the Aguilars. After a boyhood and youth devoted, not only to every manly sport and pursuit, and to the practice of arms, but to the study of letters, and more especially of the Arabic language, he made his first appearance in serious warfare on the field of Olmedo, fighting under the banner of the Marquis of Villena. On the death of Prince Alfonso, Gonsalvo returned to Cordova. His father had already died; and according to the Spanish law of primogeniture the whole of the rich estates of the family of Aguilar passed, on the death of Don Pedro, to his eldest son Alfonso, while nothing but a little personal property, a great name, a fine person, and "the hope of what he might gain by his good fortune or his valor" was inherited by his younger brother.

Cordova was obviously too small a field for Gonsalvo de Aguilar; and in the course of the eventful year 1474, having just arrived at man's estate, he proceeded to Segovia, and distinguished himself among the young nobles who crowded to the Court of Isabella, by his prowess at tournaments and all warlike games and exercises; and he soon became celebrated for his personal beauty as well as for his valor, distinguished for his fascinating manners, and, above all, by an eloquence rarely found in a young soldier of two and twenty. He was generally known as "the Prince of the Youth"; and he supported the character by an almost royal liberality and ostentatious expenditure entirely incompatible with his modest fortune.

In the war of succession between Isabella and her niece, Gonsalvo served under Alfonso de Cardenas, Grand Master of Santiago, in command of a troop of one hundred and twenty horsemen; and he particularly distinguished himself at the battle of Albuera.

And now, in the camp before Granada, he was well pleased once more to sun himself in the smiles of his queen and patroness, whose presence in the camp inspired every soldier with enthusiasm. Isabella appeared on the field superbly mounted and dressed in complete armor, and continually visited the different quarters, and held reviews of the troops. On one occasion she expressed a desire to have a nearer view of the city, and a picked body of men, among whom was Gonsalvo de Cordova, commanded by the Marquis Duke of Cadiz, escorted her to the little village of Zubia, within a short distance of Granada. The citizens, indignant at the near approach of so small a force, sallied out and attacked them. The Christians, however, stood their ground so bravely, and performed such prodigies of valor under the very eyes of Isabella herself, that no less than two thousand Moslems are said to have fallen in that memorable affray.

It happened one night, about the middle of July, that the drapery of the tent or pavilion in which Isabella was lodged took fire, and the conflagration was not extinguished until several of the neighboring tents had been consumed. The queen and her attendants escaped unhurt, but a general consternation prevailed throughout the camp, until it was discovered that no more serious loss had been experienced than that of the queen's wardrobe.

Gonsalvo, however, who on more than one occasion showed himself at least as practical a courtier as Sir Walter Raleigh, immediately sent an express to Illora, and obtained such a supply of fine clothes from his wife, Doña Maria Manrique, that the queen herself was amazed, as much at their magnificence as at the rapidity with which they had been obtained.

But this incident led to even more important results than the amiable pillage of Dona Maria's wardrobe, for in order to guard against a similar disaster, as well as to provide comfortable winter quarters for the troops, Isabella determined to construct a sufficient number of houses of solid masonry to provide quarters for the besieging army, a design which was carried out in less than three months. This martial and Christian town, which received the appropriate name of Santa Fe, may be still seen by the traveler in the Vega of Granada, and is pointed out by good Catholics as the only town in Andalusia that has never been contaminated by the Moslem.

But in spite of the attractions of all these feats of arms and exhibitions of magnificence, and of all the personal display and rash adventure which savors so much more of medieval chivalry than of modern warfare, Gonsalvo was more seriously engaged in the schemes and negotiations which contributed almost as much as the prowess of the Christian arms to the fall of Granada. He had spies everywhere. He knew what was going on in Granada better than Boabdil. He knew what was going on in the camp better than Ferdinand. His familiarity with Arabic enabled him to maintain secret communications with recreant Moors, without the dangerous intervention of an interpreter. He kept up constant communications with Illora, and having obtained the allegiance or friendship of the Moorish chief, Ali Atar, he gained possession of the neighboring fortress of Mondejar. He sent presents, in truly Oriental style, to many of the Moorish leaders in Granada who favored the party of Boabdil, and he was at length chosen by Isabella as the most proper person to conduct the negotiations that led to the treaty of capitulation, which was signed on the 25th of November, 1491.

The nature and the effect of this Convention are well known. The triumphal entry of the Christians into the old Moslem capital; "the last sigh of the Moor," and the setting up of the Cross in the palace-citadel of Alhambra, not only form one of the most glowing pages in the romance of history, but they mark an epoch in the annals of the world.

CHAPTER V

HE INQUISITION

TORQUEMADA AND ISABELLA — THE NEW TRIBUNAL — THE PENALTY OF UNSOUND OPINIONS — THREE CENTURIES OF SHAME

The history of Spain assumed a new phase when, at the fall of Granada, the attention of potentates and people ceased to be absorbed by the excitement of a great religious war. Then the past and the romance of it ended and the history of modern Spain began.

Before proceeding with the latter, a name and a tribunal detain attention. The one is Torquemada. The other is the Inquisition. Burke has described them both, as follows:

The Inquisition, established in Italy by Honorius III. in 1231, and in France by St. Louis in 1233, was formally introduced into Spain by Gregory IX. in 1235, by a Rescript of April 30th, addressed to Mongriu, Archbishop-Administrator of Tarragona, confirming and explaining previous Brief and Bulls upon the subject of the repression of heresy; and prescribing the issue of certain Instructions which had been prepared at the desire of his holiness by a Spanish saint, the Dominican Raymond of Penafort. From this time forward, Bulls on the subject of the Inquisition into heresy were frequently issued; and the followers of Dominic were ever the trusted agents of the Holy See.

The first suggestion of the serious introduction of the Tribunal of the Holy Office into Castile, at the end of the fifteenth century, is said to have come from Sicily. An Italian friar bearing the suggestive name of Dei Barberi, Inquisitor-general at Messina, paid a visit to his sovereign Ferdinand at Seville in 1477, in order to procure the confirmation of a privilege accorded to the Sicilian Dominicans by the Emperor Frederic II., in 1233, by virtue of which the Inquisitors entered into possession of one-third of the goods of the heretic whom they condemned. This dangerous charter was confirmed in due course by Ferdinand on the 2d of September, 1477, and by Isabella on the 18th of October; and very little argument was required on the part of the gratified envoy to convince his sovereign of the various temporal and spiritual advantages that would follow the introduction of the Tribunal, that had so long existed in an undeveloped form in Sicily and in Aragon, into the dominions of his pious consort, Isabella of Castile.

In the middle of the year 1480 there was as yet no court of the Holy Inquisition established in Spain. At length, pressed by the Papal Nuncio, by the Dominicans, by her confessor, most of all by her husband, Isabella gave her consent; and at length, in August, 1483, the Inquisition was established as a permanent tribunal. Tomas de Torquemada was appointed Inquisitor-general of both Castile and Aragon. Subordinate tribunals were constituted; new and more stringent regulations were made; the victims smoked from day to day on the great stone altar of the Quemadero.

The life of Tomas de Torquemada is the history of contemporary Spain. Born of a noble family, already distinguished in the Church by the reputation of the cardinal his uncle, Tomas early assumed the habit of a Dominican, and was in course of time appointed prior of an important monastery at Segovia, and confessor to the young Princess Isabella. His influence upon that royal lady was naturally great; his piety pleased her; his austerity affected her; and his powerful will directed, if it could not subdue, a will as powerful as his own. Brought up far away from a court whose frivolities had no charm for her, and where, under any circumstances, she would have been considered as a rival if not a pretender, the counsels of her confessor, both sacred and secular, were the most authoritative that she could expect to obtain. It has been constantly asserted that the friar obtained from the princess a promise that, in the event of her elevation to the throne of Castile, she would devote herself to the destruction of heretics and the increase of the power of the Church. Such a promise would have been but one of many which such a confessor would have obtained from such a penitent, and would have been but the natural result of his teaching. Nor is it surprising that in the intrigues that preceded the death of Henry IV., and the War of Succession that immediately followed it, the whole influence of the priesthood should have been cast on the side of Isabella and against her niece Joanna. For ten years, says the biographer of his Order, the skillful hand of Torquemada cultivated the intellect of Isabella; and in due course the propitious marriage with Ferdinand of Aragon, far from removing his pupil from his sacerdotal influence, brought him a new and an equally illustrious penitent. Torquemada became the confessor of the king as well as of the queen.

If the establishment of the Inquisition was the fulfillment of Isabella's vow, and the realization of the aspirations of her tutor, his appointment as Inquisitor-general, although it necessitated the choice of another confessor, did not by any means withdraw him from his old sphere of influence. He ceased not to preach the destruction of the Moslem, even as he was employed about the destruction of the Jew; and if Isabella was the active patroness of the war in Granada, there was a darker spirit behind the throne, ever preaching the sacred duty of the slaughter of the infidel and the heretic of every race and nation.

Torquemada was at once a politician and an enthusiast; rigid, austere, uncompromising; unbounded in his ambition, yet content to sacrifice himself to the cause that made him what he was. His moral superiority to the Innocents and Alexanders at Rome, his intellectual superiority to the Carrillos and the fighting bishops of Spain, gave him that enormous influence over both queen and king which his consuming bigotry and his relentless tenacity of purpose induced him to use with such dreadful effect. Aggressive even in his profession of humility, Torquemada was insolent, not only to his unhappy victims, but to his colleagues, to his sovereigns, to his Holy Father at Rome. He was, perhaps, the only man in Europe who was more masterful than Isabella, more bloodthirsty than Alexander; and he was able to impose his own will on both queen and pope. Rejecting in his proud humility every offer of the miter, he asserted and maintained his ecclesiastical supremacy even over the Primate of Spain. Attended by a body-guard of noble youths who were glad to secure at once the favor of the queen and immunity from ecclesiastical censure by assuming the habit of the Familiars of the Holy Office, the great destroyer lived in daily dread of the hand of the assassin.

Fifty horsemen and two hundred foot-guards always attended him. Nor was it deemed inconsistent with the purity of his own religious faith that he should carry about with him a talisman, in the shape of the horn of some strange animal, invested with the mysterious power of preventing the action of poison.

On the death of Torquemada in September, 1498, Don Diego Deza was promoted to the office of Inquisitor-general of Spain. Yet the activity of the Ecclesiastical Tribunal was rather increased than diminished by the change of masters, and an attempt was made soon afterward to extend its operations to Naples. But Gonsalvo de Cordova, who was then acting as viceroy, took upon himself to disregard not only the demands of the Inquisitors, but the orders of Ferdinand (June 30, 1504), and to postpone the introduction of the new tribunal into the country that he so wisely and so liberally governed. After the recall of his great representative, some six years later, Ferdinand himself made another attempt to establish the hated Tribunal in Italy in 1510. But even Ferdinand did not prevail; and Naples retained the happy immunity which it owed to the Great Captain.

If no error is more gross than to suppose that the establishment of the Inquisition was due to popular feeling in Spain, it is almost equally false to assert that it was the work of the contemporary popes. Rome was bad enough at the end of the fifteenth century; but her vast load of wickedness need not be increased by the burden of sins that are not her own. The everlasting shame of the Spanish Inquisition is that of the Catholic kings. It is not difficult to understand why the poor and rapacious Ferdinand of Aragon should welcome the establishment of an instrument of extortion which placed at his disposal the accumulated savings of the richest citizens of Castile. It is yet easier to comprehend that Isabella, who was not of a temper to brook resistance to authority in Church or State, should have consented to what her husband so earnestly desired. The queen, moreover, was at least sincerely religious, after the fashion of the day; and was constrained to follow the dictates of her confessor in matters judged by him to be within his spiritual jurisdiction, even while she was, as a civil ruler, withstanding the Pope himself on matters of temporal sovereignty. It is the height of folly to brand Isabella as a hypocrite, because we are unable to follow the workings of a medieval mind, or to appreciate the curious religious temper—by no means confined to the men and women of the fifteenth century—that can permit or compel the same person to be devoted to Popery and to be at war with the Pope, and find in the punctilious observance of ceremonial duty excuse or encouragement for the gratification of any vice and the commission of any crime. But that the nobility and people of Castile should have permitted the crown to impose upon them a foreign and an ecclesiastical despotism, is at first sight much harder to understand. No one reason, but an unhappy combination of causes, may perhaps be found to explain it.

The influence of the queen was great. Respected as well as feared by the nobles, she was long admired and beloved by the mass of the people.* The great success of her administration, which was apparent even by the end of 1480; her repression of the nobility; her studied respect for the Cortes; all these things predisposed the Castilians, who had so long suffered under weak and unworthy sovereigns, to trust themselves not only to the justice but to the wisdom of the queen. The influence of the clergy, if not so great as it was in France or Italy, was no doubt considerable, and, as a rule, though not always, it was cast on the side of the Inquisition. Last and most unhappy reason of all, the nobility and the people were divided; and, if not actually hostile, were at least ever at variance in Castile.

The first efforts of the new tribunal, too, were directed either against the converted Jews, of whose prosperity the Christians were already jealous, and for whose interested tergiversations no one could feel any respect; or against the more or less converted Moslems, toward whom their neighbors still maintained a certain hereditary antipathy. The New Christians alone were to be haled before the new tribunal. The Old Christians might trust in the queen, if

---

* Certainly in 1480, possibly not five-and-twenty years later. From curious criminal proceedings instituted against the Corregidor of Medina del Campo, we learn that that high judicial authority had not hesitated to declare that the soul of Isabella had gone direct to hell for her cruel oppression of her subjects, and that King Ferdinand was a thief and a robber, and that all the people round Medina and Valladolid, where the queen was best known, had formed the same judgment of her. "Arch. Gen. Simancas," Estado, Legajo i., f. 192; "Calendar of State Papers" (Spain), Supplement to i. and ii. (1868), p. 27.

not in their own irreproachable lineage, to protect them from hurt or harm.

The number of subordinate or subsidiary tribunals of the Holy Office was at first only four; established at Seville, Cordova, Jaen, and Ciudad Real. The number was gradually increased, during the reign of the Catholic kings, to thirteen; and over all these Ferdinand erected, in 1483, a court of supervision under the name of the Council of the Supreme, consisting of the Grand Inquisitor as President, and three other subordinate ecclesiastics, well disposed to the crown, and ready to guard the royal interests in confiscated property.

One of the first duties of this tremendous Council was the preparation of a code of rules or Instructions, based upon the Inquisitor's Manual of Eymeric, which had been promulgated in Aragon in the fourteenth century. The new work was promptly and thoroughly done; and twenty-eight comprehensive sections left but little to be provided for in the future.

The prosecution of unorthodox Spanish bishops by Torquemada on the ground of the supposed backslidings of their respective fathers is sufficiently characteristic of the methods of the Inquisition to be worthy of a passing notice. Davila, bishop of Segovia, and Aranda, bishop of Calahorra, were the sons of Jews who had been converted and baptized by St. Vincent Ferrer. No suspicion existed as to the orthodoxy of the prelates, both of whom were men distinguished for their learning and their piety. But it was suggested that their fathers had relapsed into Judaism before they died. They had each, indeed, left considerable fortunes behind them: and it was sought to exhume and burn their mortal remains; and to declare the property —long in the enjoyment of their heirs and successors—forfeited to the crown; and, in spite of a brief of Innocent VIII., of the 25th of September, 1487, the attempt was made by the Spanish Inquisitors. Both prelates sought refuge and protection by personal recourse to Rome (1490). Bishop Davila, in spite of the urgent remonstrances of Isabella herself, ultimately secured the protection of Alexander VI. and was invested with additional dignities and honors. Bishop Aranda was less fortunate. He was stripped of his office and possessions, and died a prisoner in the castle of St. Angelo in 1497.

It was not only living or dying heretics who paid the penalty of their unsound opinions. Men long dead, if they were represented by rich descendants, were cited before the Tribunal, judged, condemned, and the lands and goods that had descended to their heirs passed into the coffers of the Catholic kings. The scandal was so great that Isabella actually wrote to the Bishop of Segovia to defend herself against an accusation that no one had ever presumed to formulate. "I have," said the queen, "caused great calamities, I have depopulated towns and provinces and kingdoms, for the love of Christ and of His Holy Mother, but I have never touched a maravedi of confiscated property; and I have employed the money in educating and dowering the children of the condemned." This strange apology, which seems to have to some extent imposed upon Prescott, is shown by more recent examination of the State papers to be a most deliberate and daring falsehood, and would go far to justify the suggestion of Bergenroth that if Ferdinand never scrupled to tell direct untruths and make false promises whenever he thought it expedient, Queen Isabella excelled her husband in "disregard of veracity."

If the Holy Office had existed in Aragon in an undeveloped state from the thirteenth to the fifteenth century, and if it was actually introduced into Castile at the suggestion of an Inquistor of the Aragonese island of Sicily, the old independence of the inhabitants once more asserted itself when the time arrived for the introduction of the brand-new Castilian Tribunal into the old kingdom that is watered by the Ebro. Saragossa, indeed, may be nearer to Rome than Toledo; but the Catalan has ever been less submissive than his brother or cousin in Castile; less obedient to authority; more impatient of royal and ecclesiastical oppression. Yet Aragon, which had defied Innocent at Muret, and vanquished Martin at Gerona, was no match for the inquisitors of Ferdinand the Catholic. The Inquisition, as we have seen, had once before been established in Aragon; but in one most important particular the new institution differed from the old. In former days, even in the rare cases when the heretic paid the penalty of his heterodoxy with his life, his property passed to his heirs. The ecclesiastical tribunal of Ferdinand was not only more efficient in the matter of burning or otherwise disposing of accused persons; but the property of all doubtful Catholics, even of those who were graciously permitted to live after their trial, was absolutely forfeit to the crown. And the number of rich men, not only converted Jews but prosperous Christians, whose orthodoxy failed to come up to the new standard, was even in those days considered remarkable.

Ferdinand at all times hated popular assemblies. He spent the greater part of his time in Castile; and he saw as little as possible of the people of Aragon. But in April, 1484, he summoned a Cortes at Saragossa, and decreed by royal ordinance the establishment of the new tribunal. The old constitutional spirit of the Aragonese seems to have evaporated; and a degenerate justiciary was found to swear to support the jurisdiction of the Inquisitors. Yet envoys and delegates of the Commons of Aragon were dispatched to Castile, whither Ferdinand had promptly retired, and also to Rome, to remonstrate against the new Institution, and more especially against the new provisions for the forfeiture of the property of the convicted. If these provisions, contrary to the laws of Aragon, were repealed or suspended, the deputies "were persuaded," and there was a grim humor in the suggestion, "that the Tribunal itself would soon cease to exist."

But the repression of heresy was far too profitable an undertaking to be lightly abandoned; nor was Ferdinand of Aragon the man to abandon it; and the envoys returned from an unsuccessful mission to Valladolid to find a Quemadero already blazing at Saragossa.

Yet the Aragonese were not at once reduced to subjection. A popular conspiracy led to the assassination of the Inquisitor-general, Pedro de Arbues, in spite of his steel cap and coat of mail, as he stood one day at matins in the Cathedral of Saragossa (15th September, 1457); but this daring crime served only to enrage Ferdinand and to strengthen the power of the Inquisition. A most rigorous and indefatigable inquiry, which was extended from Saragossa into every part of Aragon, was at once undertaken; and an immense number of victims, chosen not only from among the people, but from almost every noble family in

Aragon, if it did not appease the vengeance of the Inquisitors, gratified at least the avarice of Ferdinand. Among the accused, indeed, was Don Jayme of Navarre, a nephew of the King of Aragon—a son of Eleanor, queen of Navarre, and her husband, Gaston de Foix—who was actually arrested and imprisoned by the Holy Office; and discharged only after having done public penance, as convicted of having in some way sympathized with the assassination of Arbues. But it may be noted that the young prince was anything but a favorite with his uncle, to whom this bit of ecclesiastical discipline was no doubt very gratifying.

But it was not only at Saragossa that opposition was offered to the establishment of the new Tribunal. In every part of Aragon and of Valencia; at Lerida, at Teruel, at Barcelona, the people rose against this new exhibition of royal and priestly tyranny. And it was not for fully two years, and after the adoption of the most savage measures of repression both royal and ecclesiastical, that the Inquisition was finally accepted in the kingdom of Aragon, and that Torquemada, fortified by no less than two special Bulls, made his triumphal entry as Inquisitor-general into Barcelona on the 27th of October, 1488.

Among all the tens of thousands of innocent persons who were tortured and done to death by the Inquisition in Spain, it is instructive to turn to the record of one man at least who broke through the meshes of the ecclesiastical net that was spread abroad in the country; for the mode of his escape is sufficiently instructive. Ready money at command, but not exposed to seizure, was the sole shield and safeguard against the assaults of Church and State. Don Alfonso de la Caballeria was a Jew by race, and a man who was actually concerned in the murder of the Inquisitor Arbues; but his great wealth enabled him to purchase not only one but two Briefs from Rome, and to secure the further favor of Ferdinand. He was accused and prosecuted in vain by the Holy Office of Aragon. He not only escaped with his life, but he rose to a high position in the State, and eventually mingled his Jewish and heretic blood with that of royalty itself.

Various attempts were made by the Commons of Aragon to abate the powers of the Inquisition; and at the Cortes of Monzon, in 1510, so vigorous a remonstrance was addressed to Ferdinand that he was unable to do more than avoid a decision, by a postponement on the ground of desiring fuller information; and two years later, at the same place, he was compelled to sanction a declaration or ordinance, by which the authority assumed by the Holy Office, in defiance of the Constitution of Aragon, was specifically declared to be illegal; and the king swore to abolish the privileges and jurisdiction of the Inquisition. Within a few months, however, he caused himself to be absolved from this oath by a Papal Brief; and the Inquisition remained unreformed and triumphant. But the Aragonese had not yet entirely lost their independence, and a popular rising compelled the king not only to renounce the Brief, so lately received, but to solicit from the Pope a Bull (May 12, 1515), exonerating him from so doing, and calling upon all men, lay and ecclesiastical, to maintain the authority of the Cortes. Aragon was satisfied. And the people enjoyed for a season the blessings of comparative immunity from persecution.

To recall the manifold horrors of the actual working of

the Inquisition in Spain would be a painful and an odious task. To record them in any detail is surely superfluous; even though they are entirely denied by such eminent modern writers as Hefele, in Germany, or Menendez Pelayo, in Spain. The hidden enemy, the secret denunciation, the sudden arrest, the unknown dungeon, the prolonged interrogatory, the hideous torture, the pitiless judge, the certain sentence, the cruel execution, the public display of sacerdotal vengeance, the plunder of the survivors, innocent even of ecclesiastical offense—all these things are known to every reader of every history. All other considerations apart, it is an abuse of language to speak of the proceedings before the Inquisition as a trial, for the tribunal was nothing but a Board of Conviction. One acquittal in two thousand accusations was, according to Llorente, who had access to all the records of the Holy Office in Spain, about the proportion that was observed in their judicial findings.

Statistics, as a rule, are not convincing, and figures are rarely impressive; yet it may be added that, according to Llorente's cautious estimate, over ten thousand persons were burned alive during the eighteen years of Torquemada's supremacy alone; that over six thousand more were burned in effigy either in their absence or after their death, and their property acquired by the Holy Office; while the number of those whose goods were confiscated, after undergoing less rigorous punishments, is variously computed at somewhat more or somewhat less than one hundred thousand. But it is obvious that even these terrible figures give but a very feeble idea of the vast sum of human suffering that followed the steps of this dreadful institution. For they tell no tale of the thousands who died, and the tens of thousands who suffered, in the torture chamber. They hardly suggest the anguish of the widow and the orphan of the principal victims, who were left, bereaved and plundered, to struggle with a hard and unsympathetic world, desolate, poor, and disgraced.

Nor does the most exaggerated presentment of human suffering tell of the disastrous effects of the entire system upon religion, upon morals, upon civil society at large. The terrorism, the espionage, the daily and hourly dread of denunciation, in which every honest man and woman must have lived, the boundless opportunities for extortion and for the gratification of private vengeance and worldly hatred, must have poisoned the whole social life of Spain. The work of the Inquisition, while it tended, no doubt, to make men orthodox, tended also to make them false, and suspicious, and cruel. Before the middle of the sixteenth century, the Holy Office had profoundly affected the national character; and the Spaniard, who had been celebrated in Europe during countless centuries for every manly virtue, became, in the new world that had been given to him, no less notorious for a cruelty beyond the imagination of a Roman emperor, and a rapacity beyond the dreams of a republican proconsul.

Torquemada and Ferdinand may have burned their thousands and plundered their ten thousands in Spain. Their disciples put to death millions of the gentlest races of the earth, and ravaged without scruple or pity the fairest and most fertile regions of the new Continent which had been given to them to possess.

As long as the Inquisition confined its operations to the

Jews and the Moors, the Old Christians were injured and depraved by the development of those tendencies to cruelty and rapacity that lie dormant in the heart of every man. But this was not the end. For when Spain at length sheltered no more aliens to be persecuted and plundered in the name of religion, and murder and extortion were forced to seek their easy prey in the new world beyond the Atlantic Ocean, the Holy Office turned its attention to domestic heresy; and the character of the Spaniard in Europe became still further demoralized and perverted. Every man was suspected. Every man became suspicious. The lightest word might lead to the heaviest accusation. The nation became somber and silent. Religious life was but a step removed from heresy. Religion died. Original thought was above all things dangerous. The Spaniard took refuge in Routine. Social intercourse was obviously full of peril. A prudent man kept himself to himself, and was glad to escape the observation of his neighbors. Castile became a spiritual desert. The Castilian wrapped himself in his cloak, and sought safety in dignified abstraction.

The Holy Office has done its work in Spain. A rapacious government, an enslaved people, a hollow religion, a corrupt Church, a century of blood, three centuries of shame, all these things followed in its wake. And the country of Viriatus and Seneca, of Trajan and Marcus Aurelius, where Ruy Diaz fought, and Alfonso studied, and where two warrior kings in two successive centuries defied Rome temporal and Rome spiritual, and all the crusaders of Europe—Spain, hardly conquered by Scipio or by Cæsar, was enslaved by the dead hand of Dominic.

CHAPTER VI

THEIR CATHOLIC MAJESTIES

THE BANISHMENT OF THE JEWS—INTERNATIONAL NEGOTIATIONS—THE SPANIARDS IN ITALY—THE VICTORIES OF GONSALVO—THE BEGINNING OF A NEW ERA

The fall of Granada left the Catholic sovereigns free to turn their attention more completely to the domestic affairs of the kingdom; and it seems moreover to have increased the bigotry both of the Church and of the Court, and to have added new zeal to the fury of the Inquisition.

The conquest of the Moorish kingdom was said by pious ecclesiastics to be a special sign or manifestation of the approval by Heaven of the recent institution of the Holy Office. The knights and nobles, proud of their military successes, may have attributed the victory to causes more flattering to their valor, their skill, and their perseverance. The common people, as yet not demoralized, but gorged with plunder, and invited to occupy without purchase the fairest province in the Peninsula, were little disposed to quarrel with the policy of Ferdinand; and far from feeling any pity for the sufferings of the vanquished Moors, they sighed for new infidels to pillage. And new infidels were promptly found.

The Inquisition so far had troubled itself but little with Christian heretics. The early Spanish Protestantism of the thirteenth century had died away. The later Spanish Prot-

VIEW OF CADIZ

Spain.

estantism of the sixteenth century had not yet come into existence. Few men had done more than Averroes of Cordova and Ramon Lull of Palma to awaken religious thought in Medieval Europe; yet speculative theology has never been popular among the Spanish people. It was against the Jews, renegade or relapsed, even more than the avowedly unconverted, that the Holy Office directed all its exertions until the end of the fifteenth century. By April, 1492, although a great number of the unfortunate Hebrews had already found their way to the Quemadero, there was still a very large Jewish population in Spain, the most industrious, the most intelligent, the most orderly, but, unhappily for themselves, the most wealthy of all the inhabitants of the Peninsula.

The Spanish Jews, as we have seen, were treated on the arrival of the Arab conquerors not only with consideration, but with an amount of favor that was not extended to them under any other government in the world; nor was this wise liberality, as time went on, displayed only by the Moslem in Spain. At the Christian courts of Leon, of Castile, and of Catalonia, the Jews were welcomed as lenders of money and as healers of diseases, and as men skilled in many industrial arts; and they supplied what little science was required in northern Spain, while their brethren shared in the magnificent culture and extended studies of Cordova. When the rule of the Arab declined, and Alfonso el Sabio held his court at southern Seville, the learned Jews were his chosen companions. They certainly assisted him in the preparation of his great astronomical tables. They probably assisted him in his translation of the Bible

Nor does this court favor appear to have caused any serious jealousy among Christian Spaniards. The fellow-student of Alfonso X., the trusted treasurer of Peter the Cruel, the accommodating banker of many a king and many a noble—the Jew was for some time a personage of importance rather than a refugee in the Peninsula. And during the whole of the thirteenth century, while the Jews were exposed throughout western Europe to the most dreadful and systematic persecutions, they enjoyed in Spain not only immunity, but protection, not only religious freedom, but political consideration.

Under Alfonso XI. they were particularly regarded, and even under Peter the Cruel, who, though he tortured and robbed his Hebrew treasurer, did not at any time display his natural ferocity in any form of religious persecution. Yet, as we are told that his rival and successor, Henry of Trastamara, sought popular favor by molesting the Jews, it would seem that already by the end of the fourteenth century they were becoming unpopular in Castile. But on the whole, throughout the Peninsula, from the time of James I. of Aragon, who is said to have studied ethics under a Jewish professor, to the time of John II. of Castile, who employed a Jewish secretary in the compilation of a national "Cancionero," or ballad book, the Jews were not only distinguished, but encouraged, in literature and abstract science, as they had always been in the more practical pursuits of medicine and of commerce.

But in less than a century after the death of Alfonso X. the tide of fortune had turned. Their riches increased overmuch in a disturbed and impoverished commonwealth, and public indignation began to be displayed, rather at their un-Christian opulence than at their Jewish faith. Inquisition was made rather into their strong-boxes than into their theology; and it was their debtors and their rivals, rather than any religious purists, who, toward the end of the fourteenth century, and more especially in Aragon, stirred up those popular risings against their race that led to the massacres and the wholesale conversions of 1391. The first attack that was made upon the persons and property of the Jews was in 1388, and it was no doubt provoked by the preaching of the fanatic archdeacon Hernando Martinez at Seville. But it was in nowise religious in its character, and was aimed chiefly at the acquisition and destruction of the property of the rich and prosperous Hebrews. The outbreaks which took place almost simultaneously in all parts of Spain were disapproved both by kings and councils. Special judges were sent to the disturbed cities, and a considerable amount of real protection was extended to the plundered people. No one said a word about conversion; or at least the conversion was that of ancient Pistol, the conversion of the property of the Jews into the possession of the Christians. When the Jewish quarter of Barcelona was sacked by the populace, and an immense number of Hebrews were despoiled and massacred throughout the country, John of Aragon, indolent though he was, used his utmost endeavors to check the slaughter. He punished the aggressors, and he even caused a restitution of goods to be made to such of the victims as survived.

The preaching of St. Vincent Ferrer, during the early part of the fifteenth century, was addressed largely to the Jews in Spain, but little or no religious persecution seems to have been directed against them in consequence of his harangues. On the contrary, we read of friendly conferences or public disputations between Jewish and Christian doctors in Aragon, where the Inquisition was, at least, nominally established. Such conferences could hardly be expected to convince or convert the advocates of either faith, but they tell at least of an amount of toleration on the part of the Christian authorities of the day that was certainly not to be found in Spain at the close of the century; and there is no doubt that they were followed by a very large number of conversions of the more malleable members of the Hebrew community. But it is a far cry from St. Vincent Ferrer to the uncanonized Tomas de Torquemada.

Yet, even in outward conformity to the established religion, the Jews, as time went on, found no permanent safety from persecution and plunder. John II. indeed had little of the bigot in his composition; it was Politics and not Persecution that, under his successor, engrossed the attention of clergy and laity in Castile; but, as soon as the power of Isabella was formally established, the destruction of all that was not orthodox, Catholic, and Spanish, became the key-note of the domestic policy of the new government of Spain.

The earliest efforts of the Spanish Inquisition were directed, as we have seen, almost exclusively against those converted Jews, or the sons and daughters of converts, who were known by the expressive name of New Christians, a title applied also to Christianized Moslems, and which distinguished both classes from the Old Christians or Cristianos Viejos, who could boast of a pure Castilian ancestry. These New Christians, as a whole, at the end of the fifteenth century, were among the richest, the most industrious, and the most intelligent of the population, and they were regarded with considerable envy by their poorer neighbors, whose blue blood did not always bring with it either wealth or fortune. The Rules and Regulations for the guidance of the Inquisitors were therefore specially framed to include every possible act or thought that might bring the members of the classes specially aimed at within the deadly category of the Relapsed. If the "New Christian" wore a clean shirt, or spread clean table-linen on a Saturday (Art. 4), if he ate meat in Lent (7), observed any of the Jewish fasts (8-17), or sat at table with any Jew of his acquaintance (19); if he recited one of the Psalms of David without the addition of the Doxology (20), if he caused his child to be baptized under a Hebrew name (23), he was to be treated as a renegade and condemned to the flames.

With every act of his life thus at the mercy of spies and informers, his last end was not unobserved by the Dominicans and the Familiars of the Holy Office. If in the article of death he turned his weary face (31) to the wall of his chamber, he was adjudged relapsed, and all his possessions were forfeit; or if the sorrowing children of even the most unexceptionable convert had washed his dead body with warm water (32) they were to be treated as apostates and heretics, and were at least liable to suffer death by fire, after their goods had been appropriated by the Holy Office or by the Crown.

In the sentences which condemned to the stake, to confiscation, and to penances which were punishments of the severest description, we find enumerated such offenses as the avoiding the use of fat, and especially of lard; preparing amive, a kind of broth much appreciated by the Jews; or eating "Passover bread"; reading, or even possessing, a Hebrew Bible; ignorance of the Pater noster and the Creed; saying that a good Jew could be saved, and a thousand other equally harmless deeds or words.

But with the professed and avowed Jew, unpopular as he may have been with his neighbors, and exposed at times to various forms of civil and religious outrage, the Holy Office did not directly concern itself. The Hebrew, like the Moslem, was outside the pale even of Christian inquiry.

There is no doubt that it was the success of the operations against the Moors of Granada that suggested to Ferdinand and Isabella the undertaking of a campaign, easier by far, and scarcely less lucrative, against the unhappy descendants of Abraham who had made their home in Spain.

The annual revenue that was derived by the Catholic sovereigns from the confiscations of the Inquisition amounted to a considerable income; and the source as yet showed no signs of drying up. Yet cupidity, marching hand in hand with intolerance—the Devil, as the Spanish proverb has it, ever lurking behind the Cross—the sovereigns resolved upon the perpetration of an act of State more dreadful than the most comprehensive of the Autos da Fe.

The work of the Holy Office was too slow. The limits of the Quemadero were too small. Half a million Jews yet lived unbaptized in Spain. They should be destroyed at a single blow. The Inquisition might be left to reckon with the New Christians whose conversion was unsatisfactory.

As soon as the Spanish Jews obtained an intimation of what was contemplated against them, they took steps to propitiate the sovereigns by the tender of a donative of thirty thousand ducats, toward defraying the expenses of the Moorish war; and an influential Jewish leader is said to have waited upon Ferdinand and Isabella, in their quarters at Sante Fe, to urge the acceptance of the bribe. The negotiations, however, were suddenly interrupted by Torquemada, who burst into the apartment where the sovereigns were giving audience to the Jewish deputy, and drawing forth a crucifix from beneath his mantle, held it up, exclaiming, "Judas Iscariot sold his master for thirty pieces of silver; Your Highnesses would sell him anew for thirty thousand; here he is, take him and barter him away." The extravagant presumption of the inquisitor-general would not perhaps have been as successful as it was, had it not been obvious to the rapacious Ferdinand that thirty thousand ducats was a trifle compared with the plunder of the entire body of Jews in Spain. Yet the action of Torquemada was no doubt calculated to affect the superstitious mind of Isabella, and even the colder spirit of Ferdinand.

Whatever may have been the scruples of the Spanish sovereigns, the fanaticism of the Spanish people had been at this critical juncture stirred up to an unusual pitch of fury by the proceedings and reports of the Holy Office in a case which has attracted an amount of attention so entirely disproportionate to its apparent importance that it merits something more than a passing notice.

In June, 1490, a converted Jew of the name of Benito Garcia, on his way back from a pilgrimage to Compostella, was waylaid and robbed near Astorga, by some of the Christian inhabitants. A Jew, converted or otherwise, was a legitimate object of plunder. The contents of his knapsack not being entirely satisfactory, and the ecclesiastical authorities sniffing sacrilege in what was supposed to be a piece of the consecrated wafer, Garcia, and not the robbers, was arrested, subjected to incredible tortures, and finally handed over to the local inquisitors.

His case was heard with that of other Conversos; first at Segovia and afterward at Avila. Tortures were repeated. Spies were introduced in various guises and disguises, but no confession could be extorted.

At length, after a year and a half of such practices, the endurance of one of the accused gave way—the dreadful story affords some slight notion of the methods of the Inquisition—and the unhappy man invented a tale in accordance with what was demanded of him; the crucifixion of a Christian child; the tearing out of his heart, the theft of the Host from a Christian Church, and a magical incantation over the dreadful elements, directed against Christianity, and more particularly against the Holy Office. The Tribunal having been thus satisfied of the guilt of the accused, a solemn Auto da Fe was held at Avila, on the 16th of November, 1491, when two of the convicts were torn to death with red-hot pincers; three who had been more mercifully permitted to die under the preliminary tortures were burned in effigy; while the remaining prisoners were visited only with the slight punishment of strangulation before their consignment to the inevitable fire. That no boy, with or without a heart, could be found or invented, by the most rigorous examination; that no Christian child had disappeared from the neighborhood of the unhappy Jews at the time of their arrest—this surprised no one. In matters of Faith such evidences were wholly superfluous. Secura judicat Ecclesia.

That these poor Hebrews should have suffered torture and death for an imaginary sacrilege upon the person of an imaginary boy, was indeed a thing by no means unexampled in the history of religious fanaticism. But the sequel is certainly extraordinary. With a view of exciting the indignation of the sovereigns and of the people against the Jews at an important moment, Torquemada devoted much attention to the publication throughout Spain of the dreadful story of the murdered boy, the Niño of La Guardia, the village where the crime is supposed to have taken place. As to the name of the victim, the authorities did not agree. Some maintained that it was Christopher, while others declared for John. But the recital of the awful wickedness of the Jews lost none of its force by adverse criticism. The legend spread from altar to altar throughout the country. The Nuno de la Guardia at once became a popular hero, in course of time, a popular saint; miracles were freely worked upon the spot where his remains had not been found, and something over a century later (1613) his canonization was demanded at Rome.

His remains, it was asserted by Francisco de Quevedo, could not be found on earth, only because his body as well as his soul had been miraculously carried up to heaven, where it was the most powerful advocate and protector of the Spanish monarchy. The story, moreover, has been twice dramatized—once by Lope de Vega—and no less than three admiring biographies of this imaginary martyr have been published in Spain within the last forty years of this nineteenth century.

At length from conquered Granada, on the 30th of March, 1492, the dreadful edict went forth. By the 30th of July not a Jew was to be left alive in Spain. Sisenand, indeed, nine hundred years before, had promulgated such an edict. But the Visigoth had been too tender-hearted to enforce it. Isabella, whose gentleness and goodness historians are never tired of applauding, was influenced by no such considerations, and the sentence was carried out to the letter. With a cruel irony, the banished people were permitted to sell their property, yet forbidden to carry the money out of the kingdom, a provision which has obtained the warm approval of more than one modern Spanish historian, by whom it is accepted as a conclusive proof that this wholesale depopulation did not and could not diminish the wealth of Spain!

Thus two hundred thousand Spaniards, men, women, and children of tender years, rich and poor, men of refinement and of position, ladies reared in luxury, the aged, the sick, the infirm, all were included in one common destruction, and were driven, stripped of everything, from their peaceful homes, to die on their way to some less savage country. For the sentence was carried out with the most relentless ferocity. Every road to the coast, we read, was thronged with the unhappy fugitives, struggling to carry off some shred of their ruined homes. To succor them was death; to pillage them was piety. At every seaport, rapacious shipmasters exacted from the defenseless travelers the greater part of their remaining possessions, as the price of a passage to some neighboring coast; and in many cases the passenger was tossed overboard ere the voyage was completed, and his goods confiscated to the crew. A rumor having got abroad that the fugitives were in the habit of swallowing jewels and gold pieces in order to evade the royal decree, thousands of unhappy beings were ripped up by the greedy knife of the enemy, on land or sea, on the chance of discovering in their mutilated remains some little store of treasure.

And thus, north, south, east, and west, the Jews straggled and struggled over Spain; and undeterred by the manifold terrors of the sea, a vast multitude of exiles, whose homes in Spain once lay in sunny Andalusia, sought and found an uncertain abiding place in neighboring Africa.

Of all Christian countries, it was in neighboring Portugal that the greatest number of the exiles found refuge and shelter; until, after five brief years of peace and comparative prosperity, the heavy hand of Castilian intolerance once more descended upon them, and they were driven out of the country, at the bidding of Isabella and her too dutiful daughter, the hope of Portugal and of Castile.

But to every country in Europe the footsteps of some of the sufferers were directed. Not a few were permitted to abide in Italy and Southern France; some of the most distinguished found a haven in England; many were fortunate enough to reach the Ottoman dominions, where, under the tolerant government of the Turk, they lived and prospered, and where their descendants, at many of the more important seaports of the Levant, are still found to speak the Castilian of their forefathers.

That the edict of banishment was meant to be, as it so constantly was, a doom of death, and not merely a removal of heretics, is clear from the action of the Spanish sovereigns, who, at the instigation of Torquemada, procured from the pliant Innocent VIII. a Bull enjoining the authorities of every country in Christian Europe to arrest and send back to Spain all *fugitive* Jews under penalty of the Greater Excommunication.

More than once, indeed, the demand for extradition was made. But save in the case of the Portuguese Jews, on the second marriage of the Princess Isabella to the reigning sovereign of that country, no foreign prince appears to have paid any heed to this savage edict. Nor was it, as a rule, of any material advantage, either at Rome or at Seville, that it should be put in force.

Avarice was perhaps the besetting sin of Rome in the fifteenth century; nor was bigotry unknown throughout western Europe. But in Spain, as the century drew to a close, avarice and bigotry joined hand in hand, and flourished under royal and noble patronage, preached by religion, practiced by policy, and applauded by patriotism. It was not strange that, under such teaching, the people of Castile should have rapidly become demoralized, and that the great race should have begun to develop that sordid and self-satisfied savagery which disgraced the name of the Spaniard, in the heartless and short-sighted plunder of the new world that lay before him.

Yet in all human affairs there is something that too often escapes our observation, to explain, if not to excuse, what may seem the most dreadful aberrations of the better nature of man. And it may be that the uncompromising religious spirit, which has had so enormous an influence for evil and for good upon the Spanish people, is to some extent the result of their Semitic environment of eight hundred years.

Religious controversy indeed, between rival branches of the Christian Church in the days of the Visigoths, developed religious animosities before the first Moslem landed at Tarifa; yet the Arab and the Moor, fired with the enthusiasm of a new and living faith, brought into their daily life in Spain, in peace and in war, a deep and all-pervading religious spirit—an active recognition of the constant presence of one true God—unknown to the Roman or the Visigoth, which must have had an enormous influence upon the grave and serious Spaniards who lived under the rule of the Arab.

Nor was the Moslem the only factor in this medieval development. In no other country in Europe was the Jew, as we have seen, more largely represented, and more powerful, for the first fifteen centuries of our era, than in Spain, whether under Christian or Moslem masters. But the direct and simple monotheism of the Hebrew and the Arab, while it had so great a direct influence upon Spanish Christianity, provoked as part of the natural antagonism to the methods of the rival and the enemy, the counter development of an excessive Hagiolatry, Mariolatry, and Sacerdotalism.

It would be strange enough if the religious fervor which doomed to death and torment so many tens of thousands of Semites in Spain should be itself of Semitic suggestion. It is hardly less strange that the Greek Renaissance, which revolutionized the Christian world, and whose anti-Semitic influence to the present day is nowhere more marked than in every department of religious thought, should by the irony of fate have been forestalled by a writer, at once Spanish and Semitic; and when, by the sixteenth century, the rest of modern Europe had been led by the teaching of Averroes to accept the philosophy of Aristotle, Spain, the earliest home of Hellenism, new born in Europe, had already turned again to a religious Philistinism or Phariseeism of the hardest and most uncompromising type, Semitic in its thoroughness, Greek only in its elaborate accessories, and Spanish in its uncompromising vigor.

Thus it was that the Arab and the Jew, parents, in some sense, of the religious spirit of Ximenez and of Torquemada, became themselves the objects of persecution more bitter than is to be found in the annals of any other European nation. The rigors of the Spanish Inquisition, and the policy that inspired and justified it, are not to be fully explained by the rapacity of Ferdinand, the bigotry of Isabella, the ambition of Ximenez, or the cruelty of Torquemada. They were in a manner the rebellion or outbreak of the old Semitic spirit against the Semite, the ignorant jealousy of the wayward disciple against the master whose teaching has been but imperfectly and unintelligently assimilated—perverted, distorted, and depraved by the human or devilish element which is to be found in all religions, and which seems ever striving to destroy the better, and to develop the worser part of the spiritual nature of man.

We now enter upon a period of European history which is but feebly characterized by the term interesting, and which has been too accurately chronicled and too severely investigated to be called romantic; when a well-founded jealousy, or fear of the growing power of France, alone supplies the key to the ever-changing foreign policy of the sovereigns of Spain. Genuine State papers of the fifteenth century are by no means numerous. In such of them, however, as are still extant, we find the fear expressed over and over again that the kings of France would render themselves "masters of the world," would "establish a universal empire," or "subject the whole of Christendom to their dictation." The best means to avert such a danger appeared to contemporary statesmen to be the foundation of another European State as a counterpoise. Ferdinand the Catholic, ambitious, diplomatic, and capable, was the first prince who undertook the enterprise.

Within less than three years after the Inquisition had been established at Seville, Louis XI. of France, the old rival and colleague of John II. of Aragon, had died in Paris, August 30, 1483. He was succeeded by his son Charles VIII., a young prince whose ignorance was only equaled by his vanity, and was if possible exceeded by his presumption. With such an antagonist, Ferdinand of Aragon was well fitted to deal, with advantage to himself and to Spain. To win over the Duchess of Bourbon, who had virtually succeeded to the government of France on the death of Louis XI., and to marry his eldest daughter Isabella to the young King Charles VIII., were accordingly the first objects of his negotiations. But in spite of all the flattery lavished on the duchess, Ferdinand did not succeed in obtaining the crown for the Infanta. A more richly dowered bride was destined for the King of France, to whom the acquisition of the province of Brittany was of far greater importance than the doubtful friendship of Spain; and after much public and private negotiation, the Spanish embassador was reluctantly withdrawn from Paris in the summer of 1487 (29th of July).

Disappointed in his dealing with the court of France, the ever-watchful and persistent Ferdinand turned his eyes to England; and in the last days of the year 1487 an embassador from the Spanish sovereigns, Roderigo de Puebla, doctor of canon and civil law, arrived at the court of London. Henry VII., who greatly desired to establish a closer alliance with Spain, succeeded in flattering the new envoy, and rendering him almost from the first subservient to his personal interests. Yet the King of England and the Spanish embassador together were no match for Ferdinand of Aragon. The negotiations between the sovereigns were prolonged for two years, and in the end Henry was worsted at every point. He had signed a treaty of offensive alliance with Spain against France, with which power he wisely desired to maintain friendly relations, and he had been prevailed upon to send some English troops into Brittany to co-operate with a Spanish contingent which never arrived, in the expulsion of the French from that country. He had concluded further treaties of friendship and alliance with the King of the Romans, who was actually encouraging Perkin Warbeck to assert his claim to the crown of England, and with the Archduke Philip, whom he personally and independently hated. And he had been forced to content himself with the promise of a very modest dowry with the Spanish princess who was affianced to his son Arthur, Prince of Wales.

Relatively too, as well as positively, he had been falsely borne in hand. Maximilian, who had been no less ready than Henry with his promises to Ferdinand, did not send a single soldier into Brittany, but endeavored to overreach Henry, Charles, and Ferdinand by a hasty marriage—by proxy—with the young duchess, without the consent or knowledge of either England or Spain. Yet this diplomatic victory over the very astute Englishman did not satisfy Ferdinand and Isabella, who, fearful lest they should "become the victims of their honesty" if they permitted Maximilian to surpass them in political perfidy, immediately renewed secret negotiations with France, and declared themselves ready to abandon the king, the duchess, and the emperor. Charles, they promised, should obtain what he wished, without risking the life of a single soldier, if only he would marry a Spanish Infanta. And they offered him, not Isabella, their eldest born, but their second daughter, Joanna.

Charles, however, had other views, and finding no cohesion or certainty in Ferdinand's league against him, strengthened his cause and his kingdom by marrying the Duchess Anne of Brittany himself, and uniting her hereditary dominions forever to the crown of France, a fair stroke of policy for a foolish sovereign in the midst of crafty and unscrupulous adversaries. (December 13, 1491.)

Ferdinand replied by calling on Henry VII. to fulfill his engagements and invade France. Henry accordingly, on the 1st of October, 1492, landed an army at Calais, and marched on Boulogne; while Ferdinand, without striking a blow either for Spain or for England, took advantage of the English expedition to extort from the fears and folly of Charles VIII. the favorable conditions of peace and alliance that were embodied in the celebrated Convention which was signed at Barcelona on the 19th of January, 1493. By this instrument it was provided that each of the high contracting parties should mutually aid each other against all enemies, the Vicar of Christ alone excepted, that the Spanish sovereigns should not enter into an alliance with any other power, to the prejudice of the interests of France, and finally, that the coveted provinces of Roussillon and Cerdagne, whose recovery had long been one of the chief objects of Ferdinand's ambition, should be immediately handed over to Spain.

The services of England being no longer needed by the peninsular sovereigns, Ferdinand abruptly broke off all further negotiations with Henry VII.; the signatures of Ferdinand and Isabella to the treaty which had already been ratified were disposed of by the simple but effective expedient of cutting them out of the parchment with a pair of scissors; and the contract of marriage between Arthur, Prince of Wales, and the Infanta Catharine having served its immediate diplomatic purpose — was removed, for the time being,* from the sphere of practical politics.

It is sufficiently characteristic of both parties, that in the treaty of Barcelona, between Charles and Ferdinand, Naples, the true objective of the young king of France, was not even mentioned. Ferdinand, well content with the immediate advantages obtained by the treaty, was by no means imposed upon by such vain reticence, while Charles, pluming himself upon the success of his diplomacy in his treaties with England, with France, and with the empire, looked forward to establishing himself with-

---

* From January, 1493, till October, 1497.

out opposition on the throne of Naples, on his way to assume the Imperial purple at Constantinople.

The kingdom of Naples, on the death of Alfonso the Magnanimous of Aragon, had passed, we have already seen, to his illegitimate son Ferdinand, who proved to be a tyrant of the worst Italian type, worthless, contemptible and uninteresting. To expel this hated monarch, for whom not one of his Neapolitan subjects would have been found to strike a blow in anger, seemed but a chivalrous and agreeable pastime to the vain and ignorant youth who had succeeded Louis XI. upon the throne of France. His more experienced neighbors indeed smiled with some satisfaction at his presumption. Yet, strange to say, the judgment of the vain and ignorant youth was just; and the wise men, who ridiculed his statesmanship, and scoffed at his military ineptitude, were doomed to great and astounding disappointment.

Before the French preparations for the invasion of Italy were fairly completed, in the early spring of 1494, Ferdinand of Naples died, and was succeeded by his son Alfonso I., the cousin-german of Ferdinand of Aragon. This change of rulers altered in no way the wild schemes of Charles of France, nor, although the new king of Naples was far less odious than his father had been in his own dominions, did it make any important change in the condition of Italian politics. By the month of June, 1494, the French preparations were so far advanced that Charles judged it opportune to acquaint his Spanish allies with his designs on Naples, and to solicit their active co-operation in his undertaking.

That Ferdinand should, under any possible circumstances, have been found to spend the blood and treasure of Spain in assisting any neighbor, stranger, or ally, in any enterprise, without direct advantage to himself, was a supposition entirely extravagant. But that he should assist a feather-headed Frenchman to dispossess a son of Aragon of a kingdom from which his own ancestors had thrice driven a French pretender, and where, if any change were to be made in the sovereignty, his own rights of succession were far superior to the shadowy claims derived from the hated Angevins: this was a thing so grotesquely preposterous that it is hard to suppose that even Charles of France should have regarded it as being within the bounds of possibility. Ferdinand contented himself for the moment with expressions of astonishment and offers of good advice, while Charles pushed forward his preparations for the invasion of Italy. Don Alfonso de Silva, dispatched by the court of Spain as a special envoy, came up with the French army at Vienne, on the Rhone, toward the end of June, 1494. But he was instructed rather to seek, than to convey, intelligence of any sort; nor was it to be supposed that his grave remonstrances or his diplomatic warnings should have had much effect upon the movements of an army that was already on the march.

In August, 1494, thirty thousand men, hastily equipped, yet well provided with the new and dreadful weapon that was then first spoken of as a cannon, crossed the Alps, and prepared to fight their way to Naples. But no enemy appeared to oppose their progress. The various States of Italy, jealous of one another, if not actually at war, were unable or unwilling to combine against the invader; the roads were undefended; the troops fled; the citizens of the isolated cities opened their gates, one after the other, at the approach of the strange and foreign invader. The French army, in fine, after a leisurely promenade militaire through the heart of Italy, marched unopposed into Rome on the last day of the year 1494.

Ferdinand and Isabella had, in the first instance, offered no serious opposition to the French enterprise, which appeared to them to be completely impracticable; and they had awaited with diplomatic equanimity the apparently inevitable disaster, which, without the loss of a single Spanish soldier or the expenditure of a single maravedi, would at once have served all the purposes of Ferdinand, and permitted him to maintain his reputation for goodwill toward Charles, which might have been useful in future negotiations. The astonishing success of the French invasion took the Spanish sovereigns completely by surprise, and it became necessary for Ferdinand to adopt, without haste, but with prudent promptitude, a new policy at once toward France and toward the various parties in Italy.

The boldest and the most capable of all the sovereigns of Italy, in these trying times, was the Spanish Pontiff, who by a singular fate has been made, as it were, the whipping boy for the wickedness of nineteen centuries of popes at Rome, and who is known to every schoolboy and every scribbler as the infamous Alexander VI. Roderic Lenzuoli, or Llançol, was the son of a wealthy Valencian gentleman, by Juana, a sister of the more distinguished Alfonso Borja, bishop of his native city of Valencia.

Born at Valencia about 1431, Roderic gave evidence from his earliest years of a remarkable strength of character, and of uncommon intellectual powers. While still a youth, he won fame and fortune as an advocate. But his impatient nature chafed at the moderate restraint of a lawyer's gown; and he was on the point of adopting a military career, when the election of his uncle to the Supreme Pontificate as Calixtus III. in 1455 opened for him the way to a more glorious future. At the instance of the new Pope, Roderic adopted his mother's name, in the Italian form already so well known and distinguished at the court of Rome, and taking with him his beautiful mistress, Rosa Vanozza, whose mother he had formerly seduced, he turned his back upon his native Valencia, and sought the fortune that awaited him at the capital of the world.

Unusually handsome in his person, vigorous in mind and body, masterful, clever, eloquent, unscrupulous, absolutely regardless of all laws, human or divine, in the gratification of his passions and the accomplishment of his designs, Roderic, the Pope's nephew, was a man made for success in the society in which he was to find himself at Rome. On his arrival at the Papal court in 1456 he was received with great kindness by his uncle, and was soon created Archbishop of Valencia, Cardinal of St. Nicholas *in Carcere Tulliano*, and Vice-Chancellor of the Holy Roman Church. On the death of Calixtus, in 1458, the Cardinal Roderic Borgia sank into comparative insignificance; and during the reigns of Pius II., Paul II., Sixtus IV. and Innocent VIII. we hear little of him but that he was distinguished for his amours, for his liberality in the disposal of his fortune, and for his attention to public business. Having thus secured the goodwill of many of the cardinals and the affection of the Roman people, he had no difficulty, on the death of Innocent VIII. in July, 1492, in making a bargain with a majority of the members of the Sacred College, in accordance with which he was elected Pope, and took the title of Alexander VI. on the 26th of August, 1492.

His election was received by the Roman people with the utmost satisfaction, and celebrated with all possible demonstrations of joy. His transcendent abilities and his reckless methods could not fail to render him obnoxious to his companions and his rivals in Italy; but it is due rather to his foreign origin, his Valencian independence of character, and above all his insolent avoidance of hypocrisy in the affairs of his private life, that he has been made a kind of ecclesiastical and Papal scapegoat, a Churchman upon whose enormous vices Protestant controversialists are never tired of dilating, and whose private wickedness is ingenuously admitted by Catholic apologists as valuable for the purposes of casuistic illustration, as the one instance of a divinely infallible judge whose human nature yet remained mysteriously impure, and whose personal or individual actions may be admitted to have been objectively blamable.

To measure the relative depths of human infamy is an impossible as well as an ungrateful task. It is not given to mortals to know the secrets of the heart. But bad as Alexander undoubtedly was, he was possibly no worse than many of his contemporaries in the Consistory, less wicked than some of his predecessors at the Vatican. The guilt of greater and more vigorous natures passes for superlative infamy with the crowd; but when dispassionately compared with that of his immediate predecessors, Sixtus IV. and Innocent VIII., the character of Alexander VI. is in almost every respect less flagitious and more admirable.

So unblushing was the venality of the Holy See in the

fourteenth century that sacred dialecticians and jurists of high authority were found seriously to argue that the Pope was not subjectively capable of committing the offense of Simony. It might have been contended with equal justice that in every other respect he was at once above, or without, the scope of the entire moral law. Nor can it be said that the fifteenth century brought any serious amendment.

From the death of Benedict XI., in 1303, to the death of Alexander VI., in 1503, the night was dark before the inevitable dawn; and in every phase of human depravity, in every development of human turpitude, in arrogance, in venality, in cruelty, in licentiousness, medieval Popes may be found pre-eminent among contemporary potentates. Thus, if the wickedness of Alexander was extravagant, it was by no means unparalleled, even among the Popes of a single century. His cruelty was no greater than that of Urban VI., or of Clement VII., or of John XXII. His immorality was, at least, more human than that of Paul II. and of Sixtus IV., nor were his amours more scandalous than those of Innocent VIII. His sacrilege was less dreadful than that of Sixtus IV. His covetousness could hardly have exceeded that of Boniface IX.; his arrogance was less offensive than that of Boniface VIII. If he was unduly subservient to Ferdinand and Isabella in his toleration of the enormities of Torquemada, his necessities as an Italian sovereign rendered the Spanish alliance a matter of capital importance. As a civil potentate and as a politician, he was not only wiser, but far less corrupt than Sforza, less rapacious than Ferdinand, more constant than Maximilian of Germany, less reckless than Charles of France. His administrative ability, his financial enlightenment, his energy as regards public works, were no less remarkable than his personal liberality, his affability, and his courage. His division of the New World by a stroke of the pen was an assumption of imperial power which was at least justified by the magnitude of its success. As he sat in his palace on the Mons Vaticanus, he was the successor, not of Caligula, but of Tiberius—not of Commodus, but of Diocletian.

Of the misfortunes of his eldest son, created by Ferdinand Duke of Gandia; of the wickedness of his second son, the fifteenth century Cæsar, who succeeded his father as Cardinal Archbishop of Valencia; of the profligacy of his daughter, so unhappily named Lucretia; of the marriage of his youngest son Geoffrey to a daughter of Alfonso of Naples, as a part of the treaty of alliance between the kingdom of the Two Sicilies and the States of the Church, in 1494; of the alliance between Alexander and Bajazet, and the poisoning of the Sultan's brother, Zem, after thirteen years' captivity, on receipt of an appropriate fee; of the elevation of a facile envoy to the full rank of Cardinal, to please the Grand Turk; of all these things nothing need be said in this place.

We are more immediately concerned to know that on New Year's Day, 1495, Pope Alexander VI., a refugee, if not actually a prisoner, in the Castle of St. Angelo, was fain to accept the terms that were imposed upon him by the victorious Frenchmen—masters for the nonce of Italy, and of Rome.

As Charles VIII. was marching through Italy, and was approaching, all unopposed, the sacred city of Rome, Alexander VI., anxious at all hazards to obtain the assistance

of his countrymen in the hour of danger, had sent an
envoy to the Spanish court representing the critical state
of affairs in Italy, assuring the king and queen of his
constant good will, in spite of certain disputes as to the
Papal authority in Spain, and conveying to them, with
other less substantial favors, the grant of the Tercias, or
two-ninths of the tithes throughout all the dominions of
Castile, an impost which, until the middle of the present
century, formed a part of the revenues of the Spanish
monarchy. He also conceded to the Spanish crown the
right of dominion over the whole of northern Africa, except Fez, which had been given to the King of Portugal.

A projected marriage between the Duke of Calabria,
eldest son of the King of Naples, and the Infanta Maria,
daughter of Ferdinand and Isabella, served to give the
King of Spain an opportunity for negotiating with the
Neapolitan court; and Ferdinand at the same time dispatched the celebrated Garcilaso de la Vega as his embassador, with instructions to return the most comforting
assurances to the Pope at Rome. Yet he refrained from
making any definite promises, or from committing himself
to any definite policy. He was not a man to do anything
rashly; and he preferred to await the course of events.
Meanwhile, having sent a second mission from Guadalajara to the French court or camp, with good advice for
his young friend and ally Charles VIII., Ferdinand betook
himself with Isabella to Madrid, where the Spanish sovereigns devoted themselves to the preparation and equipment of an army to be dispatched at an opportune moment
to any part of Italy where subsequent events might render its presence necessary. As, for various reasons, it was

impossible that either Ferdinand or Isabella should accompany their army abroad, it became necessary to select a general. Among all the skillful leaders and gallant knights who had signalized themselves in the wars of Granada, it was somewhat difficult to decide upon a commander. But Isabella had never lost sight of Gonsalvo de Cordova, in whom she discerned traces of rare military talent; and from the moment the Sicilian expedition was planned she determined that he should be captain-general of the royal forces. The greater experience and apparently superior claims of many who had distinguished themselves in battle against the Moors were urged by Ferdinand without avail. The command was given to Gonsalvo de Cordova.

But while the Spanish fleet, under the gallant Count of Trivento, was riding at anchor at Alicante, and Gonsalvo was preparing to embark his army on board the ships in that harbor, the Spanish sovereigns dispatched a final embassy to Charles in Italy. On the 28th of January, 1495, as the king was leaving Rome on his way toward Naples, the embassadors, Juan de Albion and Antonio de Fonseca, arrived at the Vatican. They found Pope Alexander smarting under the humiliation of his recent treaty with the invader, and willing to assist them in any scheme for his discomfiture. They accordingly followed the French army with all speed, overtook it within a few miles of Rome, and immediately demanded an audience of Charles, even before his troops had come to a halt. They delivered up to him their credentials as he was riding along, and peremptorily required him to proceed no further toward Naples. The haughty tone of the Spaniards, as may be supposed, excited the greatest indignation in the breast of

Charles and those who surrounded him; high words arose on both sides, and finally Fonseca, giving way to a simulated transport of rage, produced a copy of the once prized treaty of Barcelona, tore it to pieces, and threw down the fragments at Charles's feet. Paul Jove seems to think that this violent and unjustifiable conduct on the part of the Spanish embassador was entirely unpremeditated; but it is certain that the whole scene had been preconcerted with either Ferdinand or the Pope. Zurita and the other chroniclers are silent on the point, but Peter Martyr in one of his letters affirms that the mutilation of the treaty in Charles's presence was included in the secret instructions given to Fonseca by Ferdinand.

The envoys, as was expected, were promptly ordered to quit the French camp; and retiring with all speed to Rome, they hastened to transmit to Spain the earliest intelligence of the success of their mission. They were also permitted to inform their sovereigns of the new honor that had been conferred upon them by his Holiness Alexander VI., in the shape of the grant to them and to their heirs forever on the throne of Spain of the title of "Catholic Kings."

Meanwhile Charles VIII. had reached Naples, which had at once opened its gates to the invaders, and the Castel Nuovo and the Castel d'Uovo were reduced to submission by their well served artillery. King Alfonso abdicated the crown, and Fabricio Colonna ravaged the whole kingdom of Naples to the very gates of Brindisi, dispersing the little band of troops that had been collected by Don Cæsar of Aragon, illegitimate brother of the king; while Perron dei Baschi and Stuart D'Aubigny overran the whole country almost without striking a blow; and the greater part of the Neapolitan nobility gave their adhesion to the French. Nothing, however, could be more impolitic or more ungrateful than the manner in which Charles made use of his unexpectedly acquired authority, and it soon became evident that the new state of affairs in Naples would not be of very long duration. The moment for the judicious interference of Ferdinand of Aragon had not been long in arriving.

The conduct of the French at Naples showed pretty clearly to the Italian States the mistake they had made in permitting Charles to enter the country, and they were not slow to accept the suggestions of the Spanish embassador, Don Lorenzo Suarez de Mendoza y Figueras, that they should form a league with the object of expelling the French from Italy. The attitude of the Duke of Orleans, who had remained at Asti, toward the duchy of Milan, and the favorable reception accorded by Charles to Giovanni Trivulzio, Cardinal Fregosi, and Hybletto dei Fieschi, the chiefs of the banished nobles, and the sworn enemies of Ludivico Sforza, showed that prince how little he had to expect from the French alliance; and the conduct of Charles toward the Florentines, and indeed toward every government whose dominion he had traversed throughout Italy, terrified and enraged every statesman from Milan to Syracuse.

The envoys of the various states assembled at Venice. The deliberations in the council chamber were brief and decisive; and such was the secrecy with which the negotiations were conducted that the astute statesman and historian Philip de Commines, who then represented France at the court of Venice, remained ignorant that any league or convention was even contemplated by the various powers, until he was informed by the Doge Agostino Barberigo, on the morning of the 1st of April, 1495, that the treaty had been signed on the previous day. The avowed objects of this Most Holy League, which was entered into by Spain, Austria, Venice, Milan and the Court of Rome, were the recovery of Constantinople from the Turks, and the protection of the interests of the Church; but the secret articles of the treaty, as may be supposed, went much further, and provided that Ferdinand should employ the Spanish armament, now on its way to Sicily, in re-establishing his kinsman on the throne of Naples; that a Venetian fleet of forty galleys should attack the French positions on the Neapolitan coasts, that the Duke of Milan, the original summoner, should expel the French from Asti, and blockade the passage of the Alps, so as to prevent the arrival of further re-enforcements, and that the Emperor and the King of Spain should invade France on their respective frontiers, while the expense of all these warlike operations should be defrayed by subsidies from the allies. The Sultan Bajazet II., though not included in the League, offered, and was permitted, to assist the Venetians both by sea and land against the French. Thus we see the strange spectacle of the Pope and the Grand Turk—the Prince of Christendom and the Prince of Islam—united against the first Christian Power of Europe, under the leadership of The Most Christian King.

Within six weeks of the signature of this important treaty, Charles VIII. of France had caused himself to be crowned at Naples, with extraordinary pomp, not only as king, but as emperor; and, having thus gratified his puerile vanity, he abandoned his fantastic empire, and flying from the dangers that threatened him in Italy he returned to Paris. His army in Naples was intrusted to his cousin, Gilbert de Bourbon, duc de Montpensier, who was invested with the title of viceroy, and instructed by the fugitive king to maintain his position in the country against all opponents.

It is not within the scope of this history to give any detailed account of the retreat of the French through Italy, of the wonderful passage of the Apennines at Pontremoli, and the still more wonderful victory of Fornovo on the Taro, when the French, whose entire force did not exceed ten thousand soldiers, completely routed the Italian army of thirty-five thousand men, under the command of Gonzago, marquis of Mantua. The French forces that remained in southern Italy were doomed to a very different fate. The command of the French army had been intrusted to the celebrated Stuart d'Aubigny, a knight of Scottish ancestry, who had been invested by Charles VIII. with the dignity of Constable of France, and who was accounted one of the most capable officers in Europe. But a greater captain than d'Aubigny was already on his way from Castile, who was in a single campaign to restore the reputation of the Spanish infantry to the proud position which they had once occupied in the armies of ancient Rome.

Landing at Reggio in Calabria, on the 26th of May, 1495, with a force of all arms not exceeding five thousand fighting men, Gonsalvo de Cordova speedily possessed himself of that important base of operations, established himself on the coast, captured several inland towns, was victorious in many skirmishes, and would soon have overrun the whole of Calabria, had not the rashness of Ferdinand, the young king of Naples, who had succeeded but a few months before to the crown which Alfonso had abdicated after a reign of less than one year, led to a disastrous check at Seminara. But Gonsalvo rapidly reorganized his army, and showing himself, like a great general, no less admirable in repairing a defeat than in taking advantage of a victory, he had kept d'Aubigny so completely in check that he had been unable even to go to the assistance of Montpensier, who was in sore straits in Naples. The citizens soon opened their gates to their lawful sovereign, and Montpensier retreated with his remaining forces to Avella, on the banks of the Lagni, twenty miles northeast of the city of Naples, whither Gonsalvo promptly marched to besiege him. Having received intelligence in the course of his march—Gonsalvo was ever well informed—that a strong body of French, with some Angevin knights and nobles, were on their way to effect a junction with d'Aubigny, he surprised them by a night attack in the fortified town of Lino, where he captured every one of the Angevin lords, no less than twenty in number, and immediately marching off to Avella with his spoils and prisoners, and an immense booty, he arrived at Ferdinand's camp early in July, just thirteen months after their separation on the disastrous field of Seminara.

On hearing of Gonsalvo's approach, the king marched out to meet him, accompanied by Cæsar Borgia, the Papal Legate, and many of the principal Neapolitan nobles and commanders, who greeted the victorious Castilian with the proud title of "The Great Captain," by which he was already known to some of his contemporaries, and by which he has ever since been distinguished by posterity. At Avella he found a re-enforcement of five hundred Spanish soldiers, a welcome addition to his small force, which amounted on his arrival to only two thousand one hundred men, of whom six hundred were cavalry. With such an army, less numerous than a modern German regiment, did Gonsalvo overrun Calabria, out-general the most renowned French commanders, and defeat their gallant and well-disciplined forces, emboldened by uninterrupted success.

The siege operations at Avella, which had been conducted without energy by the Neapolitans, received a new impetus from the presence of the Spaniard, who displayed such skill and vigor that in a few days the French, defeated at every point, were glad to sue for terms, and on the 21st of July, 1496, signed a capitulation which virtually put an end to the war. It was meet that Gonsalvo should now pay a visit to his countryman at the Vatican, and having, on his way to Rome, delivered the town of Ostia from the dictatorship of a Basque adventurer of the name of Guerri, the last remaining hope of the French in Italy, he was received by Alexander VI. with such splendor that his entry into the city is said to have resembled rather the *triumph* of a victorious general into ancient Rome than the visit of a modern grandee.

The streets were lined with enthusiastic crowds, the windows were filled with admiring spectators, the very tops of the houses were covered with lookers-on, as Gonsalvo marched into and through the city, preceded by bands of music, and accompanied by his victorious army. The entire garrison of Ostia, with Manuel Guerri at their head, mounted on a wretched horse, was led captive to the Vatican, where Roderic Borgia, in the full splendor of his tiara and pontifical robes, and surrounded by his cardinals, sat on his throne awaiting the coming of his victorious countryman. When Gonsalvo reached the foot of the throne, he knelt down to receive the pontifical benediction, but Alexander raised him in his arms, and presented to him the Golden Rose, the highest and most distinguished honor that a layman could receive from the hands of the sovereign Pontiff.

The Great Captain now returned to Naples, into which city he made an entry scarcely less splendid than that into Rome; and he received at the hands of Frederic more substantial honors than those of a golden rose, in the shape of the dukedom of Santangelo, with a fief of two towns and seven dependent villages in the Abruzzo. From Naples the new duke sailed for Sicily, which was then in a state of open insurrection, in consequence of the oppressive rule of Giovanni di Nuccia, the Neapolitan viceroy. By the intervention of Gonsalvo, the inhabitants were satisfied to return to their allegiance; and order was restored, without the shedding of a single drop of blood. After some further services to the state, and to the cause of peace, services both diplomatic and military, in Naples, in Sicily and in Calabria, adding in every case to his reputation as a soldier and a statesman, and above all as a great Castilian gentleman, Gonsalvo returned to his native Spain, where he was received with the applause and respect that is not always granted to great men by their own sovereigns, or even by their own countrymen.

His last service to King Frederic and his people, ere he quitted the country, was no less honorable than wise. Frederic was engaged in the siege of the last city in the kingdom of Naples that refused to recognize the dominion of Aragon, the ancient and noble city of Diano, whose inhabitants, vassals of that Prince of Salerno who was attached to the Angevin cause, refused to listen to the terms which were proposed. Gonsalvo took charge of the operations; and the citizens, convinced of the hopelessness of holding out any longer against so vigorous a commander, surrendered a few days afterward at discretion. Gonsalvo, whether touched at their bravery and their forlorn condition, or merely being adverse from severity for which he saw no reason, obtained from the king favorable terms for the garrison.

The expulsion of the French from Naples put an end, as might have been supposed, to The Most Holy League. For the high contracting parties, finding themselves secure from immediate danger, conceived themselves no longer bound by its provisions. Maximilian, ever penniless and generally faithless, had made no attempt to engage in any operations on the French frontier, nor had any one of the allies contributed to defray the heavy charges incurred by the Spanish sovereigns in fulfilling their part of the agreement. The Venetians were rather occupied in securing for themselves as much of the Neapolitan territory as they could acquire, by way of indemnification for their own expenses. The Duke of Milan had already made a separate treaty with Charles VIII. Each member of the league, in fact, after the first alarm had subsided, had shown himself ready to sacrifice the common cause to his own private advantage; and Ferdinand of Aragon, who had already suspended his operations on the frontiers of Spain in October, 1496, had no difficulty in agreeing to a further truce as regarded Naples and Italy, which was signed on the 5th of March, 1497.

The Spaniards had borne the entire burden of the late war. They had been virtually abandoned by their allies, and their unassisted operations had led to the deliverance of Naples, to the safety of the Italian States, and the humiliation and the defeat of the French. Their immediate objects having been thus happily accomplished, Ferdinand and Isabella proposed to Charles VIII., without shame or hesitation, that the French and Spaniards should enter into an immediate treaty of alliance, with a view to drive out the reigning sovereign of Naples, and divide his kingdom between themselves! Meanwhile the Castilian envoy to the Holy See endeavored to induce Alexander VI. to withhold the investiture of his kingdom from Frederic, the new sovereign of Naples, on the ground that he was friendly to the Angevin party in Italy, the hereditary enemies of Spain. But Alexander paid no heed to Garcilaso de la Vega. Charles showed himself not only willing but eager to treat with Fernando de Estrada; but unwilling at once to abandon all his claims to Italian sovereignty, he offered to cede Navarre to Ferdinand, and keep all Naples to himself. Proposals and counter proposals thus passed between France and Spain; but before any definite programme had been agreed to, the negotiations were cut short by the sudden death of the French monarch, in the tennis court at Amboise, on the eve of Easter, 1498.

The success of the Spanish arms under Gonsalvo de Cordova in Italy was but the beginning of a long career of triumph. From the great victory at Seminara, in 1503, to the great defeat of Rocroy, in 1648, the Spanish infantry remained unconquered in Europe. The armies of Castile had been, indeed, as Prescott has it, "cooped up within the narrow limits of the Peninsula, uninstructed and taking little interest in the concerns of the rest of Europe." But the soldiers and sailors of Aragon and Catalonia had fought with distinction, not only in Italy and in Sicily, but in the furthest east of Europe, for two hundred years before the Great Captain of the United Kingdom set foot on the shores of Calabria. Yet the victories of Gonsalvo were the beginning of a new era, and his life is interesting, not only as that of a brave soldier and an accomplished general, who flourished at a very important period of the history of Europe; but it is further and much more interesting as being the history of a man who united in himself many of the characteristics of ancient and modern civilization, and who himself appears as a sort of middle term between medieval and modern times.

In personal valor, in knightly courtesy, in gaudy display, he was of his own time. In astute generalship, and in still more astute diplomacy, an envoy not an adventurer, the servant and not the rival of kings, he belongs to a succeeding age, when the leader of a victorious army is prouder to be a loyal subject than a rash rebel. The Castilian lords of earlier days had ever been brave knights; their followers had ever been hardy and untiring combatants. But Gonsalvo was not only a tactician, but a strategist. The men whom he commanded were soldiers. Newly armed and admirably disciplined, the regiments were no longer the followers of some powerful nobleman; they formed a part of the national army of Spain. The short sword of their Celtiberian ancestors was once more found in their hands. The long lances of the Swiss mercenaries were adopted with conspicuous success. The drill-sergeant took the place of the minstrel in the camp.

Nor was this revolution in the art of war confined to the conduct of the Spanish troops in the field. Before the close of the campaign a national militia, or rather a standing army, had taken the place of the brave but irregular levies of medieval Spain. A royal ordinance regulated the equipment of every individual, according to his property. A man's arms were declared free from seizure for debt, even by the Crown, and smiths and other artificers were restricted, under severe penalties, from working up weapons of war into articles of more pacific use. In 1426 a census was taken of all persons capable of bearing arms; and by an ordinance issued at Valladolid, on February 22d of the same year, it was provided that one out of every twelve inhabitants, between twenty and forty-five years of age, should be enlisted for the service of the State, whether in the conduct of a foreign war or the suppression of domestic disorder.

CHAPTER VII

UNITED SPAIN

THE DISCOVERY OF THE NEW WORLD—VASCO DA GAMA—
THE ROYAL MARRIAGES—DREAMS OF EMPIRE—THE
DEATH OF ISABELLA—FERDINAND'S END

The reign of Ferdinand and Isabella was made immemorial through Columbus and his discovery. The man and the event will, in subsequent chapters, be considered at length. For the present it will suffice to note that on his return from the New World, after being loaded with honors, a question arose as to Isabella's right to confer the dignities thus bestowed—Portugal claiming the territory by reason of an anterior grant from the Pope, who, in common with all other parties, believed it to be part of India.

The question was referred to a Junta of learned men of both nations, at the same time that application was made to the reigning Pope, Alexander VI., concerning it. The junta decided that the discoveries of Columbus were not included in the Portuguese grant; and his Holiness finally, as he conceived, terminated the dispute by drawing a line across the Altantic, from pole to pole, and adjudging all lands discovered on the east of that line to Portugal, all on the west to Castile.

In connection with this it should be noted that in 1497 Manuel of Portugal sent Vasco da Gama with three ships to double the Cape of Good Hope, with a view to tapping

India. In the month of November, Gama successfully doubled the formidable Cape, and sailed up the eastern coast of Africa, as far as Mozambique. Here he found a Moor from Fez, who, acting as interpreter between him and the natives, facilitated the conclusion of a treaty, in virtue of which the King of Mozambique was to furnish the adventurous navigators with pilots well acquainted with the course to India. But, while they were taking in wood and water, a quarrel arose with the natives, to whom the fault is of course imputed. The pilots made their escape, and hostilities ensued. They did not last long; the terrors of the Portuguese firearms soon compelling the Africans to submit. Another, and, as the king assured Gama, a better pilot was supplied, and on the 1st of April, 1498, he sailed from Mozambique. The new pilot proved quite as ill-disposed as his predecessors, endeavoring to betray the fleet into the power of his countrymen at Mombaza; and being alarmed with apprehensions of detection, by the bustle apparent in the crew of Gama's ship, which had accidentally grounded, he also made his escape. It was not till they reached Melinda that they found really friendly natives. From that port Gama at last obtained a pilot who steered him right across the gulf to the coast of Malabar.

The first place in India made by the Portuguese was Calecut. Here Gama announced himself as an embassador sent by the King of Portugal to negotiate a treaty of alliance with the sovereign, the zamorin of Calecut, one of the most powerful princes of that part of Hindustan, to establish commercial relations, and to convert the natives to Christianity. How far this last object of his mission was agreeable to the bigoted Hindus, or the equally bigoted

Mohammedan conquerors, who were then the masters of those wealthy regions, we are not distinctly told by the Portuguese historians; but the zamorin appears in the first instance to have received Gama well, and been upon the whole pleased with his visit. This friendly intercourse was interrupted, as we are assured, by the intrigues of the Moors or Arabs, who, being in possession of the pepper trade, and indeed of the whole spice trade, were jealous of interlopers. Quarrels arose, and some acts of violence were committed. They ended, however, in Gama's gaining the advantage, and friendship was restored between him and the zamorin. He reached Portugal in July, 1499, after a two years' voyage, and was, like Columbus in Spain, loaded with honors.

We may now return to Ferdinand and Isabella. This was the brightest period of their lives. The repulse of Charles VIII., and the victories of Gonsalvo, added fresh luster to their reign. Moreover, through measures then undertaken, the unconverted Moors were subdued, and the French provinces were regained; but, over and above all, a new world had been discovered, and marriages, seemingly the most fortunate, were concluded: Ferdinand and Isabella's son and heir, Don John, having married the daughter of the Emperor Maximilian; their second daughter Joanna, Philip, the son and heir of that monarch, by Mary of Burgundy, and already, in right of his deceased mother, sovereign of the rich and fertile Netherlands; the third, Katharine, was affianced to Arthur, Prince of Wales; and Manuel, duke of Beja, having succeeded to his cousin John II. of Portugal, despite all intrigues in favor of the illegitimate Don George, solicited and obtained the hand of the eldest Infanta, the widow of the Prince of Portugal.

The first to be celebrated of all these royal marriages was that of the Princess Isabella with Alfonso, the heir to the crown of Portugal, which took place in the autumn of the year 1490, and which was apparently calculated to lead to the happiest results. But the magnificent wedding festivities at Lisbon were scarce concluded when the bridegroom died, and the widowed princess returned disconsolate to her mother (January, 1491).

The marriage of John, prince of Asturias, was the next, and apparently the most important alliance that engaged the attention of his parents; and, moved by many considerations of policy and prestige, they turned their thoughts to far-away Flanders. Maximilian of Hapsburg, the titular sovereign of the Holy Roman Empire, had, by his first wife, Mary, a daughter of Charles the Bold, and in her own right Duchess of Burgundy, been made the father of two children, Philip, born in 1478, and Margaret, in 1480. Their mother, the beautiful empress, died in 1482; and Philip, on attaining his legal majority at the age of sixteen, assumed, in her right, the government of the Low Countries in 1494. It was with this youthful sovereign, the heir to yet more splendid possessions, that the Catholic sovereigns desired to unite their younger daughter in marriage, while the hand of his sister Margaret was sought for the Prince of Asturias. The advantages to Spain of such a double marriage were enormous.

If Prince John were to marry the Archduchess Margaret, the only daughter of the emperor, he would inherit, in the event of the death of the Archduke Philip without issue, the great possessions of the Hapsburgs, Austria, Flanders, and Burgundy, with a claim to the empire that had eluded his great ancestor, Alfonso X. That the Archduke Philip shobld in his turn espouse, not Isabella, the eldest, but Joanna, the second daughter of the Catholic king, would prevent Spain from passing under the dominion of Austria, even in the unlikely event of the death of Prince John without issue, inasmuch as Isabella of Portugal would, in such a case, inherit the Spanish crown, to the prejudice of her younger sister in Flanders. And finally, if all the young wives and husbands should live to a reasonable age, and should leave children behind them at their death, one grandson of Ferdinand and Isabella would wear the imperial purple as lord of Central Europe, and another would sit upon the throne of a great united Peninsular kingdom of Castile, Portugal, and Aragon.

In the early autumn of 1496 (August 22), a splendid fleet set out from Laredo, a little port between Bilbao and Santander, which carried Joanna in safety to her expectant bridegroom. The archduke, and the princess for whom so sad a fate was reserved, were married at Lille with the usual rejoicings; and the Spanish admiral, charged a second time with a precious freight of marriageable royalty, brought back the Lady Margaret of Hapsburg with all honor to Spanish Santander, early in March, 1497. The marriage of the heir apparent took place at Burgos, on the 3d of April; and on the 4th of October of the same year, the gentle and accomplished Prince of Asturias had passed away from Spain, and from the world.

Yet, once again, and for a few months, there lived an heir to United Spain, whose brief existence is scarce remembered in history. Isabella, the widowed queen of John II. of Portugal, had been persuaded or constrained by her parents to contract a second marriage with her husband's cousin and successor Emmanuel; but the price of her hand was the price of blood. For it was stipulated that the Jews, who, by the liberality of the late king, had been permitted to find a home in his dominions, should be driven out of the country after the stern Castilian fashion of 1492, ere the widowed Isabella should wed her cousin on the throne of Portugal. Whether the princess was an apt pupil, or merely the slave of her mother and the Inquisitor that lurked behind the throne, we cannot say, but the Portuguese lover consented to the odious bargain. The marriage was solemnized at Valencia de Alcantara, in the early days of the month of August, 1497, and the stipulated Tribute to Bigotry was duly paid. But before ever the bridal party had left the town, an express had arrived with the news of the mortal illness of the bride's only brother; and in little more than a year the young queen herself, in the 23d of August, 1498, expired in giving birth to a son. The boy received the name of Miguel, and lived for nearly two years—the heir apparent of Portugal, of Aragon, and of Castile—until he too was involved in the general destruction.

But some time before the death, or even before the birth of Miguel, another royal marriage had been concluded, whose results throughout all time were no less remarkable and scarce less important than that which handed over Spain to a Flemish emperor. For after infinite negotiations and more than one rupture, after some ten years' huxtering about dowry, and a dozen changes of policy on the part of the various sovereigns interested in the alliance, Katharine, the youngest daughter of Ferdinand and Isabella, more familiarly known as Katharine of Aragon, had been married to Arthur, Prince of Wales, and the first act had been concluded of that strange and fateful drama that led to the Reformation in England.

The dignified sadness of her story as Queen Katharine —insulted, divorced, and abandoned—the unwilling heroine of the great tragic drama that was played in the reign of Henry VIII. of England, is known to all men, who extend to her, with one consent, their pity and their respect. But those only who know something of the seven dreary and disgraceful years that she spent in the palace of her father-in-law, before she was permitted to know, even for a season, the happiness of a husband's love, or to enjoy the great position of Queen of England, may alone understand the fullness of the measure of her wretchedness.

In June, 1504, Isabella, who had for some time been ailing, and who seems to have suffered from some nervous disease, was struck down suddenly by fever. She had lived a hard life. She had never spared herself, or others. The unhappy marriages of her children had cast a dark shadow over her life. But hers was not the nature to repine. Diligent, abstemious, resolute, she had borne pain and suffering, and she was not afraid to face death. Unable at length to rise from her couch, as the autumn drew to a close, she continued to transact her accustomed business, gave audience to embassadors, chatted with privileged visitors, and, in the words of an astonished stranger, governed the world from her bed.

At last, on the 26th of November, 1504, as the church

bells of Medina del Campo were ringing out the hour of noon, the spirit of Isabella of Castile flitted away from this world; and her mortal remains were conducted by a mournful company to their last resting place under the shadow of the red towers of Alhambra. Through storm and tempest, amid earthquake and inundation, across mountain and river, the affrighted travelers wended their way. For the sun was not seen by day nor the stars by night, during three long and weary weeks, as if the very forces of nature were disturbed at the death of a giant among the princes of the earth.

The character of Isabella has suffered to an uncommon extent from an ignorant glorification of virtues that she was far from possessing, and the concealment of those transcendent powers that made her not only one of the greatest rulers of Spain, but one of the greatest women in the history of the world. Until the opening of the treasure-house at Simancas displayed her correspondence to the world, she was only known from the extravagant but somewhat colorless panegyrics of contemporary chroniclers, who recognized at least that she was a royal lady, compelling their gallant admiration, and that she was immensely superior to her husband, whom it was necessary also to glorify, as the last Spanish sovereign of Spain.

Isabella was one of the most remarkable characters in history. Not only was she the most masterful, and, from her own point of view, by far the most successful ruler that ever sat upon the throne of Spain, or of any of the kingdoms of the Peninsula; she stands in the front rank of the great sovereigns of Europe, and challenges comparison with the greatest women who have ever held sway in the world. A reformer and a zealot, an autocrat and a leader of men, with a handsome face and a gracious manner, scarce concealing the iron will that lay beneath, Isabella was patient in adversity, dignified in prosperity, at all times quiet, determined, thorough.

In one particular she stands alone among the great ruling women, the conquerors and empresses of history. She is the only royal lady, save, perhaps, Maria Theresa of Hungary, who maintained through life the incongruous relations of a masterful sovereign and a devoted wife, and shared not only her bed but her throne with a husband whom she respected—a fellow-sovereign whom she neither feared nor disregarded. To command the obedience of a proud and warlike people is given to few of the great men of history. To do the bidding of another with vigor and with discretion is a task that has been but rarely accomplished by a heaven-born minister. But to conceive and carry out great designs, with one hand in the grasp of even the most loyal of companions, is a triumphant combination of energy with discretion, of the finest tact with the most indomitable resolution, that stamps Isabella of Spain as a being more vigorous than the greatest men, more discreet than the greatest women of history. Semiramis, Zenobia, Boadicea, Elizabeth of England, Catherine of Russia, not one of them was embarrassed by a partner on the throne. The partner of Isabella was not only a husband but a king, jealous, restless, and untrustworthy. It is in this respect, and in the immense scope of her political action, that the great Queen of Castile is comparable with the bold Empress-King of

Hungary rather than with any other of the great queens and royal ladies of history.

The husband of Zenobia indeed enjoyed the title of Augustus; but it was only after his assassination that the lady earned her fame as a ruler. Catherine caused her imperial consort to be executed as a preliminary to her vigorous reign in Russia; Boadicea was the successor and not the colleague of Prasutagus; and Semiramis, though herself somewhat a mythical personage, is said to have slain both her husband and his rival, in her assertion of her absolute power. Yet Isabella revolutionized the institutions of her country, religious, political, military, financial, she consolidated her dominions, humiliated her nobles, cajoled her Commons, defied the Pope, reformed the clergy; she burned some ten thousand of her subjects; she deported a million more; and of the remnant she made a great nation; she brooked no man's opposition, in a reign of thirty years, and she died in the arms of the king, her husband!

Ferdinand of Aragon was no hero. But he was a strong man; a capable ruler; a clever if a treacherous diplomatist. And to this husband and consort was Isabella faithful through life, not merely in the grosser sense of the word, to which Ferdinand for himself paid so little heed; but in every way and walk of life. She supported him in his policy; she assisted him in his intrigues; she encouraged him in his ambitious designs; she lied for him, whenever prudence required it; she worked for him at all times, as she worked for Spain. For his policy, his intrigues, his designs were all her own. Whenever the views of the king and queen were for a moment discordant, Isabella prevailed, without apparent conflict of authority. In her assumption of supremacy in the marriage contract; in her nomination of Gonsalvo de Cordova to the command of the army; in her choice of Ximenez as the Primate of Spain, she carried her point, not by petulance or even by argument, but by sheer force of character; nor did she strain for one moment, even in these manifestations of her royal supremacy, the friendly and even affectionate relations that ever subsisted between herself and her husband. The love and devotion of Isabella was a thing of which the greatest of men might have well been proud. And though Ferdinand the Catholic may not fairly be counted among the greatest, he was a man wise enough to appreciate the merits of his queen, and to accept and maintain the anomalous position in which he found himself as her consort.

In war at least it might have been supposed that the queen would occupy a subordinate position. Yet in no department of State did Isabella show to greater advantage than as the organizer of victorious armies; not as a batallador after the fashion of her distinguished ancestors in Castile and in Aragon; but as the originator of an entirely new system of military administration.

Before her time, in Spain, war had been waged by the great nobles and their retainers in attendance upon the king. There was no such thing as uniformity of action or preparation, no central organization of any kind. Each man went into battle to fight and to forage as opportunity offered. Each commander vied with his fellow nobles in deeds of bravery, and accorded to them such support as he chose. The sovereign exercised a general authority, and assumed the active command of the united multitude of soldiers, on rare and important occasions. If victory followed, as at the Navas de Tolosa, the soldiers were rewarded with the plunder, and took possession of the property of the enemy. If the Christians were defeated, the army melted away; and the king betook himself to the nearest shelter.

But Isabella had no sooner assumed the title of Queen of Castile, than she was called upon to maintain her pretensions in the field. With no experience but that of a country palace, with no training but that of a country cloister, she set herself to work to organize an army. On the 1st of May, 1474, five hundred horsemen represented the entire forces of the fair usurper. By the 19th of July she had collected over forty thousand men, had armed and equipped them ready for the field, and had sent them forward under the command of Ferdinand to the frontier. Although she was at the time in delicate health, she was constantly in the saddle, riding long distances from fortress to fortress, hurrying up recruits all day, dictating letters all night, giving her zealous personal attention to every detail of armory and equipment, showing from the first that quiet energy and that natural aptitude for command that ever so constantly distinguished her. That her levies were not victorious in no way daunted her determination. A second army was raised by her, within a few weeks after the first had melted away under Ferdinand; nor would she listen to any offers of negotiation, until the enemy had been driven out of Castile.

In the conduct of the war of Granada, with time and money at her command, her preparations were upon a very different scale. The most skillful artificers were summoned from every part of Europe to assist in the work of supplying the army with the necessary material of war. Artillery, then almost unknown to the military art, was manufactured in Spain according to the best designs. Model cannon were imported, and the necessary ammunition collected from abroad. Sword-blades were forged at home. Not only a commissariat, but a field hospital—institutions till then unheard of in Spanish warfare—were organized and maintained under the personal supervision of the queen. The presence of a lady on the day of battle would, as a rule, as she rightly judged, have been rather a hinderance than a help; but she was very far from being a mere commissioner of supply. A first-rate horsewoman, she was constantly seen riding about the camp, encouraging, inspecting, directing; and in the last days of the siege of Granada, when the spirits of the troops had begun to flag, she appeared daily in complete armor, and showed herself upon more than one occasion in a post of danger on the field. The armies with which Gonsalvo de Cordoa overran Calabria, and annihilated the French at Cerignola, were prepared and dispatched by Isabella; and if, in a subsequent campaign, the Great Captain was left without supplies or re-enforcements, it was that the queen was already sickening to her death, broken down and worn out by her constant and enormous exertions.

But with all her aptitude for military organization, Isabella had no love for war. Her first campaign was undertaken to make good her pretensions to the crown. The extermination of the Moslems was a matter of religious feeling and patriotic pride, rather than an object of military glory; but she refused to pursue her conquest across the Straits of Gibraltar. The expeditions to Italy were a part of Ferdinand's diplomacy, though the honor of victory must be shared between Isabella and her Great Captain. But the queen's ambition lay not in conquest abroad. On the contrary, as soon as the last province in Spain had been delivered from the foreign yoke of the Moor, she turned her attention to the peaceful development of the kingdom; and, unlettered warrior as she was, she bestowed her royal patronage upon students and studies, rather than upon the knights and nobles who had fought her battles before Granada.

The old foundations of the Universities, the new art of printing, scholarship, music, architecture found in her a generous patron, not so much from predilection as from policy. Men of letters and men of learning were welcomed at her court, not only from every part of Spain, but from every part of Europe. For herself she had little appreciation of literature. She neither knew nor cared what influence her beloved Inquisition would have upon science. But as long as the queen lived, learning was honored in Spain.

In this, as in all other things, her judgment of men was unerring. The queen who made Gonsalvo the commander-in-chief of her armies, and Ximenez the president of her council, who selected Torquemada as her grand inquisitor, and Talavera as her archbishop of Granada, made no mistake when she invited Peter Martyr to instruct her son in polite letters, and commissioned Lebrija to compose the first Castilian Grammar for the use of her court.

Her beauty of face and form are familiar. Yet vanity was unknown to her nature. Simple and abstemious in her daily life, and despising pomp for its own sake, no one could make a braver show on fitting occasions; and the richness of her apparel, the glory of her jewels, and the noble dignity of her presence, have been celebrated by subjects and strangers.

At the death of Isabella, Ferdinand, in accordance with the provisions of her will, caused his daughter, Joanna, to be proclaimed queen and himself regent. Philip, archduke of Austria, the husband of Joanna, having disputed the rights of his father-in-law and threatened an appeal to arms, the latter in disgust, with the view of again separating the crowns of Aragon and Castile, entered into negotiations with Louis XII., married Germaine de Foix, the niece of Louis (1505), and shortly afterward resigned the regency of Castile. On the death of Philip, in 1506, he resumed the administration, though not without opposition, and retained it till his death. In 1508 he joined the League of Cambray for the partition of Venice, and thus without any trouble became master of five important Neapolitan cities. In the following year (1509) the African expedition of Cardinal Ximenez was undertaken, which resulted in the conquest of Oran. In 1511 Ferdinand joined Venice and Pope Julius II. in a "holy league" for the expulsion of the French from Italy. This gave a pretext for invading Navarre, which had entered into alliance with France, and been laid under Papal interdict in consequence. Aided by his son-in-law Henry VIII. of England, who sent a squadron under the Marquis of Dorset to co-operate in the descent on Guienne, Ferdinand became master of Navarre in 1513; and on June 15, 1515, by a solemn act in Cortes held at Burgos, he incorporated it with the kingdom of Castile.

The League of Cambray, which was signed on the 10th of December, 1508, between Louis XII., the Emperor Maximilian, and Ferdinand of Aragon, at the instance of the warlike Pope Julius II., was nominally directed against the Turks, but was in reality a coalition for the destruction and partition among the confiscators of the rich State of Venice. If anything was wanted to make this league of public plunderers more corrupt and more odious than it would under any circumstances have been, it was that the kings of France and of Aragon, in order to secure the adhesion of the Medicis, sacrificed their faithful allies, the Pisans, after solemn assurances of protection and support, and actually sold that ancient city to the Florentines, their hereditary enemies, for a hundred thousand ducats.

But all their bad faith and covetousness was displayed in vain. The perfidious leaguers could not even trust one another; and the success of the French arms at Agnadel, in May, 1509, so seriously alarmed both Julius and Ferdinand that a second treaty was concluded in October, 1511, when the Pope and the King of Aragon invited the Venetian Republic, for whose destruction they had leagued themselves together with Louis XII. not three years before, to assist them in driving the French out of Italy.

Of the consummate skill with which Ferdinand, from the middle of 1509 to the end of 1511, played off his allies and rivals one against the other, until he had accomplished the central object of his diplomacy in the great Confederation against Louis XII., we may read in the history of

France and of Italy, of England and of Germany, rather than in the Chronicles of Aragon. For King Ferdinand pulled the strings that moved the puppets, while he remained wellnigh hidden himself. But by the end of 1511 the showman was compelled to make his own appearance upon the stage of European warfare; and Ferdinand was ever less successful as an actor than as an impresario. His policy for the past two years had been the formation of a league against his dearly-beloved uncle-in-law, Louis XII., by the aid of his dearly-beloved son-in-law, Henry VIII. Queen Katharine, who had already played the part of embassador to her English father-in-law, was to make use of her influence over her English husband; and if the queen should refuse to advise King Henry to go to war with France, her confessor was to tell her that she was bound as a good Christian to do so.

To coerce the confessor, Ferdinand applied to the Pope; and to control the Pope, he betrayed to him, in secret, the whole scheme of King Louis XII. as regarded the plunder of the States of the Church. It is easy to understand what an effect the communication of the French king's plans of spoliation produced upon the excitable and irascible Julius. When he had learned that he was not only to be robbed of his temporalities, but that he was to be deposed and imprisoned in case he should prove spiritually intractable, he hastened, in spite of his age and his infirmities, to traverse the snow-covered mountains, that he might meet his enemy in the field.

The King of Aragon was a diplomatist who left nothing to chance. He trusted no man. And if no man trusted him, he never deceived himself by supposing that any one was simple enough to do so. No detail, however trifling, was neglected by him in his negotiations. No contingency, however remote, was left out of sight in his intrigues. And however little we may respect his character, which was perhaps not much worse than that of some of his rivals, we cannot refuse to admire his transcendent skill, his infinite perseverance, his forethought, and his keen appreciation of every shade of political development. A little honesty would have made him a great man, a little generosity would have made him a great king. His policy, moreover, toward the close of his life, is at least worthy of an admiration which has rarely been extended to it. It was a policy which embraced all Europe in its scope; and although it had no direct relation to Spain or the Spanish people, it would be ill to conclude even a brief survey of the history of Spain without referring to the imperial dreams of the great Spaniard, first of modern diplomatists, and of his early endeavors to solve more than one of those questions that still embarrass the foreign policy of modern States: the establishment of a kingdom of Italy; the alliance between Italy and Germany, to withstand a dreaded power beyond the Danube and the Carpathians; the entanglement of England in a central European league; and the treatment of the Pope of Rome.

The Turks, the medieval bugbear in the East—for the Middle Ages had also their Eastern Question—were at this time rapidly encroaching upon Christian Europe; and it was obviously desirable to form a powerful empire, as a bulwark of Christendom, on the banks of the Danube. The opportunity of founding a great empire in central Europe actually existed. Ladislaus II., king of Bohemia and of

Hungary, had only one son, Louis, who was of so delicate a constitution that no issue could be expected of his marriage. In case he should die without children, his sister, the Princess Anne, was the heiress of both his kingdoms; and if her father could be persuaded to marry her to the heir of the Austrian principalities, Bohemia, Austria, and Hungary, thus united with the heritage of the Hapsburgs, would form by no means a contemptible State, which might itself be but the nucleus of a greater and more ambitious empire.

Naples, which had so lately been added to the Spanish dominions, was still exposed to the attacks of the French, who claimed one-half, and were always ready to appropriate to themselves the whole of the kingdom. Naples was separated from France, indeed, by a considerable extent of territory in Italy; but the smaller Italian States were too weak to render any serious resistance, and too fickle to be counted upon as friends or as foes by any Spanish sovereign. The best way to render Naples secure was, in the eyes of Ferdinand, the foundation of a great kingdom in northern Italy, powerful enough to prevent the French from marching their armies to the south. The formation of such a kingdom moreover would have greatly facilitated a peaceful division of the great Austro-Spanish inheritance between Prince Charles and his brother, the Infante Ferdinand.

If Charles could be provided not only with the kingdom of Spain, but with the possessions of Maximilian and Ladislaus and the Princess Anne, and the empire of central Europe, his younger brother Ferdinand might content himself with a kingdom to be made up of all the States of

Italy, protected against the encroachments of **France** by Spanish infantry and German landsknechts, and ready to drive the Turk out of the Mediterranean in support of the Christian empire on the Danube.

The kingdom of Italy, thus designed for his younger grandson by the far-seeing Ferdinand of Aragon, was to consist of Genoa, Pavia, Milan, and the Venetian territories on the mainland. The country of the Tyrol, being the most southern of the Austrian dominions, could, without sensibly weakening the projected empire, be separated from it and added to the new kingdom in Italy. Thus stretching from the Mediterranean to the Adriatic, and from the Gulf of Spezia to the Lake of Constance, this sixteenth century kingdom of Italy, with the whole power of the Holy Roman Empire to support it, would have been a splendid endowment for a younger son of the greatest family on earth. There was also a reasonable prospect that it might afterward be still further enlarged by the addition of Naples, and the smaller Italian States would easily have fallen a prey to their powerful neighbor. But in addition to all this, Ferdinand thought that he would render a notable service to the Catholic religion and to the peace of Europe if the Church were thoroughly reformed. What Rome herself has lost by Ferdinand's failure it is not given even to the Infallible to know. What the king's reforms were to be, we can only shrewdly surmise; and although they would most assuredly not have been Protestant, they would with equal certainty have been by no means palatable to the Vatican. For it is reasonably probable that if either Louis XII. or Ferdinand the Catholic had been permitted to carry out their designs, the Pope of Rome would have found himself deprived of his temporal power, and Garibaldi, nay, perchance Luther, would have been forestalled. It was the reforms of Ximenez that to a large extent prevented Luther in Spain. The reforms of Ferdinand might possibly have prevented him in Italy.

It was in 1516 that Ferdinand died. Seven years previous Queen Germaine had been delivered of a son, who received from his parents the name of John. But the curse that lay upon the children of Ferdinand was not yet spent; and the rival of Charles V., the heir of Aragon, Sardinia, Naples, and Sicily, was permitted to gladden the envious heart of his father by but a few hours of life. As years passed on there seemed little chance of any further issue of the King and Queen of Aragon. The unity of Spain at length appeared to be secure. But the ambition of Ferdinand was even surpassed by his jealousy. Childless, vindictive, and obstinate, he chafed at the ill-success of his personal schemes; and rather than suffer the crown of united Spain to pass over to his daughter's son and heir, he sought, at the hands of some medical impostor, the powers that were denied to his old age. The drug that was to have renewed his youth destroyed his constitution, and his death was the direct result of one of the least creditable of the many developments of his jealousy, his obstinacy, and his selfishness.

At length came the inevitable end; and at the wretched hamlet of Madrigalejo, near Guadalupe, in the mountains of Estremadura, on the 23d of January of the new year 1516, Ferdinand died; and Spain was at length a United Kingdom.

CHAPTER VIII

MODERN SPAIN

THE HOUSE OF HAPSBURG — PHILIP II. — DEFEAT OF THE INVINCIBLE ARMADA — A BOURBON AMONG THEM — THE PENINSULAR WAR — ALFONSO XIII

WITH the death of Ferdinand begins the period of uninterrupted Hapsburg rule in Spain, which lasted for nearly two centuries. In the course of this period, the monarchy obtained absolute authority, and Spain, after rising for a time to be the foremost State in Europe, sank to the position of a second-rate power, from which it has never since emerged. Aragon and Castile were distinct kingdoms, and the former was again divided into the three provinces of Aragon, Catalonia, and Valencia, each of which had its own Cortes, its own privileges, and the most warmly-cherished traditions of independence. The foreign possessions of the two crowns were a source of weakness rather than of strength. France stood ready at the earliest opportunity to contest the possession of Navarre with Castile, and that of Naples with Aragon.

The difficulties of domestic government were increased by the fact that the prospective ruler was a youthful foreigner, who had never visited Spain, and who was completely ignorant of the customs and even of the language of the country. Charles—the son of Philip, archduke of Austria, and of Jane, daughter of **Ferdinand and Isabella**

—had been born and educated in the Netherlands, of which he had been nominal ruler ever since the death of his father in 1506. All his friends and advisers were Flemings, who cared nothing for Spanish interests, and had already acquired an evil reputation for selfish greed. The first symptom of discontent in Spain was excited by Charles's demand to be recognized as king, in utter disregard of his mother. In Aragon the demand was unhesitatingly refused, but in Castile the vigorous measures of the famous Cardinal Ximenez secured Charles's proclamation. The regent, however, had great difficulties to face. The nobles, delighted to be rid of the strong government of Ferdinand, wished to utilize the opportunity to regain the privileges and independence they had lost. In this crisis the loyal devotion of Ximenez saved the monarchy. Throwing himself upon the support of the citizen class, he organized a militia which overawed the nobles and maintained order. A French invasion of Navarre was repulsed, and to avoid any danger from the discontent of the inhabitants, all the fortresses of the province, with the single exception of Pamplona, were dismantled. These distinguished services were rewarded with more than royal ingratitude by Charles, who came to Spain in 1517, and who allowed the aged cardinal to die on November 8th, without even granting him an interview.

Charles's enormous inheritance was increased by the successes of Cortes in Mexico and of Pizarro in Peru, by his own annexation of the Milanese, and by his conquests in northern Africa.

The glory of Spain was then at its apogee. After his death, which occurred in 1558, the decline set in. From this time also the House of Hapsburg became divided into its contemporary branches.

Charles was succeeded by Philip II., his only legitimate son. The administration of the latter, while successful at home, was a failure abroad. During his reign a claim to the throne of Portugal was successfully asserted, and the unity of the Peninsula was completed. Moreover, colonial possessions were greatly extended. Yet his religious intolerance excited the revolt of the Netherlands, which resulted in a loss of the seven northern provinces. His effort to obtain a preponderant influence over France was dexterously foiled by the succession and triumph of Henry IV. But his great and historical defeat was that which he experienced with the Armada.

Besides the Spanish crown, Philip succeeded to the kingdom of Naples and Sicily, the Duchy of Milan, Franche-Comte, and the Netherlands. In Africa he possessed Tunis, Oran, the Cape Verd, and the Canary Islands; and in Asia, the Philippine and Sunda Islands, and a part of the Moluccas. Beyond the Atlantic he was lord of the most splendid portions of the New World. The empires of Peru and Mexico, New Spain, and Chili, with their abundant mines of the precious metals, Hispaniola and Cuba, and many other of the American islands, were provinces of the sovereign of Spain.

Philip had also the advantage of finding himself at the head of a large standing army in a perfect state of discipline and equipment, in an age when, except some few insignificant corps, standing armies were unknown to Christendom. The renown of the Spanish troops was justly high, and the infantry in particular was considered the best in the world. His fleet, also, was far more numerous, and better appointed, than that of any other European power; and both his soldiers and his sailors had the confidence in themselves and their commanders which a long career of successful warfare alone can create.

One nation only had been his active, his persevering, and his successful foe. England had encouraged his revolted subjects in Flanders against him, and given them the aid in men and money without which they must soon have been humbled in the dust. English ships had plundered his colonies; had defied his supremacy in the New World, as well as the Old; they had inflicted ignominious defeats on his squadrons; they had captured his cities, and burned his arsenals on the very coasts of Spain. The English had made Philip himself the object of personal insult. He was held up to ridicule in their stage plays and masks, and these scoffs at the man had (as is not unusual in such cases) excited the anger of the absolute king, even more vehemently than the injuries inflicted on his power. Personal as well as political revenge urged him to attack England. Were she once subdued, the Dutch must submit; France could not cope with him, the empire would not oppose him; and universal dominion seemed sure to be the result of the conquest of that malignant island.

For some time the destination of an enormous armament which he had long been preparing was not publicly announced. Only Philip himself, the Pope Sixtus, the Duke of Guise, and Philip's favorite minister, Mendoza, at first knew its real object. Rumors were sedulously spread that it was designed to proceed to the Indies to realize vast projects of distant conquest. Sometimes hints were dropped by Philip's embassadors in foreign courts that their master had resolved on a decisive effort to crush his rebels in the Low Countries. But Elizabeth and her statesmen could not view the gathering of such a storm without feeling the probability of its bursting on their own shores. As early as the spring of 1587, Elizabeth sent Sir Francis Drake to cruise off the Tagus. Drake sailed into the Bay of Cadiz and the Lisbon Roads, and burned much shipping and military stores, causing thereby an important delay in the progress of the Spanish preparations. Drake called this "Singeing the king of Spain's beard." Elizabeth also increased her succors of troops to the Netherlanders, to prevent the Prince of Parma from overwhelming them, and from thence being at full leisure to employ his army against her dominions.

Philip had an ally in France who was far more powerful than the French king. This was the Duke of Guise, the chief of the League, and the idol of the fanatic partisans of the Romish faith. Philip prevailed on Guise openly to take up arms against Henry III. (who was reviled by the Leaguers as a traitor to the true Church, and a secret friend to the Huguenots); and thus prevent the French king from interfering in favor of Queen Elizabeth. "With this object, the commander, Juan Iniguez Moreo, was dispatched by him in the early part of April to the Duke of Guise at Soissons. He met with complete success. He offered the Duke of Guise, as soon as he took the field against Henry III., three hundred thousand crowns, six thousand infantry, and twelve hundred pikemen, on behalf of the king, his master, who would, in addition, withdraw his embassador from the court of France, and accredit an envoy to the Catholic party. A treaty was concluded on these conditions, and the Duke of Guise entered Paris, where he was expected by the Leaguers, and whence he expelled Henry III. on the 12th of May, by the insurrection of the barricades. A fortnight after this insurrection, which reduced Henry III. to impotence, and, to use the language of the Prince of Parma, did not even 'permit him to assist the Queen of England with his tears, as he needed them all to weep over his own misfortunes,' the Spanish fleet left the Tagus and sailed toward the British isles."

Meanwhile in England, from the sovereign on the throne to the peasant in the cottage, all hearts and hands made ready to meet the imminent deadly peril. A camp was formed at Tilbury; and there Elizabeth rode through the ranks, encouraging her captains and her soldiers by her presence and her words.

The ships of the royal navy at this time amounted to no more than thirty-six; but the most serviceable merchant vessels were collected from all the ports of the country; and the citizens of London, Bristol, and the other great seats of commerce, showed as liberal a zeal in equipping and manning vessels as the nobility and gentry displayed in mustering forces by land. The seafaring population of the coast, of every rank and station, was animated by the same ready spirit; and the whole number of seamen who came forward to man the English fleet was 17,472. The number of the ships that were collected was 191; and the total amount of their tonnage 31,985. There was one ship in the fleet (the "Triumph") of 1,100 tons, one of 1,000, one of 900, two of 800 each, three of 600, five of 500, five of 400, six of 300, six of 250, twenty of 200, and the residue of inferior burden. Application was made to the Dutch for assistance; and, as Stowe expresses it, "The Hollanders came roundly in, with threescore sail, brave ships of war, fierce and full of spleen, not so much for England's aid, as in just occasion for their own defense; these men foreseeing the greatness of the danger that might ensue, if the Spaniards should chance to win the day and get the mastery over them; in due regard whereof their manly courage was inferior to none."

The equipment of the Spanish forces consisted of 130 ships (besides caravels), 3,165 cannon, 8,050 sailors, 2,088 galley-slaves, 18,973 soldiers, 1,382 noblemen, gentlemen, and attendants, 150 monks, with Martin Alarco, vicar of the Inquisition—the whole under the command of the Duke of Medina-Sidonia.

While this huge armada was making ready in the southern ports of the Spanish dominions, the Prince of Parma, with almost incredible toil and skill, collected a squadron of warships at Dunkirk, and his flotilla of other ships and of flat-bottomed boats for the transport to England of the picked troops, which were designed to be the main instruments in subduing England. Thousands of workmen were employed, night and day, in the construction of these vessels, in the ports of Flanders and Brabant. One hundred of the kind called hendes, built at Antwerp, Bruges, and Ghent, and laden with provision and ammunition, together with sixty flat-bottomed boats, each capable of carrying thirty horses, were brought, by means of canals and fosses, dug expressly for the purpose, to Nieuport and Dunkirk. One hundred smaller vessels were equipped at the former place, and thirty-two at Dunkirk, provided with twenty thousand empty barrels, and with materials for making pontoons, for stopping up the harbors, and raising forts and intrenchments. The army which these vessels were designed to convey to England amounted to thirty thousand strong, besides a body of four thousand cavalry, stationed at Courtroi, composed chiefly of the ablest veterans of Europe; invigorated by rest (the siege of Sluys having been the only enterprise in which they were employed during the last campaign), and excited by the hopes of plunder and the expectation of certain conquest.

Philip had been advised by the deserter, Sir William Stanley, not to attack England in the first instance, but first to effect a landing and secure a strong position in Ireland; his admiral, Santa Cruz, had recommended him to make sure, in the first instance, of some large harbor on the coast of Holland or Zealand, where the Armada, having entered the Channel, might find shelter in case of storm, and whence it could sail without difficulty for England; but Philip rejected both these counsels, and directed that England itself should be made the immediate object of attack; and on the 20th of May the Armada left the Tagus, in the pomp and pride of supposed invincibility, and amid the shouts of thousands, who believed that England was already conquered. But steering to the northward, and before it was clear of the coast of Spain, the Armada was assailed by a violent storm, and driven back with considerable damage to the ports of Biscay and Gallicia. It had, however, sustained its heaviest loss before it left the Tagus, in the death of the veteran admiral Santa Cruz, who had been destined to guide it against England.

This experienced sailor, notwithstanding his diligence and success, had been unable to keep pace with the impatient ardor of his master. Philip II. had reproached him with his dilatoriness, and had said with ungrateful harshness, "You make an ill return for all my kindness to you." These words cut the veteran's heart, and proved fatal to Santa Cruz. Overwhelmed with fatigue and grief, he sickened and died. Philip II. had replaced him by Alonzo Perez de Gusman, duke of Medina Sidonia, one of the most powerful of the Spanish grandees, but wholly unqualified to command such an expedition. He had, however, as his lieutenants, two seamen of proved skill and bravery, Juan de Martinez Recalde of Biscay, and Miguel Orquendo of Guipuzcoa.

On the 12th of July the Armada, having completely refitted, sailed again for the Channel, and reached it without obstruction or observation by the English.

The design of the Spaniards was, that the Armada should give them, at least for a time, the command of the sea, and that it should join the squadron which Parma had collected, off Calais. Then, escorted by an overpowering naval force, Parma and his army were to embark in their flotilla, and cross the sea to England, where they were to be landed, together with the troops which the Armada brought from the ports of Spain. The scheme was not dissimilar to one formed against England a little more than two centuries afterward.

The orders of King Philip to the Duke of Medina Sidonia were, that he should, on entering the Channel, keep near the French coast, and, if attacked by the English ships, avoid an action, and steer on to Calais Roads, where the Prince of Parma's squadron was to join him. The hope of surprising and destroying the English fleet in Plymouth led the Spanish admiral to deviate from these orders, and to stand across to the English shore; but, on finding that Lord Howard was coming out to meet him, he resumed the original plan, and determined to bend his way steadily toward Calais and Dunkirk, and to keep merely on the defensive against such squadrons of the English as might come up with him.

It was on Saturday, the 20th of July, that Lord Effingham came in sight of his formidable adversaries. The Armada was drawn up in form of a crescent, which from horn to horn measured some seven miles. There was a southwest wind; and before it the vast vessels sailed slowly on. The English let them pass by; and then, following in the rear, commenced an attack on them. A running fight now took place, in which some of the best ships of the Spaniards were captured; many more received heavy damage; while the English vessels, which took care not to close with their huge antagonists, but availed themselves of their superior celerity in tacking and maneuvering, suffered little comparative loss.

The Spanish admiral showed great judgment and firmness in following the line of conduct that had been traced out for him; and on the 27th of July he brought his fleet unbroken, though sorely distressed, to anchor in Calais Roads. The Armada lay off Calais, with its largest ships ranged outside, "like strong castles fearing no assault; the lesser placed in the middle ward." The English admiral could not attack them in their position without great disadvantage, but on the night of the 29th he sent eight fire-ships among them, with almost equal effect to that of the fire-ships which the Greeks so often employed against the Turkish fleets in their war of independence. The Spaniards cut their cables and put to sea in confusion. One of the largest galeasses ran foul of another vessel and was stranded. The rest of the fleet was scattered about on the Flemish coast, and when the morning broke, it was with difficulty and delay that they obeyed their admiral's signal to range themselves round him near Gravelines. Now was the golden opportunity for the English to assail them, and prevent them from ever letting loose Parma's flotilla against England; and nobly was that opportunity used. Drake and Fenner were the first English captains who attacked the unwieldy leviathans: then came Fenton, Southwell, Burton, Cross, Raynor, and then the lord-admiral, with Lord Thomas Howard and Lord Sheffield. The Spaniards only thought of forming and keeping close together, and were driven by the English past Dunkirk, and far away from the Prince of Parma, who, in watching their defeat from the coast, must, as Drake expressed it, have chafed like a bear robbed of her whelps. This was indeed the last and the decisive battle between the two fleets.

Many of the largest Spanish ships were sunk or captured in the action of this day. And at length the Spanish admiral, despairing of success, fled northward with a southerly wind, in the hope of rounding Scotland, and so returning to Spain without a further encounter with the English fleet. Lord Effingham left a squadron to continue the blockade of the Prince of Parma's armament; but that wise general soon withdrew his troops to more promising fields of action. Meanwhile the lord-admiral himself and Drake chased the vincible Armada, as it was now termed, for some distance northward; and then, when it seemed to bend away from the Scotch coast toward Norway, it was thought best, in the words of Drake, "to leave them to those boisterous and uncouth northern seas."

The sufferings and losses which the unhappy Spaniards sustained in their flight round Scotland and Ireland are well known. Of their whole Armada only fifty-three shattered vessels brought back their beaten and wasted crews to the Spanish coast which they had quitted in such pageantry and pride.

At the death of Philip, which occurred on September 13, 1598, he left to his son and successor, Philip III., an empire nominally undiminished, but unwieldy and internally exhausted. Resources had been squandered. The attention of the masses had been turned from industry to war. The soldiery once regarded as invincible had lost their prestige in the Netherland swamps. Enormous taxes, from which nobles and clergy were exempt, were multiplied on the people. That being insufficient, Philip III. proved his orthodoxy by completing the work. In 1609 the Moors, or Moriscoes as they were called, were ordered to quit the Peninsula within three days, and the penalty of death was decreed against all who failed to obey, and against any Christians who should shelter the recalcitrants. The edict was obeyed, but it was the ruin of Spain. The Moriscoes were the backbone of the industrial population, not only in trade and manufactures, but also in agriculture. The haughty and indolent Spaniards had willingly left what they considered degrading employments to their inferiors. The Moors had introduced into Spain the cultivation of sugar, cotton, rice and silk. They had established a system of irrigation which had given fertility to the soil. The province of Valencia in their hands had become a model of agriculture to the rest of Europe. In manufactures and commerce they had shown equal superiority to the Christian inhabitants, and many of the products of Spain were eagerly sought for by other countries. All these advantages were sacrificed to an insane desire for religious unity.

The resources of Spain, already exhausted, never recovered from this terrible blow. Philip III. died in March, 1621. His reign had not been glorious or advantageous to Spain, but it contrasts favorably with those of his successors. Spanish literature and art, which had received a great impulse from the intercourse with foreign countries under previous rulers, reached their zenith during his lifetime. Three writers have obtained European fame—Cervantes, who produced the immortal "Don Quixote" between 1605 and 1613, and two of the most fertile of romantic dramatists, Lope de Vega and Calderon. In the domain of art Spain produced two of the greatest masters of the seventeenth century, Velasquez and Murillo.

Philip II. was succeeded by Philip III. After him came Philip IV. and then Charles II. Of these monarchs Mignet said: "Philip II. was merely a king. Philip III. and Philip IV. were not kings, and Charles II. was not even a man." The death of the latter precipitated the War of the Succession, the military operations of which were rendered famous by the military exploits of Eugene and Marlborough. But this is not the place to recite them. The chief scenes of hostilities were the Netherlands, Germany and Italy, and their narration belongs more properly to the histories of these lands. Suffice it to say that by the Treaty of Utrecht war was concluded in 1711, and Philip V., a Bourbon, second grandson of Louis XIV., was, in accordance with the will of Charles II., acknowledged King of Spain. By the same treaty England gained Gibraltar, while the Spanish Netherlands, Milan, Naples and Sardinia were ceded to Austria.

With the accession of a Bourbon, Spain entered into a new period of history, during which it once more played a part in the politics of Europe, as also in its wars; those, for instance, of the Polish and Austrian successions —the country meanwhile being additionally embroiled with England.

Philip V. was succeeded by Ferdinand VI., and the latter by Charles III., whose death, together with the accession of Charles IV., were contemporary with the French Revolution. The execution of Louis XVI. made a profound impression on a country where loyalty was a superstition. Charles IV. was roused to demand vengeance for the insult to his family. Godoy, the Prime Minister, could but follow the national impulse; and Spain became a member of the first coalition against France. But the two campaigns which ensued provoked the contempt of Europe. They form a catalogue of defeats. Under the circumstances it is no wonder that

Spain followed the example of Prussia and concluded a treaty of peace.

The next event of importance was Napoleon's famous coup de main—the seizure of the Spanish royal family at Bayonne—the jugglery which he performed with the crown, its transference by him from Ferdinand VII. (son of Charles IV.) to Joseph Bonaparte, and the revolt of the South American colonies which that act produced.

Then came the restoration of Spanish independence through England's aid; Wellington's famous campaign; the battles of Ciudad Rodrigo and Badajos; the entry into Madrid; the retreat of Joseph to Valencia; Napoleon's crushing defeat at Leipzig, and Ferdinand's return from captivity at Valençay.

The circumstances through which these last-mentioned events were induced or precipitated, and which are collectively known as the Peninsular War, originated at the moment when Napoleon was practically master of Europe. Its whole face was changed. Prussia was occupied by French troops. Holland was changed into a monarchy by a simple decree of the French emperor, and its crown bestowed on his brother Louis. Another brother, Jerome, became King of Westphalia, a new realm built up out of the electorates of Hesse-Cassel and Hanover. A third brother, Joseph, was made King of Naples; while the rest of Italy, and even Rome itself, was annexed to the French empire. It was the hope of effectually crushing the world-power of Britain which drove him to his worst aggression, the aggression upon Spain. He acted with his usual subtlety. In October, 1807, France and Spain agreed to divide Portugal between them; and on the advance of their forces the reigning House of Braganza fled helplessly from Lisbon to a refuge in Brazil. But the seizure of Portugal was only a prelude to the seizure of Spain. Charles IV., whom a riot in his capital drove at this moment to abdication, and his son, Ferdinand VII., were drawn to Bayonne in May, 1808, and forced to resign their claims to the Spanish crown; while a French army entered Madrid and proclaimed Joseph Bonaparte king of Spain. But this highhanded act of aggression was hardly completed when Spain rose as one man against the stranger; and desperate as the effort of its people seemed, the news of the rising was welcomed throughout England with a burst of enthusiastic joy. "Hitherto," cried Sheridan, a leader of the Whig opposition, "Bonaparte has contended with princes without dignity, numbers without ardor, or peoples without patriotism. He has yet to learn what it is to combat a people who are animated by one spirit against him." Tory and Whig alike held that "never had so happy an opportunity existed in Britain to strike a bold stroke for the rescue of the world"; and Canning at once resolved to change the system of desultory descents on colonies and sugar islands for a vigorous warfare in the Peninsula.

The furious and bloody struggle which ensued found its climax at Vittoria, but it would be difficult to find in the whole history of war a more thrilling chapter than that which tells of the six great campaigns of which the war itself was composed.

The Peninsular War was perhaps the least selfish conflict ever waged. It was not a war of aggrandizement or of conquest. It was fought to deliver Europe from the despotism of Napoleon. At its close the fleets of Great

Britain rode triumphant, and in the Peninsula between 1808–14 her land forces fought and won nineteen pitched battles, made or sustained ten fierce and bloody sieges, took four great fortresses, twice expelled the French from Portugal and once from Spain. Great Britain expended in these campaigns more than one hundred million pounds sterling on her own troops, besides subsidizing the forces of Spain and Portugal. This "nation of shopkeepers" proved that when kindled to action it could wage war on a scale and in a fashion that might have moved the wonder of Alexander or of Cæsar, and from motives too lofty for either Cæsar or Alexander so much as to comprehend. It is worth while to tell afresh the story of some of the more picturesque incidents in that great strife.

On April 6, 1812, Badajos was stormed by Wellington; and the story forms one of the most tragical and splendid incidents in the military history of the world. Of "the night of horrors at Badajos," Napier says, "posterity can scarcely be expected to credit the tale." No tale, however, is better authenticated, or, as an example of what disciplined human valor is capable of achieving, better deserves to be told. Wellington was preparing for his great forward movement into Spain, the campaign which led to Salamanca, the battle in which "forty thousand Frenchmen were beaten in forty minutes." As a preliminary he had to capture, under the vigilant eyes of Soult and Marmont, the two great border fortresses, Ciudad Rodrigo and Badajos. He had, to use Napier's phrase, "jumped with both feet" on the first-named fortress, and captured it in twelve days with a loss of twelve hundred men and ninety officers.

But Badajos was a still harder task. The city stands on a rocky ridge which forms the last spur of the Toledo range, and is of extraordinary strength. The river Rivillas falls almost at right angles into the Guadiana, and in the angle formed by their junction stands Badajos, oval in shape, girdled with elaborate defenses, with the Guadiana, five hundred yards wide, as its defense to the north, the Rivillas serving as a wet ditch to the west, and no less than five great fortified outposts—Saint Roque, Christoval, Picurina, Pardaleras, and a fortified bridge-head across the Guadiana—as the outer zone of its defenses. Twice the English had already assailed Badajos, but assailed it in vain. It was now held by a garrison five thousand strong, under a soldier, General Phillipson, with a real genius for defense, and the utmost art had been employed in adding to its defenses. On the other hand, Wellington had no means of transport and no battery train, and had to make all his preparations under the keen-eyed vigilance of the French. Perhaps the strangest collection of artillery ever employed in a great siege was that which Wellington collected from every available quarter and used at Badajos. Of the fifty-two pieces, some dated from the days of Philip II. and the Spanish Armada, some were cast in the reign of Philip III., others in that of John IV. of Portugal, who reigned in 1640; there were 24-pounders of George II.'s day, and Russian naval guns; the bulk of the extraordinary medley being obsolete brass engines which required from seven to ten minutes to cool between each discharge.

Wellington, however, was strong in his own warlike genius and in the quality of the troops he commanded.

He employed eighteen thousand men in the siege, and it may well be doubted whether—if we put the question of equipment aside—a more perfect fighting instrument than the force under his orders ever existed. The men were veterans, but the officers on the whole were young, so there was steadiness in the ranks and fire in the leading. Hill and Graham covered the siege, Picton and Barnard, Kempt and Colville led the assaults. The trenches were held by the third, fourth, and fifth divisions, and by the famous light division. Of the latter it has been said that the Macedonian phalanx of Alexander the Great, the Tenth Legion of Cæsar, the famous Spanish infantry of Alva, or the iron soldiers who followed Cortes to Mexico, did not exceed it in warlike quality. Wellington's troops, too, had a personal grudge against Badajos, and had two defeats to avenge. Perhaps no siege in history, as a matter of fact, ever witnessed either more furious valor in the assault, or more of cool and skilled courage in the defense. The siege lasted exactly twenty days, and cost the besiegers five thousand men, or an average loss of two hundred and fifty per day. It was waged throughout in stormy weather, with the rivers steadily rising, and the tempests perpetually blowing; yet the thunder of the attack never paused for an instant.

Wellington's engineers attacked the city at the eastern end of the oval, where the Rivillas served it as a gigantic wet ditch; and the Picurina, a fortified hill, ringed by a ditch fourteen feet deep, a rampart sixteen feet high, and a zone of mines, acted as an outwork. Wellington, curiously enough, believed in night attacks, a sure proof of his faith in the quality of the men he commanded; and on the eighth night of the siege, at nine o'clock, five hundred men of the third division were suddenly flung on the Picurina. The fort broke into a ring of flame, by the light of which the dark figures of the stormers were seen leaping with fierce hardihood into the ditch and struggling madly up the ramparts, or tearing furiously at the palisades. But the defenses were strong, and the assailants fell literally in scores. Napier tells how "the axmen of the light division, compassing the fort like prowling wolves," discovered the gate at the rear, and so broke into the fort. The engineer officer who led the attack declares that "the place would never have been taken had it not been for the coolness of these men" in absolutely walking round the fort to its rear, discovering the gate, and hewing it down under a tempest of bullets. The assault lasted an hour, and in that period, out of the five hundred men who attacked, no less than three hundred, with nineteen officers, were killed or wounded! Three men out of every five in the attacking force, that is, were disabled, and yet they won!

There followed twelve days of furious industry, of trenches pushed tirelessly forward through mud and wet, and of cannonading that only ceased when the guns grew too hot to be used. Captain MacCarthy, of the Fiftieth Regiment, has left a curious little monograph on the siege, full of incidents, half tragic and half amusing, but which show the temper of Wellington's troops. Thus he tells how an engineer officer, when marking out the ground for a breaching-battery very near the wall, which was always lined with French soldiers in eager search of human targets, "used to challenge them to prove the perfection of their shooting by lifting up the skirts of his coat in defiance several times in the course of his survey; driving in his stakes and measuring his distances with great deliberation, and concluding by an extra shake of his coat-tails and an ironical bow before he stepped under shelter!"

On the night of April 6, Wellington determined to assault. No less than seven attacks were to be delivered. Two of them—on the bridge-head across the Guadiana and on the Pardaleras—were mere feints. But on the extreme right Picton with the third division was to cross the Rivillas and escalade the castle, whose walls rose, time-stained and grim, from eighteen to twenty-four feet high. Leith with the fifth division was to attack the opposite or western extremity of the town, the bastion of St. Vincente, where the glacis was mined, the ditch deep, and the scarp thirty feet high. Against the actual breaches Colville and Andrew Barnard were to lead the light division and the fourth division, the former attacking the bastion of Santa Maria and the latter the Trinidad. The hour was fixed for ten o'clock, and the story of that night attack, as told in Napier's immortal prose, is one of the great battle-pictures of literature; and any one who tries to tell the tale will find himself slipping insensibly into Napier's cadences.

The night was black; a strange silence lay on rampart and trench, broken from time to time by the deep voices of the sentinels that proclaimed all was well in Badajos. "Sentinelle garde à vous," the cry of the sentinels, was translated by the British private, as "All's well in Badahoo!" A lighted carcass thrown from the castle discovered Picton's men standing in ordered array, and compelled them to attack at once. MacCarthy, who acted as guide across the tangle of wet trenches and the narrow bridge that spanned the Rivillas, has left an amusing account of the scene. At one time Picton declared MacCarthy was leading them wrong, and, drawing his sword, swore he would cut him down. The column reached the trench, however, at the foot of the castle walls, and was instantly overwhelmed with the fire of the besieged. MacCarthy says we can only picture the scene by "supposing that all the stars, planets, and meteors of the firmament, with innumerable moons emitting smaller ones in their course, were descending on the heads of the besiegers." MacCarthy himself, a typical and gallant Irishman, addressed his general with the exultant remark, "'Tis a glorious night, sir —a glorious night!" and, rushing forward to the head of the stormers, shouted, "Up with the ladders!" The five ladders were raised, the troops swarmed up, an officer leading, but the first files were at once crushed by cannon fire, and the ladders slipped into the angle of the abutments. "Dreadful their fall," records MacCarthy of the slaughtered stormers, "and appalling their appearance at daylight." One ladder remained, and, a private soldier leading, the eager red-coated crowd swarmed up it. The brave fellow leading was shot as soon as his head appeared above the parapet; but the next man to him—again a private—leaped over the parapet, and was followed quickly by others, and this thin stream of desperate men climbed singly, and in the teeth of the flashing musketry, up that solitary ladder, and carried the castle.

In the meanwhile the fourth and light divisions had flung themselves with cool and silent speed on the breaches. The storming party of each division leaped into the ditch. It was mined, the fuse was kindled, and the ditch, crowded with eager soldiery, became in a moment a sort of flaming crater, and the storming parties, five hundred strong, were in one fierce explosion dashed to pieces. In the light of that dreadful flame the whole scene became visible—the black ramparts, crowded with dark figures and glittering arms, on the one side; on the other, the red columns of the British, broad and deep, moving steadily forward like a stream of human lava. The light division stood at the brink of the smoking ditch for an instant, amazed at the sight. "Then," says Napier, "with a shout that matched even the sound of the explosion," they leaped into it and swarmed up to the breach. The fourth division came running up and descended with equal fury, but the ditch opposite the Trinidad was filled with water; the head of the division leaped into it, and, as Napier puts it, "about one hundred of the fusiliers, the men of Albuera, perished there." The breaches were impassable. Across the top of the great slope of broken wall glittered a fringe of sword-blades, sharp-pointed, keen-edged on both sides, fixed in ponderous beams chained together and set deep in the ruins. For ten feet in front the ascent was covered with loose planks, studded with sharp iron points. Behind the glittering edge of sword-blades stood the solid ranks of the French, each man supplied with three muskets, and their fire scourged the British ranks like a tempest.

Hundreds had fallen, hundreds were still falling; but the British clung doggedly to the lower slopes, and every few minutes an officer would leap forward with a shout, a swarm of men would instantly follow him, and, like leaves blown by a whirlwind, they swept up the ascent. But under the incessant fire of the French the assailants melted away. One private reached the sword-blades, and actually thrust his head beneath them till his brains were beaten out, so desperate was his resolve to get into Badajos. The breach, as Napier describes it, "yawning and glittering with steel, resembled the mouth of a huge dragon belching forth smoke and flame." But for two hours, and until two thousand men had fallen, the stubborn British persisted in their attacks. Currie, of the 52d, a cool and most daring soldier, found a narrow ramp beyond the Santa Maria breach only half-ruined; he forced his way back through the tumult and carnage to where Wellington stood watching the scene, obtained an unbroken battalion from the reserve, and led it toward the broken ramp. But his men were caught in the whirling madness of the ditch and swallowed up in the tumult. Nicholas, of the engineers, and Shaw of the 43d, with some fifty soldiers, actually climbed into the Santa Maria bastion, and from thence tried to force their way into the breach. Every man was shot down except Shaw, who stood alone on the bastion. "With inexpressible coolness he looked at his watch, said it was too late to carry the breaches," and then leaped down! The British could not penetrate the breach; but they would not retreat. They could only die where they stood. The buglers of the reserve were sent to the crest of the glacis to sound the retreat; the troops in the ditch would not believe the signal to be genuine, and struck their own buglers who attempted to repeat it. "Gathering in dark groups, and leaning on their muskets," says Napier, "they looked up in sullen desperation at Trinidad, while the enemy, stepping out on the ramparts, and aiming their shots by the light of fire-balls, which they threw over, asked as their victims fell, 'Why they did not come into Badajos.' "

All this while, curiously enough, Picton was actually in Badajos, and held the castle securely, but made no attempt to clear the breach. On the extreme west of the town, however, at the bastion of San Vincente, the fifth division made an attack as desperate as that which was failing at the breaches. When the stormers actually reached the bastion, the Portuguese battalions, who formed part of the attack, dismayed by the tremendous fire which broke out on them, flung down their ladders and fled. The British, however, snatched the ladders up, forced the barrier, jumped into the ditch, and tried to climb the walls. These were thirty feet high, and the ladders were too short. A mine was sprung in the ditch under the soldiers' feet; beams of wood, stones, broken wagons, and live shells were poured upon their heads from above. Showers of grape from the flank swept the ditch.

The stubborn soldiers, however, discovered a low spot in the rampart, placed three ladders against it, and climbed with reckless valor. The first man was pushed up by his comrades; he, in turn, dragged others up, and the unconquerable British at length broke through and swept the bastion. The tumult still stormed and raged at the eastern breaches, where the men of the light and fourth division were dying sullenly, and the men of the fifth division marched at speed across the town to take the great eastern breach in the rear. The streets were empty, but the silent houses were bright with lamps. The men of the fifth pressed on; they captured mules carrying ammunition to the breaches, and the French, startled by the tramp of the fast-approaching column, and finding themselves taken in the rear, fled. The light and fourth divisions broke through the gap hitherto barred by flame and steel, and Badajos was won!

In that dreadful night assault the English lost three thousand five hundred men. "Let it be considered," says Napier, "that this frightful carnage took place in the space of less than a hundred yards square—that the slain died not all suddenly, nor by one manner of death—that some perished by steel, some by shot, some by water; that some were crushed and mangled by heavy weights, some trampled upon, some dashed to atoms by the fiery explosions—that for hours this destruction was endured without shrinking, and the town was won at last. Let these things be considered, and it must be admitted a British army bears with it an awful power. And false would it be to say the French were feeble men. The garrison stood and fought manfully and with good discipline, behaving worthily. Shame there was none on any side. Yet who shall do justice to the bravery of the British soldiers or the noble emulation of the officers? . . . No age, no nation, ever sent forth braver troops to battle than those who stormed Badajos."

In addition to Badajos, the siege of Ciudad Rodrigo and of San Sebastian deserve mention. The annals of strife nowhere record assaults more daring than those which raged in turn around these three great fortresses. Of them all that of Badajos was the most picturesque and bloody; that of San Sebastian the most sullen and exasperating; that of Ciudad Rodrigo the swiftest and most brilliant. A great siege tests the fighting quality of any army as nothing else can test it. In the night watches in the trenches, in the dogged toil of the batteries, and the crowded perils of the breach, all the frippery and much of the real discipline of an army dissolves. The soldiers fall back upon what may be called the primitive fighting qualities—the hardihood of the individual soldier, the daring with which the officers will lead, the dogged loyalty with which the men will follow. As an illustration of the warlike qualities in a race by which empire has been achieved, nothing better can be desired than the story of how the breaches were won at Ciudad Rodrigo.

At the end of 1811 the English and the French were watching each other jealously across the Spanish border. The armies of Marmont and of Soult, sixty-seven thousand strong, lay within touch of each other, barring Wellington's entrance into Spain. Wellington, with thirty-five thousand men, of whom not more than ten thousand men were British, lay within sight of the Spanish frontier. It was the winter time. Wellington's army was wasted by sickness, his horses were dying of mere starvation, his men had received no pay for three months, and his muleteers none for eight months. He had no siege train, his regiments were ragged and hungry, and the French generals confidently reckoned the British army as, for the moment at least, une quantite negligeable.

And yet at that precise moment, Wellington, subtle and daring, was meditating a leap upon the great frontier fortress of Ciudad Rodrigo, in the Spanish province of Salamanca. Its capture would give him a safe base of operations against Spain; it was the great frontier place d'armes for the French; the whole siege-equipage and stores of the army of Portugal were contained in it. The problem of how, in the depth of winter, without materials for a siege, to snatch a place so strong from under the very eyes of two armies, each stronger than his own, was a problem which might have taxed the warlike genius of a Cæsar. But Wellington accomplished it with a combination of subtlety and audacity simply marvelous.

He kept the secret of his design so perfectly that his own engineers never suspected it, and his adjutant-general, Murray, went home on leave without dreaming anything was going to happen. Wellington collected artillery ostensibly for the purpose of arming Almeida, but the guns were transshipped at sea and brought secretly to the mouth of the Douro. No less than eight hundred mule-carts were constructed without anybody guessing their purpose. Wellington, while these preparations were on foot, was keenly watching Marmont and Soult, till he saw that they were lulled into a state of mere yawning security, and then, in Napier's expressive phrase, he "instantly jumped with both feet upon Ciudad Rodrigo."

This famous fortress, in shape, roughly resembles a triangle with the angles truncated. The base, looking to the south, is covered by the Agueda, a river given to sudden inundations; the fortifications were strong and formidably armed; as outworks it had to the east the great fortified Convent of San Francisco, to the west a similar building called Santa Cruz; while almost parallel with the northern face rose two rocky ridges called the Great and Small Teson, the nearest within six hundred yards of the city ramparts, and crowned by a formidable redoubt called

Francisco. The siege began on January 8. The soil was rocky and covered with snow, the nights were black, the weather bitter. The men lacked intrenching tools. They had to encamp on the side of the Agueda furthest from the city, and ford that river every time the trenches were relieved. The 1st, 3d, and light divisions formed the attacking force; each division held the trenches in turn for twenty-four hours. Let the reader imagine what degree of hardihood it took to wade in the gray and bitter winter dawn through a half-frozen river, and, without fire or warm food, and under a ceaseless rain of shells from the enemy's guns, to toil in the frozen trenches, or to keep watch, while the icicles hung from eyebrow and beard, over the edge of the battery for twenty-four hours in succession.

Nothing in this great siege is more wonderful than the fierce speed with which Wellington urged his operations. Massena, who had besieged and captured the city the year before in the height of summer, spent a month in bombarding it before he ventured to assault. Wellington broke ground on January 8, under a tempest of mingled hail and rain; he stormed it on the night of the 19th.

He began operations by leaping on the strong work that crowned the Great Teson the very night the siege began. Two companies from each regiment of the light division were detailed by the officer of the day, Colonel Colborne, for the assault. Colborne (afterward Lord Seaton), a cool and gallant soldier, called his officers together in a group and explained with great minuteness how they were to attack. He then lanched his men against the redoubt with a vehemence so swift that, to those who watched the scene under the light of a wintry moon, the column of redcoats, like the thrust of a crimson swordblade, spanned the ditch, shot up the glacis, and broke through the parapet with a single movement. The accidental explosion of a French shell burst the gate open, and the remainder of the attacking party instantly swept through it. There was fierce musketry fire and a tumult of shouting for a moment or two, but in twenty minutes from Colborne's lanching his attack every Frenchman in the redoubt was killed, wounded, or a prisoner.

The fashion in which the gate was blown open was very curious. A French sergeant was in the act of throwing a live shell upon the storming party in the ditch, when he was struck by an English bullet. The lighted shell fell from his hands within the parapet, was kicked away by the nearest French in mere self-preservation; it rolled toward the gate, exploded, burst it open, and instantly the British broke in.

For ten days a desperate artillery duel raged between the besiegers and the besieged. The parallels were resolutely pushed on in spite of rocky soil, broken tools, bitter weather, and the incessant pelting of the French guns. The temper of the British troops is illustrated by an incident which George Napier—the youngest of the three Napiers—relates. The three brothers were gallant and remarkable soldiers. Charles Napier in India and elsewhere made history; William, in his wonderful tale of the Peninsular War, wrote history; and George, if he had not the literary genius of the one nor the strategic skill of the other, was a most gallant soldier. "I was a field-officer of the trenches," he says, "when a 13-inch shell from the town fell in the midst of us. I called to the men to lie down flat, and they instantly obeyed orders, except one of them, an Irishman and an old marine, but a most worthless drunken dog, who trotted up to the shell, the fuse of which was still burning, and striking it with his spade, knocked the fuse out; then taking the immense shell in his hands, brought it to me, saying, 'There she is for you now, yer 'anner. I've knocked the life out of the crater.'"

The besieged brought fifty heavy guns to reply to the thirty light pieces by which they were assailed, and day and night the bellow of eighty pieces boomed sullenly over the doomed city and echoed faintly back from the nearer hills, while the walls crashed to the stroke of the bullet. The English fire made up by fierceness and accuracy for what it lacked in weight; but the sap made no progress, the guns showed signs of being worn out, and, although two apparent breaches had been made, the counterscarp was not destroyed. Yet Wellington determined to attack, and, in his characteristic fashion, to attack by night. The siege had lasted ten days, and Marmont, with an army stronger than his own, was lying within four marches. That he had not appeared already on the scene was wonderful.

In a general order issued on the evening of the 19th Wellington wrote, "Ciudad Rodrigo *must* be stormed this evening." The great breach was a sloping gap in the wall at its northern angle, about a hundred feet wide. The French had crowned it with two guns loaded with grape, the slope was strewn with bombs, hand-grenades and bags of powder; a great mine pierced it beneath; a deep ditch had been cut between the breach and the adjoining ramparts, and these were crowded with riflemen. The third division, under General Mackinnon, was to attack the breach, its forlorn hope being led by Ensign Mackie, its storming party by General Mackinnon himself. The lesser breach was a tiny gap, scarcely twenty feet wide, to the left of the great breach; this was to be attacked by the light division, under Craufurd, its forlorn hope of twenty-five men being led by Gurwood, and its storming party by George Napier. General Pack, with a Portuguese brigade, was to make a sham attack on the eastern face, while a fourth attack was to be made on the southern front by a company of the 83d and some Portuguese troops. In the storming party of the 83d were the Earl of March, afterward Duke of Richmond; Lord Fitzroy Somerset, afterward Lord Raglan; and the Prince of Orange—all volunteers without Wellington's knowledge!

At seven o'clock a curious silence fell suddenly on the battered city and the engirdling trenches. Not a light gleamed from the frowning parapets, not a murmur arose from the blackened trenches. Suddenly a shout broke out on the right of the English attack; it ran, a wave of stormy sound, along the line of the trenches. The men who were to attack the great breach leaped into the open. In a moment the space between the hostile lines was covered with the stormers, and the gloomy, half-seen face of the great fortress broke into a tempest of fire.

Nothing could be finer than the vehement courage of the assault, unless it were the cool and steady fortitude of the defense. Swift as was the upward rush of the stormers, **the race of** the 5th, 77th, and 94th **regiments** was almost swifter. Scorning to wait for the ladders, they leaped into the great ditch, outpaced even the forlorn hope, and pushed vehemently up the great breach, while their red ranks were torn by shell and shot. The fire, too, ran through the tangle of broken stones over which they climbed; the hand-grenades and powder-bags by which it was strewn exploded. The men were walking on fire! Yet the attack could not be denied. The Frenchmen—shooting, stabbing, yelling—were driven behind their intrenchments. There the fire of the houses commanding the breach came to their help, and they made a gallant stand. "None would go back on either side, and yet the British could not get forward, and men and officers falling in heaps choked up the passage, which from minute to minute was raked with grape from two guns flanking the top of the breach at the distance of a few yards. Thus striving, and trampling alike upon the dead and the wounded, these brave men maintained the combat."

It was the attack on the smaller breach which really carried Ciudad Rodrigo; and George Napier, who led it, has left a graphic narrative of the exciting experiences of that dreadful night. The light division was to attack, and Craufurd, with whom Napier was a favorite, gave him command of the storming party. He was to ask for one hundred volunteers from each of the three British regiments—the 43d, 52d, and the rifle corps—in the division. Napier halted these regiments just as they had forded the bitterly cold river on their way to the trenches. "Soldiers," he said, "I want one hundred men from each regiment to form the storming party which is to lead the light division to-night. Those who will go with me come forward!" Instantly there was a rush forward of the whole division, and Napier had to take his three hundred men out of a tumult of nearly one thousand five hundred candidates. He formed them into three companies, under Captains Ferguson, Jones, and Mitchell. Gurwood, of the 52d, led the forlorn hope, consisting of twenty-five men and two sergeants. Wellington himself came to the trench and showed Napier and Colborne, through the gloom of the early night, the exact position of the breach. A staff-officer, looking on, said, "Your men are not loaded. Why don't you make them load?" Napier replied, "If we don't do the business with the bayonet we shall not do it at all. I shall not load." "Let him alone," said Wellington; "let him go his own way." Picton had adopted the same grim policy with the third division. As each regiment passed him, filing into the trenches, his injunction was, "No powder! We'll do the thing with the *could* iron."

A party of Portuguese carrying bags filled with grass were to run with the storming party and throw the bags into the ditch, as the leap was too deep for the men. But the Portuguese hesitated, the tumult of the attack on the great breach suddenly broke on the night, and the forlorn hope went running up, leaped into the ditch a depth of eleven feet, and clambered up the steep slope beyond, while Napier with his stormers came with a run behind them. In the dark for a moment the breach was lost, but found again, and up the steep quarry of broken stone the attack swept.

About two-thirds of the way up, Napier's arm was

smashed by a grape-shot, and he fell. His men, checked for a moment, lifted their muskets to the gap above them, whence the French were firing vehemently, and forgetting their pieces were unloaded, snapped them. "Push on with the bayonet, men!" shouted Napier, as he lay bleeding. The officers leaped to the front, the men with a stern shout followed; they were crushed to a front of not more than three or four. They had to climb without firing a shot in reply up to the muzzles of the French muskets.

But nothing could stop the men of the light division. A 24-pounder was placed across the narrow gap in the ramparts; the stormers leaped over it, and the 43d and 52d, coming up in sections abreast, followed. The 43d wheeled to the right toward the great breach, the 52d to the left, sweeping the ramparts as they went.

Meanwhile the other two attacks had broken into the town; but at the great breach the dreadful fight still raged, until the 43d, coming swiftly along the ramparts, and brushing all opposition aside, took the defense in the rear. The British there had, as a matter of fact, at that exact moment pierced the French defense. The two guns that scourged the breach had wrought deadly havoc among the stormers, and a sergeant and two privates of the 88th—Irishmen all, and whose names deserve to be preserved—Brazel, Kelly, and Swan—laid down their firelocks that they might climb more lightly, and, armed only with their bayonets, forced themselves through the embrasure among the French gunners. They were furiously attacked, and Swan's arm was hewed off by a saber stroke; but they stopped the service of the gun, slew five or six of the French gunners, and held the post until the men of the 5th, climbing behind them, broke into the battery.

So Ciudad Rodrigo was won, and its governor surrendered his sword to the youthful lieutenant leading the forlorn hope of the light division, who, with smoke-blackened face, torn uniform, and staggering from a dreadful wound, still kept at the head of his men.

In the eleven days of the siege Wellington lost one thousand three hundred men and officers, out of whom six hundred and fifty men and sixty officers were struck down on the slopes of the breaches. Two notable soldiers died in the attack—Craufurd, the famous leader of the light division, as he brought his men up to the lesser breach; and Mackinnon, who commanded a brigade of the third division, at the great breach. Mackinnon was a gallant Highlander, a soldier of great promise, beloved by his men. His "children," as he called them, followed him up the great breach till the bursting of a French mine destroyed all the leading files, including their general. Craufurd was buried in the lesser breach itself, and Mackinnon in the great breach—fitting graves for soldiers so gallant.

Alison says that with the rush of the English stormers up the breaches of Ciudad Rodrigo "began the fall of the French empire." That siege, so fierce and brilliant, was, as a matter of fact, the first of that swift-following succession of strokes which drove the French in ruin out of Spain, and it coincided in point of time with the turn of the tide against Napoleon in Russia.

But, as already noted, the climax of the war occurred at Vittoria. Wellington, overtaking the French at that place, inflicted on them a defeat which drove in utter rout one hundred and twenty thousand veteran troops from Spain. There is no more brilliant chapter in military history; and, at its close, to quote Napier's clarion-like sentences, "the English general, emerging from the chaos of the Peninsular struggle, stood on the summit of the Pyrenees a recognized conqueror. From those lofty pinnacles the clangor of his trumpets pealed clear and loud, and the splendor of his genius appeared as a flaming beacon to warring nations."

The victory not only freed Spain from its invaders; it restored the spirit of the allies. The close of the armistice was followed by a union of Austria with the forces of Prussia and the Czar; and in October a final overthrow of Napoleon at Leipzig forced the French army to fall back in rout across the Rhine. The war now hurried to its close. Though held at bay for a while by the sieges of San Sebastian and Pampeluna, as well as by an obstinate defense of the Pyrenees, Wellington succeeded in the very month of the triumph at Leipzig in winning a victory on the Bidassoa which enabled him to enter France. He was soon followed by the allies. On the last day of 1813 their forces crossed the Rhine; and a third of France passed, without opposition, into their hands. For two months more Napoleon maintained a wonderful struggle with a handful of raw conscripts against their overwhelming numbers; while in the south, Soult, forced from his intrenched camp near Bayonne and defeated at Orthes, fell back before Wellington on Toulouse. Here their two armies met in April in a stubborn and indecisive engagement. But though neither leader

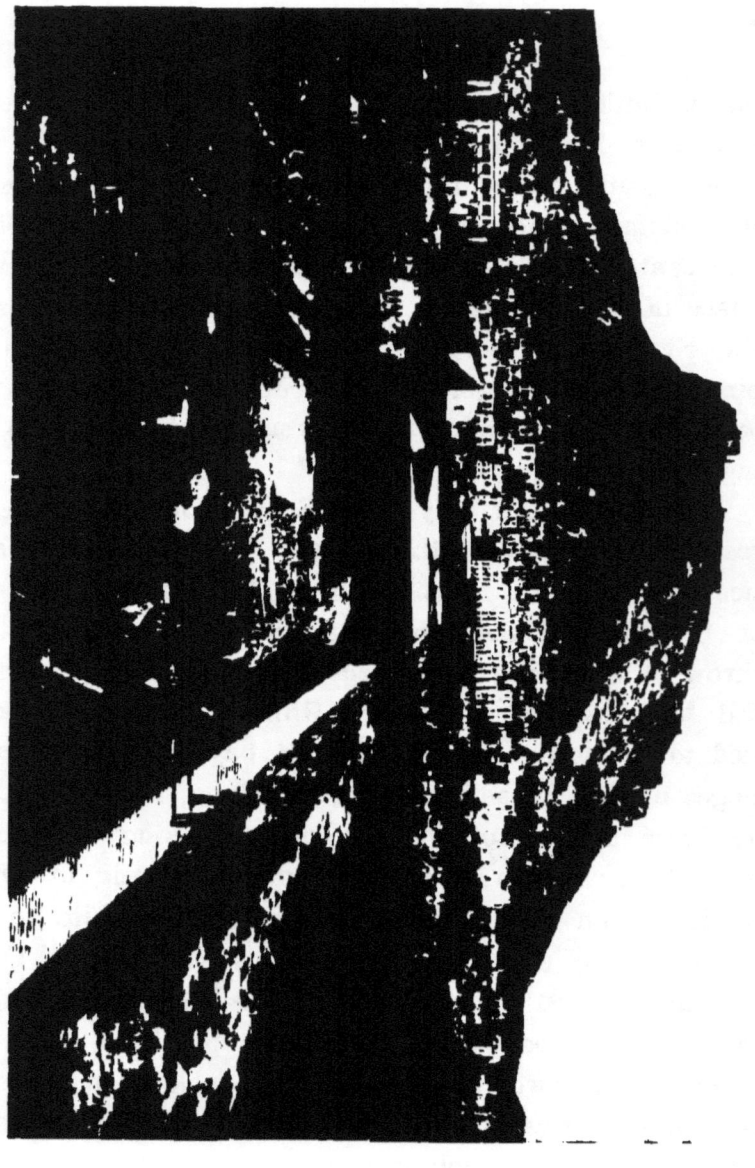

ALICANTI

Spain.

knew it, the war was even then at an end. The struggle of Napoleon himself had ended at the close of March with the surrender of Paris; and the submission of the capital was at once followed by the abdication of the emperor and the return of Ferdinand.

After the convulsions it had endured Spain, required a period of firm but conciliatory government; but the ill-fate of the country gave the throne at this crisis to the worst of her Bourbon kings. Ferdinand VII. had never possessed the good qualities which popular credulity had assigned to him, and he had learned nothing in his four years' captivity except an aptitude for lying and intrigue. He had no conception of the duties of a ruler; his public conduct was regulated by pride and superstition, and his private life was stained by the grossest sensual indulgence.

But Spain was not allowed to work out its own salvation. Europe was dominated at this time by the Holy Alliance, which disguised a resolution to repress popular liberties and to maintain despotism under a pretended zeal for piety, justice and brotherly love. At the Congress of Verona (October, 1822), France, Austria, Russia and Prussia agreed upon armed intervention in Spain, in spite of the protest of Canning on the part of England. Spain was to be called upon to alter her constitution and to grant greater liberty to the king, and if an unsatisfactory answer were received France was authorized to take active measures. The demand was unhesitatingly refused, and a French army, 100,000 strong, at once entered Spain under the Duke of Angouleme (April, 1823). No effective resistance was made, and Madrid was entered by the invaders (May 23). The Cortes, however, had carried off the king to Seville, whence they again retreated to Cadiz. The bombardment of that city terminated the revolution and Ferdinand was released (October 1). His first act was to revoke everything that had been done since 1819. The Inquisition was not restored, but the secular tribunals took a terrible revenge upon the leaders of the rebellion. The protest of the Duke of Angouleme against these cruelties was unheeded. Even the fear of revolt, the last check upon despotism, was removed by the presence of the French army, which remained in Spain till 1827. But Spain had to pay for the restoration of the royal absolutism, as Canning backed up his protest against the intervention of France by acknowledging the independence of the Spanish colonies.

Ferdinand VII. was enabled to finish his worthless and disastrous reign in comparative peace. In 1829 he married a fourth wife, Maria Christina of Naples, and at the same time he issued a "Pragmatic Sanction" abolishing the Salic law in Spain. No one expected any practical results from this edict, but a formal protest was made against it by the king's brothers, Carlos and Francisco, and also by the French and Neapolitan Bourbons. In the next year, however, the queen gave birth to a daughter, Isabella, who was proclaimed as queen on her father's death in 1833, while her mother undertook the office of regent. Don Carlos at once asserted his intention of maintaining the Salic law, and rallied round him all the supporters of absolutism, especially the inhabitants of the Basque Provinces. Christina was compelled to rely upon the Liberals, and to conciliate them by the grant of a constitution, the estatuto real, which established two chambers chosen by indirect election. But this constitution, drawn up under the influence of Louis Philippe of France, failed to satisfy the advanced Liberals, and the Christinos split into two parties, the Moderados and Progresistas. In 1836 the latter party extorted from the regent the revival of the constitution of 1812. All this time the government was involved in a desperate struggle with the Carlists, who at first gained considerable successes under Zumalacarregui and Cabrera. But the death of Zumalacarregui in 1835 and the support of France and England ultimately gave the regent the upper hand, and in 1839 her general, Espartero, forced the Basque Provinces to submit to Isabella. Don Carlos renounced his claims in favor of his eldest son, another Carlos, and retired to Trieste, where he died in 1855. Christina now tried to sever herself from the Progresistas, and to govern with the help of the moderate party who enjoyed the patronage of Louis Philippe. But England, jealous of French influence at Madrid, threw the weight of her influence on to the side of the Radicals, who found a powerful leader in Espartero. In 1840 Christina had to retire to France, and Espartero was recognized as regent by the Cortes. But his elevation was resented by the other officers, while his subservience to England made him unpopular, and in 1843 he also had to go into exile. Isabella was now declared of age. Christina returned to Madrid, and the Moderados under Narvaez obtained complete control over the government. This was a great victory for France, and Louis Philippe abused his success by negotiating the infamous "Spanish marriages." A husband was found for Isabella in her cousin, Francis of Assis, whose recommendation in French eyes was the improbability of his begetting children. On the same day the queen's sister, Maria Louisa, was married to Louis Philippe's son, the Duke of Montpensier. By this means it was hoped to secure the reversion of the Spanish throne for the House of Orleans. The scheme recoiled on the heads of those who framed it. The alienation of England gave a fatal impulse to the fall of Louis Philippe, while the subsequent birth of children to Isabella deprived the Montpensier marriage of all importance.

Spanish history during the reign of Isabella II. presents a dismal picture of faction and intrigue. The queen herself sought compensation for her unhappy marriage in sensual indulgence, and tried to cover the dissoluteness of her private life by a superstitious devotion to religion and by throwing her influence onto the side of the clerical and reactional party. Every now and then the Progresistas and Moderados forced themselves into office, but their mutual jealousy prevented them from acquiring any permanent hold upon the government. In 1866 Isabella was induced to take vigorous measures against the Liberal opposition. Narvaez was appointed chief minister; and the most prominent Liberals, Serrano, Prim and O'Donnell, had to seek safety in exile. The Cortes were dissolved, and many of the deputies were transported to the Canary Islands. The ascendency of the court party was maintained by a rigorous persecution, which was continued after Narvaez's death (April, 1868) by Gonzales Bravo. Common dangers succeeded at last in combining the various sections of the Liberals for mutual defense, and the people, disgusted by the scandals of the court and the contemptible camarilla which surrounded the queen, rallied to their side. In September, 1868, Serrano and Prim returned to Spain, where they raised the standard of revolt and offered the people the bribe of universal suffrage. The revolution was speedily accomplished and Isabella fled to France, but the successful rebels were at once confronted with the difficulty of finding a successor for her. During the interregnum Serrano undertook the regency and the Cortes drew up a new constitution by which an hereditary king was to rule in conjunction with a senate and a popular chamber. As no one of the Bourbon candidates for the throne was acceptable, it became necessary to look around for some foreign prince. The offer of the crown to Leopold of Hohenzollern-Sigmaringen excited the jealousy of France, and gave Napoleon III. the opportunity of picking a quarrel, which proved fatal to himself, with the rising state of Prussia. At last a king was found (1870) in Amadeus of Aosta, the second son of Victor Emmanuel, who made an honest effort to discharge the difficult office of a constitutional king in a country which was hardly fitted for constitutional government. But he found the task too hard and too distasteful, and resigned in 1873. A provisional republic was now formed, of which Castelar was the guiding spirit. But the Spaniards, trained to regard monarchy with superstitious reverence, had no sympathy with republican institutions. Don Carlos seized the opportunity to revive the claim of inalienable male succession, and raised the standard of revolt in the Basque Provinces, where his name was still a power. The disorders of the democrats and the approach of civil war threw the responsibility of government upon the army. The Cortes were dissolved by a military *coup d'état;* Castelar threw up his office in disgust; and the administration was undertaken by a committee of officers. Anarchy was suppressed with a strong hand, but it was obvious that order could only be restored by reviving the monarchy. Foreign princes were no longer thought of, and the crown was offered to and accepted by Alfonso XII., the young son of the exiled Isabella (1874). His first task was to terminate the Carlist war, which still continued in the north, and this was successfully accomplished in 1876. Time was required to restore the prosperity of Spain under a peaceful and orderly government and to consolidate by prescription the authority of the restored dynasty. Unfortunately a premature death carried off Alfonso XII. in 1885, before he could complete the work which circumstances laid upon him. The regency was intrusted to his widow, Christina of Austria, and the birth of a posthumous son (May 17, 1886), who is now the titular king of Spain, has excited a feeling of pitying loyalty which may help to secure the Bourbon dynasty in the last kingdom which is left to it.

CHAPTER IX

COLONIAL SPAIN

COLUMBUS — SIGHTING OF SAN SALVADOR — RETURN OF COLUMBUS — FOUNDING OF AN EMPIRE — MEXICO AND PERU — THE WEST INDIES — GERMS OF REBELLION

In August, 1492, Columbus sailed on his voyage of discovery. In September, 1898, his remains were conveyed from the New World to the Old. Between those two dates an empire rose and fell. The causes which led to the one and the effects which precipitated the other may now be conveniently considered.

In earlier years Cadiz was a famous seaport. Her sons were immemorial explorers. The presentiment of a land across the sea was theirs by intuition. Constantly they extended their expeditions, and would have extended them still further had not the Church interfered. The spirit of enterprise, checked as heretical, revived centuries later in a neighboring land. It was Portugal that it inspired. There the work of exploration and discovery was resumed. The island of Madeira was reached in 1420, the Azores annexed in 1431. But it was along the African coast that Portuguese effort was mainly directed. Tradition asserted that the entire continent had been circumnavigated centuries before by voyagers from Phœnicia; but, as no details were recorded, the adventure was regarded as something more than dubious. However, the west coast began now to be systematically explored. Nuño Tristao entered the Senegal River in 1445; a year later Diniz Dias, a fellow-navigator, sailed as far as Cape Verd. The equator was not crossed until 1471, the Congo was revealed in 1484; and in 1486 the crowning feat of all was accomplished, when Bartholomew Diaz rounded the Stormy Cape, soon to become known as the Cape of Good Hope, and opened up communication with the East by water, instead of overland or by the indirect route of the Red Sea, which necessitated the transshipment of all merchandise conveyed that way.

The expedition to the west which Columbus ultimately directed was conceived by him in 1474, and unfolded to John II., king of Portugal, by whom, however, it was rejected; whereupon Columbus dispatched his brother Bartholomew to enter into negotiations with Henry VII. of England, and after assuring himself that neither Genoa nor Venice were likely to lend him a willing ear, much less ready help, he repaired to the south of Spain in 1485.

Had Bartholomew not fallen into the hands of pirates, and so been prevented from reaching his destination for several years, it is more than probable that the credit as well as the profit of the discovery of America would have fallen at once to England, as Henry had both the means and the inclination to indulge in some such venture, provided it was not too costly, and showed any reasonable prospect of success. As it was, Christopher was left to pursue his pleadings before the Spanish Court.

It was an unfortunate time to put forward any proposals calculated to divert the wealth and strength of the kingdom beyond its own borders; for Ferdinand and Isabella were then in the very midst of the campaign which ended in the final overthrow of the Moorish dominion in the Peninsula.

Ultimately, however, after the fall of Granada and eighteen years of waiting, his proposals were accepted by Isabella and his hopes realized. A royal edict constituted him perpetual and hereditary admiral and viceroy of any territories discovered, together with a tenth of any profits derived therefrom. With this edict and funds advanced by the receiver of ecclesiastical revenues, Columbus hastened to the port of Palos. There, two brothers by the name of Pinzon aiding, he got together a crew of a hundred and twenty men, a scratch armada of three leaky tubs—the "Santa Maria," the "Pinta" and the "Nina"—and, on the 3d of August, 1492, weighed anchor for pastures new.

Columbus, as admiral of the fleet, commanded the "Santa Maria"; the two Pinzons, Martin Alonzo and Vicente Yanez, the "Pinta" and "Nina" respectively. The expressed object of the voyage was to convert the Grand Khan, supposed to be the great potentate of the Far East, to Christianity; and Columbus never doubted but that in due course he would arrive at Japan, or Zipangu, as it had been named by the Venetian explorer, Marco Polo, who had reached it by an overland route more than a century before, and had described its wonders, together with those of Cathay or China, through which he passed on his way. The one condition imposed was, that the squadron should not touch at any place on the African continent, claimed to be under Portuguese jurisdiction, as that would have led to immediate hostilities between the two countries.

The details of the voyage are sufficiently familiar to dispense with narration here. It will suffice to note that after seventy days the island of San Salvador, as it was then named, hove in sight; that on the 28th of October, sixteen days later, Cuba was discovered, and that on the 6th of December Hayti was reached.

Several circumstances then made it advisable for Columbus to return to Spain without further delay. He had seen enough to be convinced that a much larger force than he had under his command would be necessary to make the subjugation of these newly acquired territories effective; news of the discovery might reach Europe before him, and be taken advantage of by some other sovereign than the one to whom he was devoted; and he had now sufficient treasure of various kinds to convince the most skeptical of the complete success of his enterprise. After constructing a small fort, and leaving a portion of the crew, at their own desire, to garrison it until he should return, he set sail for home with the "Nina" on the 4th of January, 1493.

Reaching Palos on the 13th of March, Columbus was immediately summoned to Barcelona, where Ferdinand and Isabella were then domiciled, made a triumphal entry into the city, and, on his arrival at the royal residence, was welcomed by the king and queen in person, who commanded him to be seated by their side, while he related the account of his adventures.

Meanwhile the report of the discovery had spread. Portugal sought to take advantage of it through the theory that all heathen countries were in the gift of the Pope, which gift a Bull had already confirmed. But, Spain protesting, a subsequent Bull confirmed the Portuguese in their existing possessions, and granted them all territory that should be discovered east of a line drawn from north to south, one hundred leagues west of the Azores, while the Spaniards were to enjoy exclusive dominion over everything west of it.

This was regarded as so unsatisfactory by Portugal, that at its instigation, negotiations between the two countries were opened, and resulted the following year in the conclusion of the Treaty of Tordesillas, by which it was agreed to move the line three hundred and seventy leagues west of the Azores; a most important change, because by it Portugal subsequently established its claim to the Brazils, a portion of which was found to fall east of the line of demarcation, while it could urge the further plea of having been first in the field, through the accidental deviation of Cabral. At any rate, the whole world outside Europe was leased in perpetuity to Spain and Portugal; and had the pretensions of the Holy See in things temporal as well as spiritual continued to be recognized, neither England, France, nor Germany could to-day own a square yard of territory in the three greatest continents of the world.

While the negotiations were in progress, preparations for a second expedition on a vastly greater scale were rapidly pushed forward. The direction of them was intrusted to a cleric named Fonseca, a capable man of business, but who for some reason or other conceived a violent dislike to Columbus, and threw every obstacle in his way. The eagerness to embark on this second voyage was far more marked than the reluctance exhibited in the first, and the best blood of Spain pressed into the service. The number of adventurers was originally limited to a thousand; but the applications were so numerous, from those who believed that fortunes were waiting to be picked up in the New World, that this was raised to twelve hundred, and fifteen hundred actually sailed in seventeen vessels from the Bay of Cadiz on the 25th of September, 1493. All was keen anticipation during the voyage, the disappointments only commenced at its termination.

"Into these," says Mr. R. J. Root, whose account we quote, "there is no occasion to enter now. The main point of interest is, that a sufficiently large force of Spaniards had taken part in the enterprise to confirm the possession of the New World to their country, and defeat any attempts that Portugal might be likely to make to filch it away. After establishing a settlement at Isabella on the north of Hayti, or Hispaniola, as it was then named, Columbus was free to prosecute further explorations, the principal one being to sail along the southern shores of Cuba; but, after continuing his voyage to within a few miles of its western extremity, he arrived at the conclusion that it was the mainland, and reported to that effect—nor was it until after his death that it was proved to be an island. Everything was claimed for the Spanish crown; and, as there were absolutely no competitors, it can well be understood how the entire group of islands constituting the West Indies became Spanish colonies.

"Various causes compelled Columbus to relinquish his exploration and return, first to Hispaniola and then to

Spain. For one thing, the two vessels with which he set sail were ill-provisioned. With that confidence in his own judgment which was so characteristic of the man, he relied upon encountering at no great distance those civilized, or at least semi-civilized, nations of which he had come in search, but instead he met only the fierce tribes of Cuba and Jamaica, who offered resistance, not welcome, and arrows in lieu of food.

"On his return to the colony, affairs were in a most unsatisfactory condition. The last thing most of the colonists dreamed of when they left their native shores was work. They had gone out, as they fondly imagined, to pick up the gold as it lay at their feet, and when they had accumulated sufficient, meant to return and enjoy it. Though Columbus had never promised, nor even suggested anything of the sort, his brilliant descriptions and anticipations were undoubtedly responsible for the ideas so freely indulged, and the indignation against him rose just as rapidly as hopes were blasted. Complaints were finding their way to Spain, and lest he should be prejudiced in the eyes of his sovereigns, he determined to embark thence and render a personal account of his stewardship.

"The voyage home was, if anything, more protracted, and entailed greater hardships, than the previous one. Columbus arrived at Cadiz on the 1st June, 1496, and met with a warmer reception than he had dared to hope for. But intrigue was busy, and his arch-enemy Fonseca, who was by this time in almost undisputed control of colonial affairs, threw numerous and persistent obstacles in the way of his fitting out another expedition. The stories told by returned colonists of the want and suffering they had endured were not conducive to others volunteering for the service, and it was only on the 30th May, 1498, that the admiral was again able to set sail from San Lucar with a small fleet of six vessels, manned almost entirely by convicts specially released.

"A more southerly course was taken than on either of the previous occasions, and the first place touched was the island of Trinidad. Sailing round it from the southwest, the ships were suddenly caught and swept along by a mighty current, which Columbus discovered to be of fresh water, and rightly judged to be poured out of some vast river. He had, in fact, reached the coast of South America, and was in the waters of the Orinoco as they rushed to mingle with the ocean. The natives proved of a more friendly disposition as well as of superior type to those encountered in many of the islands; and as they possessed gold, and also something still more precious, pearls, every encouragement was given them to trade. They were just as eager after the trumpery toys of the Old World as the inhabitants of San Salvador had been the first time they were ever exhibited in the New, and we may be sure the bargains made were very profitable to the Spaniards. Still, these were not the people Columbus had come in search of, and his inquiries and labors were diligently directed to the discovery of a passage which should lead him still further west to the dominions of the Grand Khan.

"After some time vainly spent in exploring the coast with this object, an affection of the eyes compelled him to desist and make once more for Hispaniola, where he had left his brother Bartholomew as governor during his absence. A strange welcome awaited him, however. In response to the continued complaints of the colonists, a commissioner had been dispatched from Spain to inquire into their grievances, and certain powers were intrusted to him to assume authority in the island in case of necessity. Deeply impressed with a sense of his own importance, Francisco Bobadilla, the officer appointed, immediately on his arrival began to act in the most reckless and arbitrary manner; and the discoverer of the New World, without any warning, found himself arrested, loaded with chains, thrown into prison, and finally sent home to Spain in this ignominious fashion.

"Great was the public, still greater the royal indignation, when he arrived in this sorry plight; every effort was made to soothe the feelings so deeply wounded by this dire insult, and Bobadilla would have paid dearly for his temerity had he survived to answer for his misdeeds. But news had reached Spain of the wonderful riches of the Gulf of Paria some time before the arrival of Columbus, and the malignant and untiring Fonseca, in direct contravention of the charter conveying the rights to the admiral, stimulated private enterprise to follow in the track, taking the utmost possible advantage of whatever information he had gained in his official capacity, and imparting it to others. An expedition was fitted out under Alonso de Ojeda, one of the most dare-devil adventurers who ever quitted the shores of his own or any other country, and whose marvelous exploits in Hispaniola had already excited the wonder and admiration of men long accustomed to feats of skill and courage. Accompanying him was Amerigo Vespucci, a Venetian navigator, who strangely enough was destined to give his name to the whole of the vast continent which he was about to visit for the first time, though he never accomplished anything of practical importance in it. Several other ships were fitted out, including a caravel of fifty tons' burden by Pedro Alonso Nino, which performed the most lucrative voyage of any vessel or squadron equipped up to that time, and returned home well freighted with pearls and other costly treasure. This was quite sufficient to stimulate ambition as well as greed, and when Columbus arrived he had the mortification of learning that others were actively exploiting his preserves.

"While these events were happening, another enterprise was undertaken quite beyond the cognizance of the Spanish authorities. Bartholomew Columbus, it will be remembered, had proceeded on a mission to Henry VII. some years previous; and when the English monarch learned that the most sanguine anticipations had been realized, he was anxious to share in the results. As early as 1495 he endeavored to equip and dispatch a squadron of his own, but it was not until two years later that Sebastian Cabot, despite the existence of the Papal Bull, set sail from Bristol. Steering a direct westerly course, he struck the coast of Newfoundland, and leisurely sailed south almost to the extreme point of Florida, ere he resumed his homeward journey. The Spanish government naturally protested against this infringement of its rights, and Henry found it politic to listen, as he was then in close alliance, and engaged in negotiating the marriage between his son and Katharine of Aragon, which subsequently proved so pregnant to the religious and ecclesiastical destinies of England. It was at a later period, and under totally different circumstances, that the Anglo-Saxon race was to occupy and overrun the northern continent.

"Columbus himself was spared to undertake one more voyage, and this time it was to be confined exclusively to the continent, he being absolutely forbidden to land at Hispaniola, where Nicolas Ovando, with a force of all sorts and conditions of men, numbering two thousand five hundred, had been installed as governor; and so jealous was he of any interference with his prerogatives that, when the admiral was driven by stress of weather to take shelter in the harbor of San Domingo, he was ordered to quit instantly.

"This proved the most disastrous of all his voyages. After exploring the coasts of Honduras and Central America generally, in search of the non-existent channel, until the provisions were in such a state that they could only be eaten in the dark, it was decided to land, despite the fierce opposition of the natives, and plant a permanent settlement under Bartholomew, who accompanied his brother. This, however, had to be abandoned; and on the way back the only remaining vessel ran aground in Dry Harbor in Jamaica, and became a total wreck, the most incredible suffering, aggravated by constant mutiny, being experienced, until the remnant of the crew was eventually relieved.

"Columbus having shown the way to the mainland, as well as the islands, it was left to others to reveal the vast extent and natural wealth of what he had discovered, and he died on the 20th May, 1506, in complete ignorance of many of the most important facts which his genius and tenacity permitted to be made known for the first time to the civilized world.

"Columbus and his immediate followers hit upon the most unpromising part of the American Continent, where the damp, hot atmosphere, with its resulting rank and profuse vegetation, makes human existence intolerable if not wellnigh impossible. As the land was known to contain gold, however, the most persistent efforts were made to settle in it, and two regular governments were established under Alonzo de Ojeda and Diego de Nicuessa respectively. Nothing but disaster resulted for many a long year, and the greatest difficulties were experienced in extending or enlarging them in any direction but coastwise.

"Narrow as the isthmus is in the part selected, it appeared impenetrable, until eventually the magic word gold encouraged a few bold spirits to overcome every obstacle. Wherever the adventurers went inland they heard of a great sea and vast abundance of the precious metal in an unknown land beyond. After incredible hardships, Vasco Nunez de Balboa and a handful of followers forced their way through the thickets and swamps, scaled the mountain range which runs like a backbone along the isthmus, and were rewarded for their pains when they reached the summit by the sight of the great southern sea lying at their feet. This occurred on the 26th September, 1513, and on the following day the party descended the western slopes; Vasco Nunez, as its leader and commander, taking possession of the Pacific Ocean on behalf of the King of Spain, with all the ceremonies and formalities customary on those occasions.

"How to take advantage of it was the question? Far

south, beyond where vision could reach, lay the golden land. They were without ships or means of conveyance of any sort, and the shore upon which they were now stranded was dangerous as well as inhospitable. The observant and ingenious mind of Nunez, inferior only to that of Columbus, evolved the idea of transporting material across the isthmus for the construction of a fleet to undertake the subjugation of all countries bordering on the Southern Sea; and such was the work eventually accomplished, though not by Nunez, who fell a victim to the jealousy and treachery of Pedrarias Davila, a new governor dispatched from Spain. It was left to one of his lieutenants, Francisco Pizarro, to set forth on a definite expedition more than ten years later; and it was not until nearly twenty years had elapsed that Peru was discovered, and the rich kingdom of the Incas added to the spoils of the Castilian monarch.

"Meanwhile, exploration had been busy on the eastern side of the continent. Cuba, realized at length to be an island, was regularly colonized in 1511, and the governor, Diego Velasquez, being an enterprising and ambitious man, dispatched an expedition westward. The great peninsula of Yucatan was reached, and the officers of the little squadron were struck by the much higher state of civilization exhibited by the natives than by any others hitherto met with either in the islands or on the mainland. The news of this led to the subsequent expedition of Cortes, the story of whose conquest of Mexico reads more like a fairy tale than the narrative of actual events and hard realities.

"The years 1519, 1520 and 1521 were occupied by this,

the greatest of all the enterprises undertaken by Spain in the New World. Nor was there any lack of activity in other directions. Juan Ponce sailed from Porto Rico in 1512, in search of a spring whose waters insured perennial youth to whoever drank of them, and found and annexed Florida instead. More than one navigator cruised southward as far as the Rio de la Plata, and in 1520 Magellan reached the extremity of the southern continent, and passed through the straits which bear his name. Nor was Cortes idle after he had accomplished his great work. North and south he sought to add to the territory of New Spain, until all the countries of Central America on one side, and the peninsula of California on the other, were brought under its sway. In less than half a century from the day Columbus first set foot on San Salvador, the entire continent, from Labrador to Patagonia, had been visited, and by far the greater part of it annexed to, and nominally ruled by, the Castilian crown.

"To return, however, to Hispaniola. The rapid exhaustion which mismanagement produced there, joined to the absence of gold, led to the creation of other colonies. The discovery of the fisheries, first at Paria, and then in the islands of the Pacific, opened up an unexpected source of wealth; but it was not until Montezuma offered his munificent gifts to Cortes, to induce the latter to quit the shores of Mexico, that the first great reservoir of the precious metals was tapped. Still, it must be remembered that the great stores of gold discovered, first in Mexico, and subsequently in Peru, did not in themselves imply that these countries were capable of continuing to produce unlimited quantities. They were the accumulations of many years, possibly of many centuries; for, as there was no foreign trade, everything produced which could not be consumed had necessarily to be preserved or destroyed.

"It may be wondered what value gold possessed in the ideas of these people. That it was held in nothing like the same esteem as by Europeans is certain; but in Peru, at any rate, its production and preservation were assured, from the fact that it was regarded as tears wept by the sun, which was the god of the people, whose Incas, or rulers, were called the Children of the Sun. In neither case, then, is it surprising that the treasure was not clung to with more tenacity. Both Montezuma and Atahualpa set a higher value upon many other things; and the quantities seized by Cortes and Pizarro and their respective followers, vast though it appeared in their eyes, and as it really was in those days, was parted with, with scarcely a pang of regret. That secured by Pizarro was by far the greater spoil, and was supposed to be the price of the freedom of the Inca himself, who offered to fill a room 35 feet by 17, and as high as a man could reach, with gold plate in exchange for it. He did not quite succeed, because Pizarro treacherously put him to death before the task was completed, yet the amount realized for distribution was equivalent to something like three and a half millions sterling ($17,500,000) of the money of to-day, and enriched the commonest foot-soldier beyond the dreams of avarice.

"It was silver, not gold, moreover, which eventually made both countries at once the wonder and the envy of the civilized world. The richest mines were unknown to the Indians, having only been discovered after the Spanish conquest. Those of Zacotecas in Mexico were first worked in 1532, while the more famous Potosi lode in Peru was laid bare in 1545, by a native scrambling up the side of a mountain in pursuit of some llamas which had strayed from his flock, and uprooting the shrubs to which he clung for support.

"In the West Indies, meanwhile, the larger islands, like Porto Rico, Cuba and Jamaica, were gradually colonized, but the smaller ones were left alone; it can well be understood that in the absence of any proved deposits of gold they were scarcely worth attention, and it was sufficient to keep a watch over them to defend them from the incursions of other nations. With the conquest of Mexico, however, the center of gravity was moved further west, and still more so when followed by that of Peru, because the only known route from the latter was by Panama and across the isthmus.

"These territories were altogether too great for efficient oversight; that of Mexico stretching from California in the north to Venezuela in the south, and including not only the West Indies, but the far removed Philippines, while that of Lima embraced the whole of South America both east and west of the Andes. The great territories included in the present Republics of Argentina, Uruguay and Paraguay were looked upon as of little value, as they contained neither gold nor silver; and as every attempt made to settle them only seemed to end in failure, little attention was given to their affairs. They became, indeed, a distinct source of loss to Spain, as they were found useful for purposes of contraband trade; and eventually the gold and silver, which could not be safely smuggled through the ordinary ports of shipment, were conveyed across the Andes and down the rivers to places of embarkation on the Amazon or Rio de la Plata, where foreign ships awaited the spoil and were ready to barter the coveted produce and manufactures of Europe in exchange. When these two viceroyalties were eventually subdivided, it was not into east and west, but north and south, and New Granada became the center of one; while the territories now included in the United States were separated from Mexico, and constituted the other.

"In Spain everybody, from the king in his palace to the peasant in his hut, regarded the colonies simply as a source of revenue and profit to himself, and when they ceased to be this, they would be useless. The most stringent regulations were adopted, therefore, against trading or even communicating among themselves, or of engaging in any industry, manufacturing or agricultural, which was not indigenous to the country; indeed, Spain insisted upon supplying everything it could grow or make which would stand the sea voyage, at its own price. The cultivation of neither the olive nor the vine was permitted in the New World, and severe penalties were inflicted upon any one who had the temerity to disobey. Peru and Chili, however, were specially exempted, owing to their immense distance, and the damaged condition in which liquids generally arrived there, but they were not allowed to export the produce to any neighboring country, and must consume it themselves. The duties of the colonists were, in fact, strictly limited to obtaining as much gold and silver as they could, while the Spaniards at home were to take care that they retained as little of it as possible. For all that, many fortunes were realized, principally by bullion being smuggled out of the country; and had there not been some such inducement, few men would have cared to expatriate themselves, and live amid such uncomfortable surroundings.

"Precisely similar principles were observed in all matters relating to government. Every office of profit under the crown, almost every emolument, however trivial, was reserved for persons of pure Spanish birth. As a consequence, the official class was migratory, and remained in the colonies no longer than was necessary to accumulate a fortune or a competence, according to the taste of each individual member of it. Though there were honest and honorable men to be found among them, notably those filling the most exalted positions, that did not prevent the vast majority from preying on the colonists, many of whom, by virtue of the grants of territory they had received, attained to great influence and wealth. Their descendants were, nevertheless, debarred from all participation in either the legislative or executive functions of government, though they might have nothing but the purest Spanish blood flowing in their veins. Nor could they become dignitaries of the Church without much difficulty. In the days when the Holy See found it politic to be on good terms with the Spanish sovereign, the whole ecclesiastical patronage of the New World was vested in him and his successors; and though many Popes endeavored to get this privilege back into their own hands, they always failed, and were compelled to confirm the nominations of the secular ruler. Both Mexico and Peru were rapidly overrun with clergy, secular as well as regular, and monastic establishments sprang up everywhere like mushrooms, yet preferment was always reserved for their brethren in Spain; and out of nearly four hundred bishops and archbishops consecrated up to the middle of the seventeenth century, scarce a dozen were taken from the Spanish-American community known as Creoles.

"A system so rigid is bound to break. Federation is all very well and may accomplish much that is beneficial to all concerned. But its first condition is elasticity, so that every section within its embrace may enjoy full freedom of expansion. There must be no jealousies, no recriminations, and, above everything, no attempts to get all and give nothing. These conditions are possible under an arrangement entered into freely by all parties; they are unattainable when imposed by the strong upon the weak. That is why Spain never won the gratitude of its colonies, why each and every one eagerly seized the opportunity of throwing off the yoke, and fought desperately for independence, and why, to-day, her colonial power is ended."

CHAPTER X

THE FALL OF AN EMPIRE

THE SUPREMACY OF SPAIN—ENCROACHMENTS OF OTHER NATIONS—CAUSES WHICH LED TO COLONIAL REVOLT —BIRTH OF THE SOUTH AMERICAN REPUBLICS—INSURRECTIONS IN CUBA—ROBAMOS TODOS

THE population of Hayti at the advent of Columbus was estimated to have been a million, yet, before many years had elapsed, the colonists were forcibly depopulating the smaller islands to provide a supply of labor sufficient for their limited requirements. It was the people of the mainland who might have been expected and who actually did offer the stoutest resistance. No more wonderful campaign is recorded in military history than that conducted by Cortes against the Mexicans, and it may be doubted whether there was another man living who could have carried it to a successful issue.

Conspicuous as a general, he was unmatched as a diplomatist, whether in dealing with his own soldiers, his allies, or his enemies. Who else in that age would have dreamed, after defeating the Tlascalans against fearful odds, of enlisting them against their deadly foes the Aztecs, and so humoring them that they never swerved in their loyalty? Or who could have traded on the superstition of Montezuma, so as to gain complete control over his mind, and extract his treasures, valued at something like seven and a half million dollars, without a blow? But Montezuma once removed, the people, who had long been accustomed to render him an unquestioned obedience, and to submit themselves to his slightest command, were free to follow leaders who evinced more spirit; and the death of that monarch was speedily followed by the *noche triste* with all its attendant horrors. To be captured alive, as many of the Spanish soldiers were, meant the most terrible of all ends, for they were hurried away to the temples, and their palpitating hearts torn from their living bodies, to be offered as a propitiation to the national deities. Yet even this did not disconcert Cortes and his brave adherents, who began immediately to concert another plan of campaign. The difficulties they had first encountered were as nothing compared to those they had still to face, for they had to deal with a victorious and determined foe, instead of a beaten and depressed one. Every obstacle, however, was overcome; and with the energetic assistance of allies, who little dreamed they were sealing their own doom and forever sacrificing their independence, the powerful and rich kingdom of Mexico was finally brought into complete subjection to the Castilian crown.

Of totally different and vastly inferior fiber was the conqueror of Peru. Pizarro was without either education or address—a rough, ambitious, and avaricious soldier. He, too, was favored by internal dissensions, of which he could not possibly have known anything when he set forth on his errand. After a long period of peaceful and undisputed sway, the Inca dynasty was split by a feud between two brothers, one of whom, Atahualpa, had just asserted his superiority by force of arms, when the European conquerors appeared on the scene. A word from him, and not a man of them would have escaped alive. But at the critical moment an unaccountable paralysis overtook him, whether or not arising from a curiosity to see and interview the strangers it is impossible to say. He realized his danger too late, for Pizarro, imitating Cortes, seized the person of the Inca, and the rest was rendered comparatively easy. Accustomed, like Montezuma, to exact unqualified obedience, he employed his subjects in collecting his ransom instead of fighting for his deliverance; and when the debt was almost paid, he found himself doomed to death instead of released from captivity. The forces of the empire were then scattered, and without a leader who could assume full authority. Still, many a desperate bid was subsequently made for freedom, but each time with less prospect of success, as the conquerors secured a firmer grip upon the country, until the execution of Tapac Amara, the last direct descendant of the Incas, in 1571, left that solitude which Cæsar called peace.

But after all it was not the opposition of the Indians, whether of the islands, of Mexico, or Peru, that proved the greatest danger to Spanish sovereignty. Enmity to Columbus, who was the accredited representative of the crown and legal governor of the Indies, did not necessarily infer enmity to the crown itself; indeed, those who rebelled against him were loud in their protestations of loyalty. Nevertheless, the turbulent factions fought for their own hand, and would have been equally opposed to any other governor who sought to place the necessary restraint upon their license. By permitting, and even compelling, many of the discontented to return home, as well as by the temporary removal of Columbus himself, something like quiet was restored; but it is more than probable that had not the colonists been largely dependent upon Spain for many necessaries, not excluding food, they would have cut themselves adrift and refused to submit to the exactions upon their industry, or rather upon that of the natives from which they profited. More than once in the early days, the home government had to step cautiously, and commissions were dispatched to ascertain where the grievances lay, and if possible redress them. They were mostly connected with labor; the majority of the clergy, to their credit be it said, ranging themselves on the side of humanity, and using all their influence to obtain ordinances favorable to the natives. This difficulty was smoothed away to a great extent by the introduction of the African negro, which began as early as the year 1503.

The followers of Cortes were remarkably loyal to him in prosperity and adversity alike; and though for a long time he was unaware how his proceedings would be received at court, he remained consistent in his devotion to his sovereign. His dispatches breathe an almost effusive submission to their will and interests, and only his enemies ever laid any charges against him, while his own actions too obviously refuted them. It was only when some of his officers were removed from his influence and intrusted with commissions of their own that they thought of kicking over the traces, and then it invariably happened that they were not in situations where any great harm could result. Mexico once subdued, long rendered the most willing obedience of any of the colonies, partly perhaps because under the direct influence of good and great viceroys, who acted both with intelligence and discretion.

It was far otherwise in Peru, where the duplicity of Pizarro in excluding Almagro from his proper share in the governorship roused the suspicion, then the ire, and finally the opposition of that honest and gallant soldier. When Pizarro returned from his visit to Spain, he was either accompanied or immediately followed by several of his brothers, who, among them, formed a family compact for the protection and promotion of their own interests. To rid themselves of the rivalry of Almagro, they obtained for him the governorship of the country which now comprises the Republic of Chili. This, however, had still to be conquered, and the obstacles which presented themselves to the enterprise appeared so insurmountable that Almagro and his followers abandoned it and returned to Cuzco, the rich capital of Peru, which, the former maintained, fell within the latitude of the patent granted to him. This assertion was naturally contested by the Pizarros, and in the civil war that followed both Francisco Pizarro, the eldest and foremost of the brothers, and Almagro met with violent deaths. The Indians looked on with amazement at this strife between the white men, but failed to profit by it. Had they shown anything like the energy displayed in the warfare among themselves, or that of their Mexican brothers, they must inevitably have recaptured their kingdom, which it would have been extremely difficult to reconquer; but having allowed the golden opportunity to slip, it never again offered.

But the most serious menace to the supremacy of Spain in the New World occurred shortly after the promulgation of the edicts of Charles V. in 1542. The clauses guaranteeing the Indians their freedom, and protecting them against undue imposition, either of taxation or forced labor, were so obnoxious to the colonists that something like a general rising was threatened. The tact of the Mexican viceroy pacified those under his rule, but Peru experienced the full force of an armed rebellion with all its evil consequences. The leader in this instance was Gonzales Pizarro, who had inherited the immense estates conferred upon the family by a grateful sovereign, and who now undoubtedly aimed at establishing a separate kingdom with himself its supreme head. Fortunately, the right man was again sent from Spain to deal effectively with this uprising, and though a cleric, Vaca de Castro exhibited the skill of a general and the diplomacy of a statesman. With the execution of Gonzales, the last of the Pizarro brothers, peace was restored; and by the middle of the sixteenth century the various governments were so effectively consolidated that not for upward of a hundred and fifty years did any revolt, Indian or Creole, meet with more than temporary success.

It was far otherwise with the Philippines, which have never been free for any length of time from disturbances of some kind. No effort indeed has ever been made to thoroughly subdue the turbulent natives; and there is no similar extent of territory under the control of a European government, about which so little is known regarding its natural resources and mineral wealth as the important islands of Luzon and Mindanao, which embrace half the total area of the archipelago. The principal ports have been strongly fortified, and reliance placed upon them to retain possession. The immunities enjoyed by the natives would, under ordinary circumstances, offer little inducement to revolt, but unfortunately the Philippines have from the very first been particularly subject to ecclesiastical influence and jurisdiction, and in its missionary and persecuting zeal the priesthood has made itself thoroughly obnoxious. The religious orders were the special object of animosity in the latest rising, and unless they are either suppressed or placed under more effective political control, there will be little prospect of peace in the islands.

In an epoch when most of the nations of Europe are struggling to add to their territories in the remotest corners of the earth, it seems almost incredible that four centuries ago a single one of them should have been permitted to annex a whole continent unchallenged. It was not so much the Pope's Bull that frightened competitors away as the fact that they were too deeply absorbed in their own affairs. The importunity of Columbus had to wear itself nearly out before the fortunate completion of the Moorish conquest won it a more ready ear; and most other countries were about the same time either engaged in, or just recovering from, some similar internecine strife. Moreover, it was the energy of private adventurers rather than of the Spanish crown which won for the latter a vast empire beyond the seas; nor was it until its value became plainly apparent that it was thought worth while to go to any great amount of trouble or expense in its development.

Similarly, the first external enemies the Spanish colonies had to encounter were private and unattached adventurers. Piracy was an institution which had already flourished for many centuries. The Barbary corsairs were far more feared by the merchants of Venice and Genoa than the fiercest storms that ever visited the Mediterranean; and they had their counterpart in the Baltic, where the Hanseatic League carried on so extensive a commerce. It was only to be expected that they would sally forth from their inland seas when so much more valuable spoil was to be secured on the open ocean beyond, but strange to say, with the rapid decline of the trade which they had so long harried, their activity slackened, and their principles and profession were largely inherited by more civilized races. Some excuse was offered for this by the almost constant warfare that prevailed during the reign of Charles V., when France and Spain were at perpetual enmity, and England was found, first on one side, then on the other. The first important loss that befell Spain was the capture of the vessel conveying home the royal share of the treasures of Mexico by a French privateer, or pirate, as the Spaniards always preferred to call the ships which despoiled their fleets, a designation that was more often than not amply justified.

To begin with, these pirate ships were content to hang about the Azores, on the chance of meeting a caravel laden with treasure homeward bound. They gradually ventured further west, until they actually arrived among the West Indian Islands, where they were surprised to find that altogether undreamed-of facilities awaited them for the pursuit of their nefarious trade. Though the entire archipelago belonged nominally to Spain, only the larger islands were actually occupied, the smaller not being regarded as worthy of attention, until the Indian population of Hispaniola, Cuba and Porto Rico began to fail, and then they were raided for their inhabitants to supply the vacant places. With a scanty Spanish population, it would have been utterly impossible to fortify and inhabit all, even had colonists been found so self-denying as to banish themselves to places where the only chance of accumulating wealth was by hard work and steady application to agricultural pursuits.

For a long time these scattered islands were merely places of call, where fresh water and fruit could be obtained. No attempt was made at annexation in the name of any foreign power, and it would have been folly for any ship's company, even had they been disposed to relinquish their buccaneering career, to settle down and defy the Spanish power, whose forces would quickly have been put in motion to expel them.

Two events, designed by Philip II. to aggrandize the power of Spain at the expense of its neighbors, were eventually the means of arousing enmity against it to such an extent that the opposition of private adventurers was suddenly backed up by the full weight of the most rapidly progressing peoples and governments in the Old World.

Many previous efforts had been made to unite the crowns of Spain and Portugal, but hitherto all had failed. The heroic death of Sebastian, however, in 1580, left the throne of Portugal without a direct heir, and among the numerous claimants was Philip, who overreached all his competitors. He was probably even then meditating that descent upon the liberties of England which resulted, eight years later, in the dispatch of the renowned Armada, and the writing of one of the most brilliant pages of English history. Success in the one instance, no less than failure in the other, created the most deadly foes that Spain ever had to encounter, until the persistent antagonism of Holland and England reduced it at last to a miserable shadow of its former self.

Philip's ruling passion was an intense bigotry, and from the moment he assumed sway in Spain and the Low Countries, he sought to exterminate every trace of the Reformed faith. That brought him into conflict with the Dutch, whose principal port and city of Amsterdam was fast concentrating within itself the trade that Bruges and Antwerp had once commanded as the principal marts of the Hanseatic League. As Portugal extended its conquests in the East, Lisbon displaced Venice and Genoa, and became the great emporium of all Eastern produce, whence Amsterdam drew its supplies for distribution throughout northern Europe. With the object, therefore, of destroying Dutch trade, Philip closed the port of Lisbon to it in 1594, fondly imagining that that would ruin his rebellious subjects, and enforce submission to his will.

He had entirely mistaken Dutch character, however; for in the following year the services were enlisted of Cornelius Hautmann, who had been a pilot in the Portuguese service; and he conducted the first Dutch expedition round the Cape of Good Hope on its way to open up a direct trade with the Spice Islands and India, which of course had become the property of Spain along with its own Philippines. Thus modestly was laid the foundation of the Dutch Empire in the East Indies, and when Portugal regained its freedom in 1640, under the House of Braganza, it found itself stripped of most of its former colonies, which were never to be restored.

Not content merely with retaining their former trade, the Dutch sought to extend it in other directions; and the incorporation of their East India Company in 1602 was followed by that of the West India Company in 1621, the operations of which were to embrace the west coast of Africa as well as the whole of Spanish America, in which the Brazils had then to be included. They had been preceded many years earlier by the English, who commenced operations in good earnest some time before the date of the Armada; indeed, those two great figures in English naval history, Sir John Hawkins and Sir Francis Drake, had then already performed their greatest exploits. As early as 1572, the latter gave a good account of himself on the Spanish Main, but his most daring feat was accomplished in 1578, when he sailed through the Straits of Magellan and appeared off the coast of Peru. Francisco Draques was the terror of Spanish America, and his was the name used to frighten Spanish-American children when they were naughty.

A new danger thus became apparent, as the Spaniards had never dreamed before of reaching their West Coast possessions by the southern route. Lest other foreign adventurers should follow in the wake, an expedition under Pedro Sarmiento was dispatched from Chili to explore the Straits and the adjoining territory, with the view, if practicable, of founding a strong colony and erecting substantial fortifications. Sarmiento's zeal outran his discretion, and after accomplishing his task he sailed for Spain, where he gave an exaggerated account, not only of the danger of leaving the Straits unprotected, but of the ease with which they could be rendered impregnable to all unfriendly visitors. A colony consisting of about four hundred souls was actually sent out in 1582, though from the very first it met with nothing but dire misfortune.

The captain-general commissioned to take charge of the undertaking, Diego Flores, disliked the job, and began by chartering the worst ships he could find. His lieutenant, Sarmiento, was more discreet in the choice of the embryo colonists, most of whom were skilled mechanics; but the fleet had scarcely left San Lucar on the outward voyage, when half of them were shipwrecked and drowned. Though replaced, disaster continued to follow upon disaster, the voyage being very much a repetition of the previous one made by Magellan, only in this instance the commander was himself the leading obstructionist. Eventually, rather more than two hundred souls sailed from the Rio de la Plata, and forty-five of these were drowned ere the Straits were reached. All but eight of the survivors subsequently perished, and the last of them was taken off in 1589 by the "Delight," commanded by Sir John Cavendish, who appropriately named the spot where he found him "Port Famine."

The advent of the English and Dutch, followed half a century later by the French, led to the settlement of some of the unoccupied islands. They rapidly became something more than mere provisioning depots, though several of them, and notably the island of Tortuga, were nothing else than the lairs of desperate crews of pirates, as reckless of their own lives as of those who were unfortunate enough to fall into their clutches. But Barbadoes and St. Christopher, St. Eustatius and Curaçoa, Martinique and Guadalupe, became the center of something more legitimate, if quite as illegal, as sinking galleons and purloining their treasure, though that business was never missed either when the opportunity presented itself; and the Dutch West India Company alone is said to have been responsible for the capture of between five and six hundred Spanish vessels.

The English secured their first foothold in the neighborhood by occupying the Bermudas in 1621, though this hardly brought them into direct contact with the West Indies. This was speedily followed by settlements in some of the unoccupied islands further south. Barbadoes was taken possession of in 1625, and the same year St. Christopher, or St. Kitts, as it is now called, was divided between the English and French. The former continued to add to their territory, taking Nevis in 1628, Antigua and Montserrat in 1632; and all these islands are so essentially English, as to prove conclusively that, although once nominally owned by Spain, Spanish influence was never exerted in them.

From 1650 until the period of his death, Oliver Cromwell, having established his authority at home, pursued an active foreign policy, and it was only natural that he should find himself in conflict with Spain, whose maxims of government, both civil and religious, were so utterly at variance with his. Thus, in 1654, a somewhat formidable fleet, under the command of the admirals Penn and Venables, sailed for Barbadoes, where they would be ready for any emergency. Early the following year they made a descent upon Hispaniola, selecting the capital, San Domingo, as the object of attack. On the approach of the ships, the inhabitants, white and black alike, fled inland, but the affair was sadly mismanaged and somehow miscarried. Not wishing the expedition to prove a complete failure, the admirals set sail for the adjoining island of Jamaica, which did not then contain, at the outside, more than fifteen hundred whites, and perhaps as many blacks. This time, no difficulty was experienced, and the island was taken formal possession of, this being the first loss of occupied territory inflicted upon Spain, as well as the most important acquisition ever made in the West Indies by England. In 1658 the Spaniards attempted to drive the intruders out but failed, and in 1670 a treaty was entered into between the two countries, in which Spain recognized the rights of England both in Jamaica and the smaller islands of which possession had been previously taken.

About this time, also, the French West India Company was incorporated, the brilliant finance minister of Louis XIV., Colbert, not liking to be without a hand in the game. He began in a more legitimate fashion than his competitors, and in 1664 purchased the rights of the settlers in Martinique, Guadalupe, St. Lucia, Grenada, and a few other islands for about a million livres. Spanish tyranny, however, afforded an excuse for more highhanded proceedings, and the company secured a footing on the western side of Hispaniola, Spanish interests being concentrated almost entirely on the eastern. The settlements so established became little more than a rallying-point and shelter for buccaneers, who, in consequence of their roving habits, were difficult to eject, until eventually this intermittent occupation of a portion of the island induced France to lay claim to the whole, but the cession was only formally recognized by Spain more than a century later. Thus the four predominant powers of Europe all had a stake in the Western Hemisphere.

Nearly a hundred and fifty years elapsed without witnessing any further important changes. The very vastness of the Spanish-American empire was its principal protection. Europe was growing thoroughly accustomed to immense armies, but they could only be moved on land, and there was no means for transporting them across the sea. What chance was there then of conquering a territory which extended uninterruptedly from California to Chili, and from Florida to the Rio de la Plata, even had there been much inclination? The idea, it is true, occurred more than once, and especially in 1702, when—the death of Charles II. of Spain having brought to an end the Hapsburg dynasty, and the Wars of the Spanish Succession being entered upon—an alliance was formed between England, Holland and the German Empire for the conquest of the Spanish colonies, but like others it came to nothing. Again, in 1739, Spain, alarmed at the growing contraband trade, insisted very justifiably on searching English ships in American waters, but this was resented and led to war, in which Porto Bello was captured; and that had something to do with the permission granted a few years later to trade by the longer, but safer and more convenient route round Cape Horn.

Once more, in 1762, what was known as the Family Compact involved the rest of Europe in hostilities against the Bourbon dynasties in France, Spain, and Italy, and the war was carried both to the East and West Indies. Havana and Manila were captured by the English, and might have become English possessions, had not the Treaty of Paris, concluded in 1763, brought the campaign to an end, and made it a condition that all colonial conquests were to be restored to their original owners. Minor changes were frequent and numerous, but they were generally a mere shuffling of the cards between England, Holland, and France, leaving the Spanish possessions much as they were.

The eighteenth century, as it drew to its close, found the Spanish occupation of America almost as it had been in the first half of the seventeenth. Then a mighty upheaval was witnessed both in North America and Europe, and the War of Independence in the United States, together with the French Revolution, provide the sequel for what followed in South America. Scarcely a murmur was heard in the principal Spanish colonies while these great events were changing the destinies of the civilized world, and an onlooker who had time to think must have been astonished at their apparent loyalty to the mother country, oppressed though they had been, and still were, while everywhere else the blow for freedom was being struck. Perhaps another conclusion might have been arrived at; namely, that the ancient Spanish stock had so degenerated, and had become such a mean-spirited race, that it dare not act like its neighbors further north; but subsequent events disproved this hypothesis. The Girondists and the Mountain rose and fell; Napoleon became successively director, dictator, emperor — still no sign of movement. Then the moment arrived for the arch-disturber of Europe to overthrow the ancient monarchy of Spain, and to establish a brand-new one with his brother Joseph at its head. That was the supreme crisis to make a move, or forever to remain still. Spain almost to a man resented the affront. Spanish America joined the mother country, and refused to recognize the upstart dynasty.

Still, in the midst of this death-like calm, some presages of the coming storm were discernible. In the first place, France, by the Treaty of Basle in 1795, secured the cession of the whole of Hispaniola, only, however, in a few years to lose it again by its declaration of independence, and the formation of a black republic. In the naval conflicts so frequent during that disturbed period England both lost and gained. The Dutch and Spanish were both unwilling confederates of Napoleon, but their connection with him, nevertheless, exposed their foreign possessions to the attack of his declared enemies; and England captured Demerara and Essequibo in Guiana from the former, and the island of Trinidad from the latter. All these were trivial acquisitions, compared with the vast extent of Mexico and Central America, Peru, and New Granada, and the eastern province of Buenos Ayres. Brazil had reverted to Portugal with the firm establishment of the Braganza dynasty, and was nearly all there was left of its once great colonial empire. In March, 1808, the ill fortune of the royal family drove them from their own kingdom to find refuge beyond the seas, and Brazil became an independent empire under the fugitive Portuguese sovereign, whose descendants remained in peaceable and prosperous possession until the revolution which dethroned the late ill-fated Dom Pedro.

These changes were due entirely to foreign intervention and not to domestic unrest. The first sign of this was when Francisco Miranda, a Spanish-American who had fought under Washington, conceived the idea of freeing his fellow-countrymen, and took steps toward that end by founding a "Gran Reunion Americana" in London in 1806. But so unresponsive were the inhabitants of the Spanish Main that the first active movement of the league resulted in dead failure. It attracted the sympathy and support, however, of two active and capable men, Bolivar and San Martin, who were destined to do so much for the emancipation of South America from European bondage, and whose advent brought a rapid change in the feeling of indifference with which the movement was regarded.

Still, the loyalty of the colonists might have been proof against their blandishments had the government of Ferdinand VII., established at Cadiz in opposition to that of Joseph Bonaparte, shown itself in any way conciliatory toward them. Loyal though the Spaniards at home were to the Bourbon dynasty, they were only willing to rally round it on condition of the carrying out of many important reforms in consonance with the spirit of the age; and the colonists likewise demanded that, as the price of their adhesion, they should be put upon an equality with Spain, and be accorded perfect liberty in their agricultural and manufacturing industries; that trade should be thrown open between all the countries on the American Continent and with the Philippines; and that all restrictions and monopolies should be abolished, and fixed duties substituted in their place. Reasonable though these demands now appear, they were indignantly rejected, and with one consent nearly every country in Spanish America was ablaze with revolution.

One of the earliest outbreaks was in Mexico, the near proximity of the United States having perhaps inspired in that country a more intense longing for freedom than elsewhere. A small band of patriots had for some time been watching an opportunity for asserting themselves, and with Hidalgo and Allende at their head, took the extreme step of issuing a declaration of independence on the 16th of September, 1810. Spanish influence was still strong, and in less than a year the outbreak was suppressed, and the leaders executed. Others rose to take their places, and just three years after the declaration of independence, the first Mexican Congress was summoned to meet at the town of Chilpantzongo, which was in the hands of the insurgents. Morelos, the principal actor at this stage of the drama, was captured and shot in December, 1815; but that only imposed a temporary check on the movement. In the delusive hope of regaining full control, Ferdinand, then firmly re-established on his throne, offered concessions in 1820, but it was too late, and they failed to effect a pacification. Independence was once more declared in 1821, but this time at the instigation of a dictator who aimed at founding an empire for himself, and who did for a short period sway the destinies of his country as the Emperor Iturbide I. His reign was brief, and a republic was definitely established on the 16th of December, 1823, the subsequent career of which has been so checkered until quite recent times. Having been recognized by the principal courts of Europe, Spain itself accredited an embassador in 1839, and made no further efforts to reassert its former title.

Elsewhere the struggle was less prolonged, though, while it lasted, quite as exciting. At the instigation of Bolivar, Venezuela proclaimed its independence in July, 1811, and several years later united with New Granada as the Republic of Colombia. Buenos Ayres established a junta in 1810, a Constituent Assembly was called in January, 1813, and entire independence of Spain was declared, July, 1816. The insurrection in Chili likewise began in 1810, when a National Congress was summoned to meet at Santiago; but the Spanish interest was strong on the west coast, and it was not until San Martin crossed the Andes from La Plata in 1817 that independence was made good. Material assistance was afforded by the famous Admiral Cochrane (Lord Dundonald), who, driven in disgrace from his native country, placed his services at the disposal of the revolting Chilians, and gave them that naval pre-eminence in South America which they have ever since retained.

Peru proved an even tougher job, but the combined forces of San Martin and Cochrane proved irresistible, and both Lima and Callao were taken in 1821. Lima, however, was recaptured by the Spaniards in 1823, but Bolivar, marching against it from Colombia, was appointed dictator, and gained so decisive a victory in 1824 that the Spanish army was forced to capitulate, and by 1826 the connection with the mother country was completely and finally severed. Spain had vainly striven against these successive misfortunes, and in 1815 sent out a considerable force under Marshal Morillo, who gained a few temporary successes; but his cruelties and atrocious conduct only exasperated the colonists, and instigated them to greater exertions. The various countries of Central America were quietly federated into the Republic of Guatemala in 1823, in the absence of any Spanish troops to oppose; and thus, from the northern borders of Mexico to the southern confines of Chili and La Plata, the conquerors of the New World were forever ejected. England was the first to recognize the South American republics, and entered into commercial treaties with several of them in 1825, after which date Spain can no longer be said to have been able to claim ownership of a single acre on the American Continent.

Meanwhile of a once vast colonial empire but Cuba and Porto Rico remained. What were the forces at work which there prevented secession?

The political economist Mr. R. J. Root, to whom and to whose work on this subject we are already much indebted, states that the conditions were different. The predominant feature of the islands was negro slavery, whereas the wealth of the Spanish-American colonist lay in lands which, if subject to alienation, were at least impossible of removal. The Cuban planter reckoned as his most precious possession the flesh and blood attached to his estates, and the very words "freedom" and "independence" stank in his nostrils. Whatever inconvenience, therefore, he suffered from his political connection with an effete monarchy and a decaying or decayed empire, he at least felt that, while he clung to it, it would afford him protection for his property.

A steady flood of immigration from the mother country maintained this connection down to the recent war. The wealthiest merchants and planters have invariably been of pure Spanish blood, and their contempt for the Cuban Creoles, though many of them are as pure-blooded as themselves, and have no taint whatever of the "tar-brush," has helped to maintain them as a separate class, regarded as intruders by all of Cuban birth, and hated accordingly. They have of necessity invoked Spanish aid and relied on Spanish authority, and have, for nearly a hundred years, provided the basis for Spanish rule in the island. Many of them made their fortunes and returned home, leaving room for others to follow. Some made Cuba their permanent domicile, but invariably with fatal effects upon their offspring, for Cuban birth is almost synonymous with Cuban sympathies, and, in any rising, the father, who has been on the side of the crown, has witnessed his sons throwing in their lot with the rebels.

Ever since the emancipation of the Spanish Main, Cuba has been in a state of political unrest. Various secret societies have been constituted, and have received advice and assistance from Mexicans, Chilians, and others who had already succeeded in throwing off their own fetters. In 1823 the Society of Soles struck a blow for liberty; six years later it was the Company of the Black Eagle which attempted success where its predecessor had failed. Both were essentially Creole risings, and although those who participated in them freely gave expression to their abhorrence of slavery, no assistance was either asked or received from the negroes. For these unfortunates, however, failure meant the tightening of their bonds; and it is not surprising to find that, in 1844, goaded to despair by their sufferings, they tried an insurrection on their own account, though of course it ended disastrously.

These outbreaks were all more or less localized, and it was not until 1868 that a revolution broke out, destined to involve the entire island, and to occupy long and weary years in suppressing, if, indeed, the smoking embers can be said ever to have been quenched. It was undoubtedly instigated by the American Civil War, which had ended in the uncompromising abolition of slavery, and so raised the hopes of the friends of liberty in Cuba. Though the planters and slave-owners ranged themselves, as was natural, on the side of law and order, their enthusiasm was no longer of the keenest. They realized that the institution to which they clung so tenaciously was doomed, and it became a question with them of doing the best they could for themselves. Emancipation in the British West Indies had for a time added enormously to their prosperity, until the value of slaves underwent so great an appreciation that it no longer became profitable to purchase them, and only actual owners derived any benefit. For, it must be remembered, there was a distinct difference between the slave-trade and slavery, and long after public opinion revolted against, and prohibited the kidnaping and traffic in human flesh, it continued to tolerate its ownership, and recognized natural increase as legitimate property. That African negroes were smuggled into Cuba is tolerably certain; nevertheless, the numbers were too small to prevent the gradual increase in value of an able-bodied male slave from $250 to something like $1,750 or $2,000. This was the surest means of eventual abolition;

for while this high price set upon the black made him valuable property, and insured his better treatment, it tended to make the luxury too costly, and one that could eventually no longer be indulged in, as the point must be reached where free labor would become cheaper.

About the time of the rebellion, the number of slaves in Cuba was between 350,000 and 400,000, and their value on paper was simply enormous. The $100,000,000 voted by the British Parliament as compensation to the disinherited slave-owners in the British West Indies would have been but a drop in the ocean in any scheme for Cuban emancipation by purchase. Indeed, to do the planters justice, they never expected anything of the sort, and all the more practical of them asked, was to be let down gently. This was effected by the proclamation of what was known as the Moret Law in 1870, which at once declared free all slaves over sixty years of age, and decreed that every child born after that year should be free likewise. In the first instance, the planters registered a distinct gain, as they got rid of a number of old and decrepit dependents no longer fit for work; but this was offset by the compulsory maintenance, until their eighteenth year, of all the free offspring of their slaves. Under this law, the odious institution perished in something like twenty years, because its burdens gradually outweighed its benefits, until the low wage for which the free negro is willing to work became the more economical method of production.

Thus the strongest tie between Spain and Cuba was snapped, and the party of independence gained force, as many planters found no longer any advantage in supporting the authority of the crown. The rebellion dragged on; the Spanish troops continually poured in having to encounter the guerrilla warfare, for which the division of the island afforded so many opportunities. For, considerable though the population is, two-thirds of it has always been concentrated in the western corner, of which Havana is the capital, the remaining districts being very sparsely peopled. It is in these rebellion always throve; and the policy adopted by General Welyer, when in supreme command, was to make them a desert by destroying all sustenance, and forcibly removing the inhabitants, who, under the name of Reconcentrados, aroused so much sympathy.

Though the outbreak of 1868 was eventually suppressed, it left a legacy of bitter memories and still bitterer exactions. For, true to its policy of four centuries, Spain determined that it at least would not be a loser, and saddled the entire cost of the military operations, and nobody knows what else besides, on the unfortunate island, in the form of a debt amounting to about four hundred million dollars. Even this might have been tolerated had any attempt been made to establish an equitable system of government, because an era of prosperity set in which culminated in 1891, when the total exports were valued at no less than $100,000,000, and there was ample margin for interest on an inflated debt. But the rapacity of Catalan manufacturers, no less than of government officials, upset everything; and from the captain-general down to the humblest trader in Barcelona, all expected to pocket something out of the spoils of Cuba. Nor was the plunder limited to Spaniards. Despite the restrictions against trading by foreigners, adventurers of all nationalities managed to get a foothold in Havana, and corruption preyed on corruption. No one, in fact, was expected to be honest, and a stranger remarking upon the rascality prevailing in high places, would as likely as not be met with a shrug of the shoulders and the reply, Robamos todos, "We are all thieves."

CHAPTER XI

THE PHILIPPINES

THE FIRST JOURNEY ROUND THE WORLD — FERDINAND MAGELLAN — THE MOLUCCAS — THE ISLANDS OF THE PAINTED FACES — MANILA AND THE CHINESE — THE BRITISH INVASION — SPANISH RULE

WHILE Spain was actively engaged in exploration and annexation in the west, Portugal was equally busy in the east. Though the Cape of Good Hope had been doubled by Diaz in 1486, it was not until 1497, five years after the discovery of America, that Vasco da Gama proved the possibility of reaching India by that route. Rapid progress, for those days at any rate, was made from that time. The actual neighborhood of the Cape apparently offered no attractions; the advantages of its situation were left to be realized by the Dutch a century later; and it was not until Natal was reached on Christmas day, whence its name, that there were any thoughts of annexation or settlement. It was the East Coast of Africa which seemed to offer the greatest facilities for communication and trading with the opposite shores of India, and claimed attention accordingly; and as numerous pilots were to be found there, skilled in navigating vessels across the Indian Ocean, it was there colonies were first established, one of which at least, and the only important one remaining to Portugal, Lorenzo Marques, has been the object of envy, and the source of much contention in recent years.

From the Malabar coast in the south to Karachi in the north of India, Portuguese traders grew active, but, owing to the fierceness and determination of the natives, it was found impossible for some years to permanently occupy any territory, until Goa was established in 1510, as the center of Portuguese interests. A year earlier than this, Malacca had been subjugated, and the exploration of Sumatra undertaken; while three years later, Francisco Serrao discovered the Moluccas, the far-famed islands from which Venice and Genoa had so long drawn their stores of valuable spices by the overland route through India and Persia, or by the Red Sea and Isthmus of Suez. To divert this traffic round the Cape of Good Hope, expeditions were fitted out against Muscat and Ormuz in the Persian Gulf, and Aden at the entrance to the Red Sea. While, then, the Spanish colonists were searching for gold in sufficient quantities to make the enterprise pay, much less realize fortunes, the Portuguese tapped the source of wealth of the great mercantile communities of the Middle Ages, and, monopolizing it themselves, rendered their country for a time the richest in the world.

Of the numerous governors dispatched by Portugal to the east, the Duke of Albuquerque was the most active, and accomplished the greatest results. Serving under him in various capacities was Ferrao Magalhaes, or Maghallanes, a young nobleman who sought on every possible occasion to distinguish himself. Returning home, he did not receive the reward he considered his due; and though he continued to agitate at court, and to urge his claims, on the further ground that since his arrival from the east he had taken part in an African campaign and been permanently lamed, he was either repulsed or put off with some trifling concession. This rankling in his mind, he determined to divest himself of his nationality, and offer his services to Spain, the patron of all foreign adventurers.

By the Papal Bull, Spain was debarred from undertaking any enterprise in the East. This was, of course, well known to Magalhaes, or Ferdinand Magellan, as he now chose to call himself, but he had carefully thought the matter out, and arrived at a conclusion of his own. He had heard much of the ideas which led to the discovery of America, and though other and more important matters then engaged the attention of Spain than the discovery of Japan and China by the western route, he still considered the plan feasible. He intimated to the Emperor Charles V., then king of Spain, his desire to be intrusted with an expedition, with which he would undertake to reach the Moluccas from the west, and so prove that they belonged by right to Spain.

News of this treachery reached Portugal, where it was heard with the greatest indignation, and an angry correspondence passed between the two courts. Charles's ambitions, however, lay in European aggrandizement, for which the demands upon his exchequer were heavier than he well knew how to meet. His great possessions in the New World had hitherto been a drain upon his scanty resources, as they had been upon those of his grandfather before him; and although Ferdinand lived for a quarter of a century after the discovery of America, he left hardly sufficient money in his coffers to pay his funeral expenses. Charles, therefore, listened eagerly to the proposition by which he might acquire the teeming riches of the Spice

Islands, and, notwithstanding protests and warnings alike, terms were finally agreed to in March, 1518, which placed five ships, and a full complement of men, at the disposal of Magellan. Failing any other means of putting an end to the enterprise, a plot was formed for the assassination of Magellan, but miscarried; and he weighed anchor on the 10th of August, 1519, though delayed in his actual departure until the 20th of September following.

Instructions were sent to the Brazils, already occupied by Portugal, to waylay Magellan, and at all costs prevent the continuance of his voyage; and in case he eluded the vigilance of the governor of that settlement, a strict watch was to be kept at the Moluccas, and no quarter given him if he ever reached there, as he was declared a traitor to the crown of Portugal. He arrived at the Rio de la Plata unmolested, and entered that river, of great width at its mouth and for some distance along its course, with the idea that it offered the long-sought passage to the West. The increasing freshness of the water convinced him that it was but a river, and he returned and moved his course southward. And now his real difficulties began. Winter was setting in with all its rigor, and the further south he proceeded the more severe became the weather. His crew was most cosmopolitan in character and nationality, and included a number of Portuguese, some of whom, it began to be suspected, had been bribed to mutiny, if not indeed to murder their commander. Dissensions broke out among the captains of the different vessels on petty points of precedence and discipline; and only the most determined stand by Magellan himself, who did not hesitate to hang several of the crew as an example to the rest, prevented the total ruin of his hopes and plans.

To make matters worse, scarcity of provisions began to be experienced, and it was then decided to winter in the shelter of the river St. Julian. It was in October, 1520, before a fresh start could be made, and on the 21st of that month a channel was discovered, the careful navigation of which for thirty-eight days, amid shoals and innumerable islands, brought them, amid great rejoicing, once more into the open sea, proving the theory maintained by Columbus to his dying day to be so far, at any rate, correct.

But Magellan, like all his predecessors, sadly miscalculated the distance between the remote East and the far West, and after taking in such supplies of provisions as were obtainable, renewed his voyage with a light heart, and in full expectation of reaching land in a week or two at longest. Days grew into weeks, and the weeks passed into months, and still no break on the monotonous horizon. The sufferings of the crew were horrible, as food and water became gradually exhausted, and they had to subsist at last by gnawing anything into which they could get their teeth. To turn back was certain destruction, as they could not possibly last out the time necessary to cover the distance already traversed. To go forward, therefore, was their only chance of salvation; and after a passage of ninety-eight days land was sighted on March 18, and the most dreaded of their dangers passed. They had sailed into a group of islands, not the Moluccas as they had anticipated, but the Islas de las Pintados; so called from the custom of the natives of painting or tattooing their naked bodies, and subsequently re-christened the Philippines, in honor of the heir to the Spanish throne, who afterward reigned as Philip II.

Magellan was not destined to reap the fruits of his enterprise, nor to suffer the punishment subsequently inflicted on some of the survivors. He found the natives among whom he first landed friendly disposed, but rightly suspected them of treachery. Desirous, however, of conciliating them as far as possible, he entered into their quarrel with a tribe in a neighboring island, and, in the attack which he led against it, was slain.

Disputes arose as to who should succeed to the command; and what was left of the fleet, after many adventures and the loss of a considerable number of the crew, arrived at the island of Tidor in the Moluccas on the 8th of November, 1521. There it was decided that the "Victoria" should load a cargo of spices and make its way to Spain by the Cape of Good Hope, in direct defiance of the rights of the Portuguese, while the "Trinidad" should return the way she came. A valuable cargo, consisting of about twenty-six tons of cloves, with parcels of cinnamon, sandal wood, and nutmegs, was shipped, and after being nearly captured by the Portuguese off the African coast, and again at the Canaries, arrived in the harbor of San Lucar, as was supposed, on the 6th of September, 1522, having sailed round the world in three years all but a few days. Through all their troubles, a careful record of dates had been kept, and the officers were surprised to find that what they imagined to be the 6th was actually the 7th of September in Seville; and they were at a loss to know how the one day had been missed, being of course unaware that this is the invariable result of circumnavigating the world from East to West.

Of the total number of two hundred and eighty hands originally shipped, only a remnant remained, of whom seventeen, together with the captain, Juan Sebastian Elcano, were on board the "Victoria."

The city of Seville received them with acclamation; but their first act was to walk barefooted, in procession, holding lighted candles in their hands, to the church, to give thanks to the Almighty for their safe deliverance from the hundred dangers which they had encountered. Clothes, money, and all necessaries were supplied to them by royal bounty, and Elcano and the most intelligent of his companions were cited to appear at court to narrate their adventures. His Majesty received them with marked deference. Elcano was rewarded with a life pension of five hundred ducats (worth at that date about five hundred and sixty dollars), and as a lasting remembrance of his unprecedented feat, his royal master knighted him and conceded to him the right of using on his escutcheon a globe bearing the motto: "Primus circundedit me."

Two of Elcano's officers, Miguel de Rodas and Francisco Alva, were each awarded a life pension of fifty thousand maravedis (worth at that time about seventy dolars), while the king ordered one-fourth of that fifth part of the cargo, which by contract with Maghallanes belonged to the State Treasury, to be distributed among the crew, including those imprisoned in Santiago Island.

Meanwhile the "Trinidad" was repaired in Tidor and on her way to Panama, when continued tempests and the horrible sufferings of the crew determined them to retrace their course to the Moluccas. In this interval Portuguese ships had arrived there, and a fort was being constructed to defend Portuguese interests against the Spaniards, whom they regarded as interlopers. The "Trinidad" was seized, and the captain, Espinosa, with the survivors of his crew, were afforded a passage to Lisbon, which place they reached five years after they had set out with Maghallanes.

The enthusiasm of King Charles was equal to the importance of the discoveries which gave renown to his subjects and added glory to his crown. Notwithstanding a protracted controversy with the Portuguese court, which claimed the exclusive right of trading with the Spice Islands, he ordered another squadron of six ships to be fitted out for a voyage to the Moluccas. The supreme command was confided to Garcia Yofre de Loaisa, Knight of St. John, while Sebastian Elcano was appointed captain of one of the vessels. After passing through the Magellan Straits, the commander, Loaisa, succumbed to the fatigues and privations of the stormy voyage. Elcano succeeded him, but only for four days, when he too expired. The expedition, however, arrived safely at the Molucca Islands, where they found the Portuguese in full possession and strongly established; but the long series of combats, struggles and altercations which ensued between the rival powers, in which Captain Andres do Urdaneta prominently figured, left no decisive advantage to either nation.

But the king was in no way disheartened. A third expedition—the last under his auspices—was organized and dispatched from the Pacific coast of Mexico by the viceroy, by royal mandate. It was composed of two ships, two transports and one galley, well manned and armed, chosen from the fleet of Pedro Alvarado, late governor of Guatemala. Under the leadership of Ruy Lopez de Villalobos it sailed on the 1st of November, 1542; discovered many small islands in the Pacific; lost the galley on the way, and anchored off an island about twenty miles in circumference, which was named Antonia. They found its inhabitants very hostile. A fight ensued, but the natives finally fled, leaving several Spaniards wounded, of whom six died. Villalobos then announced his intention of remaining here some time, and ordered his men to plant maize. At first they demurred, saying that they had come to fight, not to till land, but at length necessity urged them to obedience, and a small but insufficient crop was reaped in due season. Hard pressed for food, they lived principally on cats, rats, lizards, snakes, dogs, roots and wild fruit, and several died of disease. In this plight a ship was sent to Mindanao Island, commanded by Bernado de la Torre, to seek provisions. The voyage was fruitless. The party was opposed by the inhabitants, who fortified themselves, but were dislodged and slain. Then a vessel was commissioned to Mexico with news and to solicit re-enforcements. On the way, Volcano Island (of the Ladrone Islands group) was discovered on the 6th of August, 1543. A most important event followed. A galiot was built and dispatched to the islands (it is doubtful which), named by this expedition the Philippine Islands in honor of Philip, prince of Asturias, the son of King Charles I., heir apparent to the throne of Castile, to which he ascended in 1555 under the title of Philip II., on the abdication of his father.

The craft returned from the Philippine Islands laden with abundance of provisions, with which the ships were enabled to continue the voyage.

By the royal instructions, Ruy Lopez de Villalobos was strictly enjoined not to touch at the Moluccas Islands, peace having been concluded with Portugal. Heavy gales forced him, nevertheless, to take refuge at Gilolo. The Portuguese, suspicious of his intentions in view of the treaty, arrayed their forces against his, inciting the king of the island also to discard all Spanish overtures and refuse assistance to Villalobos. The discord and contentions between the Portuguese and Spaniards were increasing; nothing was being gained by either party. Villalobos personally was sorely disheartened in the struggle, fearing all the while that his opposition to the Portuguese in contravention of the royal instructions would only excite the king's displeasure and lead to his own downfall. Hence he decided to capitulate with his rival and accepted a safe conduct for himself and party to Europe in Portuguese ships. They arrived at Amboina Island, where Villalobos, already crushed by grief, succumbed to disease. The survivors of the expedition, among whom were several priests, continued the journey home via Malacca, Cochin-China and Goa, where they embarked for Lisbon, arriving there in 1549.

In 1558, King Charles was no more, but the memory of his ambition outlived him. His son Philip, equally emulous and unscrupulous, was too narrow-minded and subtly cautious to initiate an expensive enterprise encompassed by so many hazards—as materially unproductive as it was devoid of immediate political importance. Indeed the basis of the first expedition was merely to discover a western route to the rich Spice Islands, already known to exist; the second went there to attempt to establish Spanish empire; and the third to search for and annex to the Spanish crown lands as wealthy as those claimed by and now yielded to the Portuguese.

But the value of the Philippine Islands, of which the possession was but recent and nominal, was thus far a matter of doubt.

One of the most brave and intrepid captains of the Loaisa expedition — Andres de Urdaneta — returned to Spain in 1536. In former years he had fought under King Charles I., in his wars in Italy, when the study of navigation served him as a favorite pastime. Since his return from the Moluccas his constant attention was given to the project of a new expedition to the Far West, for which he unremittingly solicited the royal sanction and assistance. But the king had grown old and weary of the world, and, while he did not openly discourage Urdaneta's pretensions, he gave him no effective aid. At length in 1553, two years before Charles abdicated, Urdaneta, convinced of the futility of his importunity at the Spanish court, and equally unsuccessful with his scheme in other quarters, retired to Mexico, where he took the habit of an Augustine monk. Ten years afterward King Philip, inspired by the religious sentiment which pervaded his whole policy, urged his viceroy in Mexico to fit out an expedition to conquer and Christianize the Philippine Islands. Urdaneta, now a priest, was not overlooked. Accompanied by five priests of his order, he was intrusted with the spiritual care of the races to be subdued by an expedition composed of four ships and one frigate well armed, carrying four hundred soldiers and sailors, commanded by a Basque navigator, Miguel Lopez de Legaspi. This remarkable man was destined to acquire the fame of having established Spanish dominion in these islands. He was of noble birth and a native of the province of Guipuzcoa in Spain. Having settled in the City of Mexico, of which place he was elected mayor, he there practiced as a notary. Of undoubted piety, he enjoyed a reputation for his justice and loyalty, hence he was appointed general of the forces equipped for the voyage.

The favorite desire to possess the valuable Spice Islands still lurked in the minds of many Spaniards—among them was Urdaneta, who labored in vain to persuade the viceroy of the superior advantages to be gained by annexing New Guinea instead of the Philippines—whence the conquest of the Moluccas would be but a facile task. However, the viceroy was inexorable and resolved to fulfill the royal instructions to the letter, so the expedition set sail from the Mexican port of Navidad for the Philippine Islands on the 21st of November, 1564.

The Ladrone Islands were passed on the 9th of January, 1565, and on the 13th of the following month the Philippines were sighted. A call for provisions was made at several small islands, including Camiguin, whence the expedition sailed to Bojol Island. A boat dispatched to the port of Butuan returned in a fortnight with the news that there was much gold, wax and cinnamon in that district. A small vessel was also sent to Cebu, and on its return reported that the natives showed hostility, having decapitated one of the crew while he was bathing.

Nevertheless, General Legaspi resolved to put in at Cebu, which was a safe port; and on the way there the ships anchored off Limasana Island (to the south of Leyte). Thence, running S.W., the port of Dapitan (Mindanao Island) was reached.

Prince Pagbuaya, who ruled there, was astonished at the sight of such formidable ships, and commissioned one of his subjects, specially chosen for his boldness, to take note of their movements and report to him. His account was uncommonly interesting. He related that enormous men with long pointed noses, dressed in fine robes, ate stones (hard biscuits), drank fire and blew smoke out of their mouths and through their nostrils. Their power was such that they commanded thunder and lightning (discharge of artillery), and that at meal times they sat down at a clothed table. From their lofty port, their bearded faces and rich attire, they might have been the very gods manifesting themselves to the natives; so the prince thought it wise to accept the friendly overtures of such marvelous strangers. Besides obtaining ample provisions in barter for European wares, Legaspi procured from this chieftain much useful information respecting the condition of Cebu. He learned that it was esteemed a powerful kingdom, of which the magnificence was much vaunted among the neighboring states; that the port was one of great safety and the most favorably situated among the islands of the painted faces.

The general resolved therefore to filch it from its native king and annex it to the crown of Castile.

He landed in Cebu on the 27th of April, 1565, and negotiations were entered into with the natives of that island. Remembering how successfully they had rid themselves of Maghallanes' party, they naturally opposed this renewed menace to their independence. The Spaniards occupied the town by force and sacked it, but for months were so harassed by the surrounding tribes that a council was convened to discuss the prudence of continuing the occupation. The general decided to remain, and, little by little, the natives yielded to the new condition of things, and thus the first step toward the final conquest was achieved. The natives were declared Spanish subjects, and hopeful with the success thus far attained, Legaspi determined to send dispatches to the king by the priest Urdaneta, who safely arrived at Navidad on the 3d of October, 1565, and proceeded thence to Spain.

The pacification of Cebu and the adjacent islands was steadily and successfully pursued by Legaspi; the confidence of the natives was assured, and their dethroned king Tupas accepted Christian baptism, while his daughter married a Spaniard.

In the midst of the invaders' felicity, the Portuguese arrived to dispute the possession, but they were compelled to retire. A fortress was constructed and plots of land were marked out for the building of the Spanish settlers' residences, and finally, in 1570, Cebu was declared a city, after Legaspi had received from his royal master the title of governor-general of all the lands which he might be able to conquer.

In May, 1570, Captain Juan Salcedo, Legaspi's grandson, was dispatched to the Island of Luzon to reconnoiter the territory and bring it under Spanish dominion.

The history of these early times is very confused, and

there are many contradictions in the authors of the Philippine chronicles, none of which seem to have been written contemporaneously with the first events. It appears, however, that Martin de Goiti and a few soldiers accompanied Salcedo to the north. They were well received by the native chiefs or petty kings Lacandola, rajah of Tondo (known as Rajah Matanda, which means in native dialect the aged rajah), and his nephew, the young Rajah Soliman of Manila.

The sight of a body of European troops, armed as was the custom in the sixteenth century, must have profoundly impressed and overawed these chieftains, otherwise it seems almost incredible that they should have consented, without protest, or attempt at resistance, to (forever) give up their territory, yield their independence, pay tribute,* and be-

---

* Legaspi and Guido Lavezares, under oath, made promises of rewards to the Lacandola family and a remission of tribute in perpetuity, but they were not fulfilled. In the following century—year 1660—it appears that the descendants of the rajah Lacandola still upheld the Spanish authority, and having become sorely impoverished thereby, the heir of the family petitioned the governor (Sabiniano Manrique de Lara) to make good the honor of his first predecessors. Eventually the Lacandolas were exempted from the payment of tribute and poll tax forever, as recompense for the filching of their domains.

In 1884, when the fiscal reforms were introduced which abolished the tribute and established in lieu thereof a document of personal identity (cedula personal), for which a tax is levied, the last vestige of privilege disappeared.

Descendants of Lacandola are still to be met with in several villages near Manila. They do not seem to have materially profited by their transcendent ancestry—one of them was serving as a waiter in a French restaurant in the capital in 1885.

come the tools of invading foreigners with which to conquer their own race, without recompense whatsoever.

A treaty of peace was signed and ratified by an exchange of drops of blood between the parties thereto. Soliman, however, soon repented of his poltroonery, and raised the war cry among some of his tribes. To save his capital (then called Maynila) falling into the hands of the invaders he set fire to it. Lacandola remained passively watching the issue. Soliman was completely routed by Salcedo, and pardoned on his again swearing fealty to the King of Spain. Goiti remained in the vicinity of Manila with his troops, while Salcedo fought his way to the Bombon Lake (Taal) district. The present Batangas Province was subdued by him and included in the jurisdiction of Mindoro Island. During the campaign Salcedo was severely wounded by an arrow and returned to Manila.

Legaspi was in the Island of Panay when Salcedo (some writers say Goiti) arrived to advise him of what had occurred in Luzon. They at once proceeded together to Cavite, where Lacandola visited Legaspi on board, and, prostrating himself, averred his submission. Then Legaspi continued his journey to Manila, and was received there with acclamation. He took formal possession of the surrounding territory, declared Manila to be the capital of the archipelago, and proclaimed the sovereignty of the King of Spain over the whole group of islands. Gaspar de San Agustin, writing of this period, says: "He (Legaspi) ordered them (the natives) to finish the building of the fort in construction at the mouth of the river (Pasig), so that his majesty's artillery might be mounted therein for the defense of the port and the town. Also he ordered them to build a large house inside the battlement walls for Legaspi's own residence—another large house and church for the priests, etc. . . . Besides these two large houses he told them to erect one hundred and fifty dwellings of moderate size for the remainder of the Spaniards to live in. All this they promptly promised to do, but they did not obey, for the Spaniards were themselves obliged to terminate the work of the fortifications."

The City Council of Manila was constituted on the 24th of June, 1571. On the 20th of August, 1572, Miguel Lopez de Legaspi succumbed to the fatigues of his arduous life, leaving behind him a name which will always maintain a prominent place in Spanish colonial history. He was buried in Manila in the Augustine Chapel of San Fausto, where hung the royal standard and the hero's armorial bearings until the British troops occupied the city in 1763.

> "Death makes no conquest of this conqueror,
> For now he lives in fame, though not in life."
> —"Richard III.," Act 3, Sc. 1.

In the meantime Salcedo continued his task of subjecting the tribes in the interior. The natives of Taytay, and Cainta, in the present military district of Morong, submitted to him on the 15th of August, 1571. He returned to the Laguna de Bay to pacify the villagers, and penetrated as far as Camarines Norte to explore the Bicol River. Bolinao and the provinces of Pangasinan and Ilocos yielded to his prowess, and in this last province he had well established himself when the defense of the capital obliged him to return to Manila.

At the same time Martin de Goiti was actively employed in overrunning the Pampanga territory, with the double object of procuring supplies for the Manila camp and coercing the inhabitants on his way to acknowledge their new liege lord. It is recorded that in this expedition Goiti was joined by the rajahs of Tondo and Manila. Yet Lacandola appears to have been regarded more as a servant of the Spaniards *nolens volens* than as a free ally; for, because he absented himself from Goiti's camp "without license from the Maestre de Campo," he was suspected by some writers of having favored opposition to the Spaniards' incursions in the Marshes of Hagonoy (Pampanga coast, northern boundary of Manila Bay).

The district which constituted the ancient province of Taal y Balayan, subsequently denominated Province of Batangas, was formerly governed by a number of caciques, the most notable of which were Gatpagil and Gatjinlintan. They were usually at war with their neighbors. Gatjinlintan, the cacique of the Batangas River at the time of the conquest, was famous for his valor. Gatsungayan, who ruled on the other side of the river, was celebrated as a hunter of deer and wild boar. These men were half-castes of Borneo and Aeta extraction, who formed a distinct race called by the natives Daghagang. None of them would submit to the King of Spain or become Christians, hence their descendants were offered no privileges.

On the death of General Legaspi, the government of the colony was assumed by the royal treasurer, Guido de Lavezares, in conformity with the sealed instructions from the Supreme Court of Mexico, which were now opened. During this period, the possession of the islands was unsuccessfully disputed by a rival expedition under the command of a Chinaman, Li-ma-hong, whom the Spaniards were pleased to term a pirate, forgetting, perhaps, that they themselves had only recently wrested the country from its former possessors by virtue of might against right. On the coasts of his native country he had indeed been a pirate. For the many depredations committed by him against private traders and property, the Celestial Emperor, failing to catch him by cajolery, outlawed him.

Born in the port of Tiuchiu, Li-ma-hong at an early age evinced a martial spirit and joined a band of corsairs, which for a long time had been the terror of the China coasts. On the demise of his chief he was unanimously elected leader of the buccaneering cruisers. At length, pursued in all directions by the imperial ships of war, he determined to attempt the conquest of the Philippines. Presumably the same incentives which impelled the Spanish mariners to conquer lands and overthrow dynasties—the vision of wealth, glory and empire—awakened a like ambition in the Chinese adventurer. It was the spirit of the age.* In his sea-wanderings he happened to fall in with a Chinese trading junk returning from Manila with the proceeds of her cargo sold there. This he seized, and the captive crew were constrained to pilot his fleet toward the capital of Luzon. From them he learned how easily the natives had been plundered by a handful of foreigners

---

* Guido de Lavezares deposed a sultan in Borneo, in order to aid another to the throne, and even asked permission of King Philip II. to conquer China, which of course was not conceded to him. *Vide* also the history of the destruction of the Aztec (Mexican) and Incas (Peruvian) dynasties by the Spaniards.

—the probable extent of the opposition he might encounter—the defenses established—the wealth and resources of the district and the nature of its inhabitants.

His fleet consisted of sixty-two warships or armed junks, well found, having on board two thousand sailors, two thousand soldiers, one thousand five hundred women, a number of artisans, and all that could be conveniently carried with which to gain and organize his new kingdom. On its way the squadron cast anchor off the province of Ilocos Sur, where a few troops were sent ashore to get provisions. While returning to the junks, they sacked the village and set fire to the huts. The news of this outrage was hastily communicated to Juan Salcedo, who had been pacifying the northern provinces since July, 1572, and was at the time in Villa Fernandina (now called Vigan). Li-ma-hong continued his course until calms compelled his ships to anchor in the roads of Caoayan (Ilocos coast), where a few Spanish soldiers were stationed under the orders of Juan Salcedo, who still was in the immediate town of Vigan. Under his direction, preparations were made to prevent the enemy entering the river, but such was not Li-ma-hong's intention. He again set sail; while Salcedo, naturally supposing his course would be toward Manila, also started at the same time for the capital with all the fighting men he could collect, leaving only thirty men to garrison Vigan and protect the State interests there.

On the 29th of November, 1574, the squadron arrived in the Bay of Manila, and Li-ma-hong sent forward his lieutenant, Sioco—a Japanese—at the head of six hundred fighting men, to demand the surrender of the Spaniards.

A strong gale, however, destroyed several of his junks, in which about two hundred men perished.

With the remainder he reached the coast at Paranaque, a village a few miles south of Manila. Thence, with tow lines, the four hundred soldiers hauled their junks up to the beach of the capital.

Already at the village of Malate the alarm was raised, but the Spaniards could not give credit to the reports, and no resistance was offered until the Chinese were within the gates of the city. Martin de Goiti, the Maestre de Campo, second in command to the governor, was the first victim of the attack.

The flames and smoke arising from his burning residence were the first indications which the governor received of what was going on. The Spaniards took refuge in the fort of Santiago, which the Chinese were on the point of taking by storm, when their attention was drawn elsewhere by the arrival of fresh troops led by a Spanish sub-lieutenant. Under the mistaken impression that these were the vanguard of a formidable corps, Sioco sounded the retreat. A bloody hand-to-hand combat followed, and with great difficulty the Chinese collected their dead and regained their junks.

In the meantime Li-ma-hong, with the reserved forces, was lying in the roadstead of Cavite, and Sioco hastened to report to him the result of the attack, which had cost the invader over one hundred dead and more than that number wounded. Thereupon Li-ma-hong resolved to rest his troops and renew the conflict in two days' time under his personal supervision. The next day Juan Salcedo arrived by sea with re-enforcements from Vigan, and prepa-

WAR MINISTRY DEPARTMENT

Spain.

rations were unceasingly made for the expected encounter. Salcedo having been appointed to the office of Maestre de Campo, vacant since the death of Goiti, the organization of the defense was intrusted to his immediate care.

By daybreak on the 3d of December, the enemy's fleet hove to off the capital, where Li-ma-hong harangued his troops, while the cornets and drums of the Spaniards were sounding the alarm for their fighting men to assemble in the fort.

Then fifteen hundred chosen men, well armed, were disembarked under the leadership of Sioco, who swore to take the place or die in the attempt. Sioco separated his forces into three divisions. The city was set fire to, and Sioco advanced toward the fort, into which hand-grenades were thrown, while Li-ma-hong supported the attack with his ships' cannon.

Sioco, with his division, at length entered the fort, and a hand-to-hand fight ensued. For a while the issue was doubtful. Salcedo fought like a lion. Even the aged governor was well at the front to encourage the deadly struggle for existence. The Spaniards finally gained the victory; the Chinese were repulsed with great slaughter; and their leader having been killed, they fled in complete disorder. Salcedo, profiting by the confusion, now took the offensive and followed up the enemy, pursuing them along the seashore, where they were joined by the third division, which had remained inactive. The panic of the Chinese spread rapidly, and Li-ma-hong, in despair, landed another contingent of about five hundred men, while he still continued afloat; but even with this re-enforcement the **morale of his army could not be regained.**

The Chinese troops therefore, harassed on all sides, made a precipitate retreat on board the fleet, and Li-ma-hong set sail again for the west coast of the island. Foiled in the attempt to possess himself of Manila, Li-ma-hong determined to set up his capital in other parts. In a few days he arrived at the mouth of the Agno River, in the province of Pangasinan, where he proclaimed to the natives that he had gained a signal victory over the Spaniards. The inhabitants there, having no particular choice between two masters, received Li-ma-hong with welcome, and he thereupon set about the foundation of his new capital some four miles from the mouth of the river. Months passed before the Spaniards came in force to dislodge the invader. Feeling themselves secure in their new abode, the Chinese had built many dwellings, a small fortress, a pagoda, etc. At length an expedition was dispatched under the command of Juan Salcedo. This was composed of about two hundred and fifty Spaniards and one thousand six hundred natives well equipped with small arms, ammunition and artillery. The flower of the Spanish colony, accompanied by two priests and the Rajah of Tondo, set out to expel the formidable foe. Li-ma-hong made a bold resistance and refused to come to terms with Salcedo. In the meantime, the Viceroy of Fokien, having heard of Li-ma-hong's daring exploits, had commissioned a ship of war to discover the whereabout of his imperial master's old enemy. The envoy was received with delight by the Spaniards, who invited him to accompany them to Manila to interview the governor.

Li-ma-hong still held out, but perceiving that an irresistible onslaught was being projected against him by Salcedo's party, he very cunningly and quite unexpectedly gave them the slip, and sailed out of the river with his ships by one of the mouths unknown to his enemies.* In order to divert the attention of the Spaniards, Li-ma-hong ingeniously feigned an assault in an opposite quarter. Of course, on his escape, he had to abandon the troops employed in this maneuver. These, losing all hope, and having, indeed, nothing but their lives to fight for, fled to the mountains. Hence, it is popularly supposed that from these fugitives descends the race of people in that province still distinguishable by their oblique eyes and known by the name of Igorrote-Chinese.

"Aide toi et Dieu t'aidera" is an old French maxim, but the Spaniards chose to attribute their deliverance from their Chinese rival to the friendly intervention of Saint Andrew. This saint was declared thenceforth to be the patron saint of Manila, and in his honor High Mass is celebrated in the Cathedral at 8 A.M. on the 30th of each November. It is a public holiday and gala-day, when all the highest civil, military and religious authorities attend the "Funcion votiva de San Andrés." This opportunity to assert the supremacy of ecclesiastical power was not lost to the Church, and for many years it was the custom, after hearing Mass, to spread the Spanish national flag on the floor of the Cathedral for the metropolitan archbishop to walk over it. It has been asserted, however, that a

---

* According to Juan de la Concepcion, in his "Hist. Gen. de Philipinas," Vol. I., page 431, Li-ma-hong made his escape by cutting a canal for his ships to pass through, but this appears highly improbable under the circumstances.

few years ago the governor-general refused to witness this antiquated formula, which, in public at least, no longer obtains. Now it is the practice to carry the royal standard before the altar. Both before and after the Mass, the bearer (Alférez Real), wearing his hat and accompanied by the mayor of the city, stands on the altar-floor, raises his hat three times, and three times dips the flag before the Image of Christ, then, facing the public, he repeats this ceremony. On Saint Andrew's eve, the royal standard is borne in procession from the Cathedral through the principal streets of the city, escorted by civil functionaries and followed by a band of music. This ceremony is known as the "Paseo del Real Pendon."

According to Juan de la Concepcion, the Rajahs* Soliman and Lacandola took advantage of these troubles to raise a rebellion against the Spaniards. The natives too of Mindoro Island revolted and maltreated the priests, but all these disturbances were speedily quelled by a detachment of soldiers.

The governor willingly accepted the offer of the commander of the Chinese man-of-war to convey embassadors to his country to visit the viceroy and make a commercial treaty. Therefore two priests, Martin Rada and Geronimo Martin, were commissioned to carry a letter of greeting and presents to this personage, who received them with great distinction, but objected to their residing in the country.

After the defeat of Li-ma-hong, Juan Salcedo again repaired to the northern provinces of Luzon Island, to

---

* Other authors assert that only Soliman rebelled.

continue his task of reducing the natives to submission. On the 11th of March, 1576, he died of fever near Vigan (then called Villa Fernandina), capital of the province of Ilocos Sur. A year afterward, what could be found of his bones were placed in the ossuary of his illustrious grandfather, Legaspi, in the Augustine Chapel of Saint Fausto, Manila. His skull, however, which had been carried off by the natives of Ilocos, could not be recovered in spite of all threats and promises. In Vigan there is a small monument raised to commemorate the deeds of this famous warrior, and there is also a street bearing his name.

For several years following these events, the question of prestige in the civil affairs of the colony was acrimoniously contested by the governor-general, the supreme court and the ecclesiastics.

The governor was censured by his opponents for alleged undue exercise of arbitrary authority. The supreme court, established on the Mexican model, was reproached with seeking to overstep the limits of its functions. Every legal quibble was adjusted by a dilatory process, impracticable in a colony yet in its infancy, where summary justice was indispensable for the maintenance of order imperfectly understood by the masses. But the fault laid less with the justices than with the constitution of the court itself. Nor was this state of affairs improved by the growing discontent and immoderate ambition of the clergy, who unremittingly urged their pretensions to immunity from State control, affirming the supramundane condition of their office.

An excellent code of laws, called the Leyes de Indias, in force in Mexico, was adopted here, but modifications in harmony with the special conditions of this colony were urgently necessary, while all the branches of government called for reorganization or reform. Under these circumstances, the bishop of Manila, Domingo Salazar, took the initiative in commissioning a priest, Fray Alonso Sanchez, to repair first to the viceroy of Mexico and afterward to the King of Spain, to expose the grievances of his party.

Alonso Sanchez left the Philippines with his appointment as procurator-general for the Augustine order of monks. As the execution of the proposed reforms, which he was charged to lay before his majesty, would, if conceded, be intrusted to the government of Mexico, his first care was to seek the partisanship of the viceroy of that colony; and in this he succeeded. Thence he continued his journey to Seville, where the court happened to be, arriving there in September, 1587. H was at once granted an audience of the king, to present his credentials and memorials relative to Philippine affairs in general; and ecclesiastical, judicial, military and native matters in particular. The king promised to peruse all the documents, but suffering from gout, and having so many and distinct State concerns to attend to, the negotiations were greatly delayed. Finally, Sanchez sought a minister who had easy access to the royal apartments, and this personage obtained from the king permission to examine the documents and hand to him a succinct resume of the whole for his majesty's consideration. A commission was then appointed, including Sanchez, and the deliberations lasted five months.

At this period, public opinion in the Spanish universities was very divided with respect to Catholic missions in the Indies.

Some maintained that the propaganda of the faith ought to be purely Apostolic, such as Jesus Christ taught to his disciples, inculcating doctrines of humility and poverty without arms or violence, and if, nevertheless, the heathens refused to welcome this mission of peace, the missionaries should simply abandon them in silence without further demonstration than that of shaking the dust off their feet.

Others opined, and among them was Sanchez, that such a method was useless and impracticable, and that it was justifiable to force their religion upon primitive races at the point of the sword if necessary, using any violence to enforce its acceptance.

Much ill-feeling was aroused in the discussion of these two and distinct theories. Juan Volante, a Dominican friar of the Convent of Our Lady of Atocha, presented a petition against the views of the Sanchez faction, declaring that the idea of ingrafting religion with the aid of arms was scandalous. Fray Juan Volante was so importunate, that he had to be heard in council, but neither party yielded. At length, the intervention of the bishops of Manila, Macao and Malacca and several captains and governors in the Indies influenced the king to put an end to the controversy, on the ground that it would lead to no good.

The king retired to the Monastery of the Escorial, and Sanchez was cited to meet him there to learn the royal will. About the same time the news reached the king of the loss of the so-called Invincible Armada, sent under the command of the incompetent Duke of Medina Sidonia to annex England. Notwithstanding this severe blow to the vain ambition of Philip, the affairs of the Philippines were delayed but a short time. On the basis of the recommendation of the junta, the royal assent was given to an important decree, of which the most significant articles are the following, namely:—The tribute was fixed by the king at ten reales per annum, payable by the natives in gold, silver, or grain, or part in one commodity and part in the other. Of this tribute, eight reales were to be paid to the treasury, one half real to the bishop and clergy, and one real and a half to be applied to the maintenance of the soldiery. Full tribute was not to be exacted from the natives still unsubjected to the crown. Until their confidence and loyalty should be gained by friendly overtures, they were to pay a small recognition of vassalage, and subsequently the tribute in common with the rest.

Instead of one-fifth value of gold and hidden treasure due to his majesty (real quinto), he would henceforth receive only one-tenth of such value, excepting that of gold, which the natives would be permitted to extract free of rebate.

A customs duty of 3 per cent ad valorem was to be paid on merchandise sold, and this duty was to be spent on the army.

Export duty was to be paid on goods shipped to New Spain (Mexico), and this impost was also to be exclusively spent on the armed forces.

The number of European troops in the colony was fixed at four hundred men-at-arms, divided into six companies, each under a captain, a sub-lieutenant, a sergeant, and two corporals. Their pay was to be as follows, namely: Captain thirty-five dollars, sub-lieutenant twenty dollars, sergeant ten dollars, corporal seven dollars, rank and file six dollars per month; besides which, an annual gratuity of ten thousand dollars was to be proportionately distributed to all.

Recruits from Mexico were not to enlist under the age of fifteen years.

The captain-general was to have a body-guard of twenty-four men (halberdiers), with the pay of those of the line, under the immediate command of a captain to be paid fifteen dollars per month.

Salaries due to State employes were to be punctually paid when due; and when funds were wanted for that purpose they were to be supplied from Mexico.

The king made a donation of twelve thousand dollars, which, with another like sum to be contributed by the Spaniards themselves, would serve to liquidate their debts incurred on their first occupation of the islands.

The governor and bishop were recommended to consider the project of a refuge for young Spanish women arrived from Spain, and to study the question of dowries for native women married to poor Spaniards.

The offices of secretaries and notaries were no longer to be sold, but conferred on persons who merited such appointments.

The governors were instructed not to make grants of land to their relations, servants or friends, but solely to those who should have resided at least three years in the islands, and have worked the lands so conceded. Any grants which might have already been made to the relations of the governors or magistrates were to be canceled.

The rent paid by the Chinese for the land they occupied was to be applied to the necessities of the capital.

The governor and bishop were to enjoin the judges not to permit costly lawsuits, but to execute summary justice verbally, and, so far as possible, fines were not to be inflicted.

The city of Manila was to be fortified in a manner to insure it against all further attacks or risings.

Four penitentiaries were to be established in the islands in the most convenient places, with the necessary garrisons, and six to eight galleys and frigates well armed and ready for defense against the English corsairs which might come by way of the Moluccas.

In the most remote and unexplored parts of the islands, the governor was to have unlimited powers to act as he should please, without consulting his majesty; but projected enterprises of conversion, pacification, etc., at the expense of the royal treasury, were to be submitted to a council, comprising the bishop, the captains, etc. The governor was authorized to capitulate and agree with the captains and others who might care to undertake conversions and pacifications on their own account, and to concede the title of Maestre de Campo to such persons, on condition that such capitulations should be forwarded to his majesty for ratification.

Only those persons domiciled in the islands would be permitted to trade with them.

A sum of one thousand dollars was to be taken from the tributes paid into the royal treasury for the foundation of the hospital for the Spaniards, and the annual sum of six hundred dollars, appropriated by the governor for its support, was confirmed. Moreover, the royal treasury of Mexico was to send clothing to the value of four hundred ducats for the hospital use.

The hospital for the natives was to receive an annual donation of six hundred dollars for its support, and an immediate supply of clothing from Mexico to the value of two hundred dollars.

Slaves held by Spaniards were to be immediately set at liberty. No native was thenceforth to be enslaved. All new born natives were declared free. The bondage of all existing slaves from ten years of age was to cease on their attaining twenty years of age. Those above twenty years of age were to serve five years longer, and then become free. At any time, notwithstanding the foregoing conditions, they would be entitled to purchase their liberty, the price of which was to be determined by the governor and the bishop.*

There being no tithes payable to the church by Spaniards or natives, the clergy were to receive for their maintenance the half real above mentioned in lieu thereof, from the tribute paid by each native subjected to the

---

* Bondage in the Philippines was apparently not so necessary for the interests of the Church as it was in Cuba, where a commission of friars, appointed soon after the discovery of the island to deliberate on the policy of partially permitting slavery there, reported "that the Indians would not labor without compulsion, and that, unless they labored, they could not be brought into communication with the whites, nor be converted to Christianity." **Vide W. H. Prescott's** "Hist. of the Conquest of Mexico."

crown. When the Spaniards should have crops, they were to pay tithes to the clergy.

A grant was made of twelve thousand ducats for the building and ornaments of the Cathedral, and an immediate advance of two thousand ducats, on account of this grant, was made from the funds to be remitted from Mexico.

Forty Austin friars were to be sent at once to the Philippines, to be followed by missionaries from other corporations. The king allowed five hundred dollars to be paid against the one thousand dollars' passage money for each priest, the balance to be defrayed out of the common funds of the clergy, derived from their share of the tribute.

Missionaries in great numbers had already flocked to the Philippines and roamed wherever they thought fit, without license from the bishop, whose authority they utterly repudiated.

Affirming that they had the direct consent of his holiness the Pope, they menaced with excommunication whosoever attempted to impede them in their free peregrination. Five years after the foundation of Manila, the city and environs were infested with niggardly mendicant friars, whose slothful habits placed their supercilious countrymen in ridicule before the natives. They were tolerated but a short time in the islands; not altogether because of the ruin they would have brought to European moral influence on the untutored tribes, but because the bishop was highly jealous of all competition against the Augustine order to which he belonged. Consequent on the representations of Fray Alonso Sanchez, his majesty ordained that all priests who went to the Philippines were, in the first place, to resolve never to quit the islands without the bishop's sanction, which was to be conceded with great circumspection and only in extreme cases, while the governor was instructed not to afford them means of exit on his sole authority.

Neither did the bishop regard with satisfaction the presence of the commissary of the Inquisition, whose secret investigations, shrouded with mystery, curtailed the liberty of the loftiest functionary, sacred or civil. At the instigation of Fray Alonso Sanchez, the junta recommended the king to recall the commissary and extinguish the office, but he refused to do so. In short, the chief aims of the bishop were to enhance the power of the friars, raise the dignity of the colonial miter, and secure a religious monopoly for the Augustine order.

Gomez Perez Dasmarinas was the next governor appointed to these islands, on the recommendation of Fray Alonso Sanchez. In the royal instructions which he brought with him were embodied all the above mentioned civil, ecclesiastical and military reforms.

At the same time, King Philip abolished the supreme court. He wished to put an end to the interminable lawsuits so prejudicial to the development of the colony. Therefore the president and magistrates were replaced by justices of the peace, and the former returned to Mexico in 1591. This measure served only to widen the breach between the bishop and the civil government. Dasmarinas compelled him to keep within the sphere of his sacerdotal functions, and tolerated no rival in State concerns. There was no appeal on the spot against the governor's authority. This restraint irritated and disgusted the bishop to such a degree, that at the age of seventy-eight years he resolved to present himself at the Spanish court. On his arrival there, he manifested to the king the impossibility of one bishop attending to the spiritual wants of a people dispersed over so many islands. For seven years after the foundation of Manila, as capital of the archipelago, its principal church was simply a parish church. In 1578 it was raised to the dignity of a cathedral, at the instance of the king. Three years after this date the Cathedral of Manila was solemnly declared to be a "Suffragan Cathedral of Mexico, under the Advocation of Our Lady of the Immaculate Conception"; Domingo Salazar being the first bishop consecrated. He now proposed to raise the Manila see to an archbishopric, with three suffragan bishops. The king gave his consent, subject to approval from Rome, and, this following in due course, Salazar was appointed first archbishop of Manila; but he died before the Papal Bull arrived, dated the 14th of August, 1595, officially authorizing his investiture.

In the meantime, Alonso Sanchez had proceeded to Rome in May, 1589. Among many other Pontifical favors conceded to him, he obtained the right for himself, or his assigns, to use a die or stamp of any form with one or more images; to be chosen by the holder, and to contain also the figure of Christ, the Very Holy Virgin, or the Saint—Peter or Paul. On the reverse was to be engraven a bust portrait of His Holiness with the following indulgences attached thereto, viz.:—"To him who should convey the word of God to the infidels, or give them notice of the holy mysteries—each time 300 years' indulgence.

To him who, by industry, converted any one of these, or brought him to the bosom of the Church—full indulgence for all sins." A number of minor indulgences were conceded for services to be rendered to the Pontificate, and for the praying so many Pater Nosters and Ave Marias. This Bull was dated in Rome the 28th of July, 1591.

Popes Gregory XIV. and Innocent IX. granted other Bulls relating to the rewards for using beads, medals, crosses, pictures, blessed images, etc., with which one could gain nine plenary indulgences every day or rescue nine souls from purgatory; and each day, twice over, all the full indulgences yet given in and out of Rome could be obtained for living and deceased persons.

Sanchez returned to Spain (where he died), bringing with him the body of Saint Policarp, a relic of Saint Potenciana, and one hundred and fifty seven martyrs; among them, twenty-seven popes, for remission to the Cathedral of Manila.

The supreme court was re-established with the same faculties as those of Mexico and Lima in 1598, and since then, on seven occasions, when the governorship has been vacant, it has acted pro tem. The following interesting account of the pompous ceremonial attending the reception of the Royal Seal, restoring this court, is given by Concepcion.* He says: "The Royal Seal of office was received from the ship with the accustomed solemnity. It was contained in a chest covered with purple velvet and trimmings of silver and gold, over which hung a cloth of purple and gold. It was escorted by a majestic accom-

---

* "Hist. Gen. de Philipinas," by Juan de la Concepcion, Vol. III., Chap. IX., page 365, pub. Manila, 1788.

paniment, marching to the sounds of clarions and cymbals and other musical instruments. The cortege passed through the noble city with rich vestments, and leg trimmings and uncovered heads. Behind these followed a horse, gorgeously caparisoned and girthed, for the president to place the coffer containing the Royal Seal upon its back. The streets were beautifully adorned with exquisite drapery. The high bailiff, magnificently robed, took the reins in hand to lead the horse under a purple velvet pall bordered with gold. The magistrates walked on either side; the aldermen of the city, richly clad, carried their staves of office in the august procession, which concluded with a military escort, standard-bearers, etc., and proceeded to the Cathedral, where it was met by the dean, holding a Cross. As the company entered the sacred edifice, the Te Deum was entoned by a band of music."

In 1886 a supreme court, exactly similar to, and independent of, that of Manila, was established in the city of Cebu. The question of precedence in official acts having been soon after disputed between the president of the court and the brigadier-governor of Visayas, it was decided in favor of the latter, on appeal to the governor-general. In the meantime, the advisability of abolishing the supreme court of Cebu was debated by the public.

Consequent on the union of the crowns of Portugal and Spain (1581 to 1640), the feuds, as between nations, diplomatically subsided, although the individual antagonism was as rife as ever.

Spanish and Portuguese interests in the Moluccas, as elsewhere, were thenceforth officially mutual. In the Moluccas group, the old contests between the then rival kingdoms had estranged the natives from their forced alliances. Anti-Portuguese and Philo-Portuguese parties had sprung up among the petty sovereignties, but the Portuguese fort and factory established in Ternate Island were held for many years, despite all contentions. But another rivalry, as formidable and more detrimental than that of the Portuguese in days gone by, now menaced Spanish ascendency.

From the close of the sixteenth century up to the year of the "Family Compact" wars (1763), Holland and Spain were relentless foes. To recount the numerous combats between their respective fleets during this period would itself require a volume. It will suffice here to show the bearing of these political conflicts upon the concerns of the Philippine colony. The Treaty of Antwerp, which was wrung from the Spaniards in 1609, twenty-eight years after the union of Spain and Portugal, broke the scourge of their tyranny, while it failed to assuage the mutual antipathy. One of the consequences of the "Wars of the Flanders," which terminated with this treaty, was that the Dutch were obliged to seek in the Far East the merchandise which had hitherto been supplied to them from the Peninsula. The short-sighted policy of the Spaniards in closing to the Dutch the Portuguese markets, which were now theirs, brought upon themselves the destruction of the monopolies which they had gained by the union. The Dutch were now free, and their old tyrant's policy induced them to independently establish their own trading headquarters in the Moluccas Islands, whence they could obtain directly the produce forbidden to them in the home ports. Hence, from those islands, the ships of a powerful Netherlands Trading Company sallied forth from time to time to meet the Spanish galleons from Mexico with silver and manufactured goods.

Previous to this, and during the Wars of the Flanders, Dutch corsairs hovered about the waters of the Moluccas, to take reprisals from the Spaniards. These encounters frequently took place at the eastern entrance of the San Bernadino Straits, where the Dutch were accustomed to hove-to in anticipation of the arrival of their prizes.

In this manner, constantly roving about the Philippine waters, they enriched themselves at the expense of their detested adversary, and, in a small degree, avenged themselves of the bloodshed and oppression which for over sixty years had desolated the Low Countries.

The Philippine colony lost immense sums in the seizure of its galleons from Mexico, upon which it almost entirely depended for subsistence. Being a dependency of New Spain, its whole intercourse with the civilized world, its supplies of troops and European manufactured articles, were contingent upon the safe arrival of the galleons. Also the dollars with which they annually purchased cargoes from the Chinese for the galleons came from Mexico.

Consequently, the Dutch usually took the aggressive in these sea-battles, although they were not always victorious. When there were no ships to meet, they bombarded the ports where others were being built. The Spaniards, on their part, from time to time fitted out vessels to run down to the Moluccas Islands to attack the enemy in his own waters.

During the governorship of Gomez Perez Dasmariuas (1590–1593), the native king of Siao Island—one of the

Moluccas group—came to Manila to offer homage and vassalage to the representative of the King of Spain and Portugal, in return for protection against the incursions of the Dutch and the raids of the Ternate natives. Dasmariñas received him and the Spanish priests who accompanied him with affability, and, being satisfied with his credentials, he prepared a large expedition to go to the Moluccas to set matters in order. The fleet was composed of several frigates, one ship, six galleys and one hundred small vessels, all well armed. The fighting men numbered one hundred Spaniards, four hundred Pampanga and Tagalog arquebusiers, one thousand Visayas archers and lancers, besides one hundred Chinese to row the galleys. This expedition, which was calculated to be amply sufficient to subdue all the Moluccas, sailed from Cavite on the 6th of October, 1593. The sailing ships having got far ahead of the galleys, they hove-to off Punta de Azufre (N. of Maricaban Island) to wait for them. The galleys arrived; and the next day they were able to start again in company. Meanwhile a conspiracy was formed by the Chinese galleymen to murder all the Spaniards. Assuming these Chinese to be volunteers, their action would appear most wanton and base. If, however, as is most probable, they were pressed into this military service to foreigners, it seems quite natural that, being forced to bloodshed without alternative, they should first fight for their own liberty.

All but the Chinese were asleep, and they fell upon the Spaniards in a body. Eighteen of the troops and four slaves escaped by jumping into the sea. The governor was sleeping in his cabin, but awoke on hearing the noise. He supposed the ship had grounded, and was coming up the companion en deshabille, when a Chinaman cleaved his head with a cutlass. The governor reached his state-room, and taking his missal and the Image of the Virgin in his hand, he died in six hours. The Chinese did not venture below, where the priests and armed soldiers were hidden. They cleared the decks of all their opponents, made fast the hatches and gangways, and waited three days, when, after putting ashore those who were still alive, they escaped to Cochin-China, where the king and mandarins seized the vessel and all she carried. On board were found twelve thousand dollars in coin, some silver, and jewels belonging to the governor and his suite.

Thus the expedition was brought to an untimely end. The King of Siao, and the missionaries accompanying him, had started in advance for Otong (Panay Island) to wait for the governor, and there they received the news of the disaster.

Among the most notable of the successful expeditions of the Spaniards was that of Pedro Bravo de Acuna, in 1606, which consisted of nineteen frigates, nine galleys and eight small craft, carrying a total of about two thousand men and provisions for a prolonged struggle. The result was, that they subdued a petty sultan friendly to the Dutch, and established a fortress on his island.

About the year 1607, the supreme court (the governorship being vacant from 1606 to 1608), hearing that a Dutch vessel was hovering off Ternate, sent a ship against it, commanded by Pedro de Heredia. A combat ensued. The Dutch commander was taken prisoner with several of his men, and lodged in the fort at Ternate, but was ransomed on payment of fifty thousand dollars to the Spanish commander. Heredia returned joyfully to Manila, where, much to his surprise, he was prosecuted by the supreme court for exceeding his instructions, and expired of melancholy. The ransomed Dutch leader was making his way back to his headquarters in a small ship, peacefully, and without hostilizing the Spaniards in any way, when the supreme court treacherously sent a galley and a frigate after him to make him prisoner a second time. Overwhelmed by numbers and arms, and little expecting such perfidious conduct of the Spaniards, he was at once arrested and brought to Manila. The Dutch returned twenty-two Spanish prisoners of war to Manila to ransom him; but while these were retained, the Dutch commander was, nevertheless, imprisoned for life.

Some years afterward, a Dutch squadron anchored off the south point of Bataan Province, not far from Punta Marivelez, at the entrance to Manila Bay. Juan de Silva, the governor (from 1609 to 1616), was in great straits. Several ships had been lost by storms, others were away, and there was no adequate floating armament with which to meet the enemy. However, the Dutch lay-to for five or six months, waiting to seize the Chinese and Japanese traders' goods on their way to the Manila market. They secured immense booty, and were in no hurry to open hostilities. This delay gave Silva time to prepare vessels to attack the foe. In the interval, he dreamed that Saint Mark had offered to help him defeat the Dutch. On awaking, he called a priest, whom he consulted about the dream, and they agreed that the nocturnal vision was a sign from Heaven denoting a victory. The priest went (from Cavite) to Manila to procure a relic of this glorious intercessor, and returned with his portrait to the governor, who adored it. In haste the ships and armament were prepared. On Saint Mark's day, therefore, the Spaniards sallied forth from Cavite with six ships, carrying seventy guns, and two galleys and two launches also well armed, besides a number of small light vessels, to assist in the formation of line of battle.

All the European fighting men in Manila and Cavite embarked—over one thousand Spaniards—the flower of the colony, together with a large force of natives, who were taught to believe that the Dutch were infidels. On the issue of this day's events perchance depended the possession of the colony. Manila and Cavite were garrisoned by volunteers. Orations were offered in the churches. The Miraculous Image of Our Lady of the Guide was taken in procession from the Hermit, and exposed to public view in the Cathedral. The saints of the different churches and sanctuaries were adored and exhibited daily. The governor himself took the supreme command, and dispelled all wavering doubt in his subordinates by proclaiming Saint Mark's promise of intercession. On his ship he hoisted the royal standard, on which was embroidered the Image of the Holy Virgin, with the motto: "Mostrate esse Matrem," and over a beautifully calm sea he led the way to battle.

A shot from the Spanish heavy artillery opened the bloody combat. The Dutch were completely vanquished, after a fierce struggle which lasted six hours. Their three ships were destroyed, and their flags, artillery, and plundered merchandise to the value of three hundred thousand dollars were seized. This famous engagement was thenceforth known as the battle of Playa Honda.

Again in 1611, under Silva, a squadron sailed to the Moluccas and defeated the Dutch off Gilolo Island.

In 1617, the Spaniards had a successful engagement off the Zambales coast with the Dutch, who lost three of their ships.

In July, 1620, three Mexican galleons were met by three Dutch vessels off Cape Espiritu Santo (Samar Island), at the entrance of the San Bernadino Straits, but managed to escape in the dark. Two ran ashore and broke up; the third reached Manila. After this the governor-general, Alonzo Fajardo de Tua, ordered the course of the State ships to be varied on each voyage.

In 1625, the Dutch again appeared off the Zambales coast, and Geronimo de Silva went out against them. The Spaniards, having lost one man, relinquished the pursuit of the enemy, and the commander was brought to trial by the supreme court.

In 1626, at the close of the governorship of Fernando de Silva, a Spanish colony was founded on Formosa Island, but no supplies were sent to it, and consequently in 1642 it surrendered to the Dutch, who held it for twenty years, until they were driven out by the Chinese adventurer Keuseng. And thus for over a century and a half the strife continued, until the Dutch concentrated their attention in the development of their Eastern colonies, which the power of Spain, growing more and more effete, was incompetent to impede.

In 1761, King George III. had just succeeded to the throne of England, and the protracted contentions with France had been suspended for a while. It was soon evident, however, that efforts were being employed to extinguish the power and prestige of Great Britain, and with this object a convention had been entered into between France and Spain known as the "Family Compact." It was so called because it was an alliance made by the three branches of the House of Bourbon; namely, Louis XV. of France, Charles III. of Spain, and his son Ferdinand, who, in accordance with the Treaty of Vienna, had ascended the throne of Naples. Spain engaged to unite her forces with those of France against England on the 1st of May, 1762, if the war still lasted, in which case France would restore Minorca to Spain. Pitt was convinced of the necessity of meeting the coalition by force of arms, but he was unable to secure the support of his Ministry to declare war, and he therefore retired from the premiership. The succeeding Cabinet was, nevertheless, compelled to adopt his policy, and, after having lost many advantages by delaying their decision, war was declared against France and Spain.

The British were successful everywhere. In the West Indies, the Caribbean Islands and Havana were captured, with great booty, by Rodney and Monckton, while a British fleet was dispatched to the Philippine Islands with orders to take Manila.

There are many versions of this event given by different historians, and among them there is not wanting an author who, following the Spanish custom, has accounted for defeat by alleging treason.

On the 14th of September, 1762, a British vessel arrived in the Bay of Manila, refused to admit Spanish officers on board, and after taking soundings she sailed again out of the harbor.

In the evening of the 22d of September, the British squadron, composed of thirteen ships, under the command of Admiral Cornish, entered the bay, and the next day two British officers were deputed to demand the surrender of the citadel, which was refused.

Brigadier-general Draper thereupon disembarked his troops, and again called upon the city to yield. This citation being defied, the bombardment commenced the next day. The fleet anchored in front of a powder-magazine, took possession of the churches of Malate, Hermita, San Juan de Bagumbayan and Santiago. Two picket guards made an unsuccessful sortie against them. The whole force in Manila at the time was the king's regiment, which mustered about six hundred men and eighty pieces of artillery. The British forces consisted of one thousand five hundred European troops (one regiment of infantry and two companies of artillery), three thousand seamen, eight hundred Sepoy fusileers and one thousand four hundred Sepoy prisoners, making a total of six thousand eight hundred and thirty men.

There was no governor-general here at the time, and the only person with whom the British commander could treat was the acting-governor, the Archbishop Manuel Antonio Rojo, who was willing to yield. His authority was, however, set aside by a rebellious war party, who placed themselves under the leadership of a magistrate of the supreme court named Simon de Anda y Salazar.

This individual, instead of heading them to battle, fled to the province of Bulacan, the day before the capture of Manila, in a prahu with a few natives, carrying with him some money and half a ream of official stamped paper. He knew perfectly well that he was defying the legal authority of the acting-governor, and was, in fact, in open rebellion against his mandate. It was necessary, therefore, to give an official color to his acts by issuing his orders and proclamations on government-stamped paper, so that their validity might be recognized if he subsequently succeeded in justifying his action at court.

On the 24th of September the Spanish batteries of San Diego and San Andres opened fire, but with little effect. A richly laden galleon—the "Philipino"—was known to be on her way from Mexico to Manila, but the British ships which were sent in quest of her fell in with another galleon—the "Trinidad"—and brought their prize to Manila. Her treasure amounted to about two million five hundred thousand dollars.

A Frenchman resident in Manila, Monsieur Faller, made an attack on the British, who forced him to retire, and he was then accused by the Spaniards of treason. Artillery fire was kept up on both sides. The archbishop's nephew was taken prisoner, and an officer was sent with him to hand him over to his uncle. However, a party of natives fell upon them and murdered them all. The officer's head having been cut off, it was demanded by General Draper. Excuses were made for not giving it up, and the general determined thenceforth to continue the warfare with vigor and punish this atrocity. The artillery was increased by another battery of three mortars, placed behind the Church of Santiago, and the bombardment continued.

Five thousand native recruits arrived from the provinces, and out of this number two thousand Pampangos were selected. They were divided into three columns, in order to advance by different routes and attack respectively the Church of Santiago, Malate and Hermita, and the troops on the beach. At each place they were driven back. The leader of the attack on Malate and Hermita—Don Santiago Orendain—was declared a traitor. The two first columns were dispersed with great confusion and loss. The third column retreated before they had sustained or inflicted any loss. The natives fled to their villages in dismay, and on the 5th of October the British entered the walled city. After a couple of hours' bombardment the forts of San Andres and San Eugenio were demolished, the artillery overturned, and the enemy's fusileers and sappers were killed.

A council of war was now held by the Spaniards. General Draper sustained the authority of the archbishop against the war-party, composed chiefly of civilians, who determined to continue the defense in spite of the opinion of the military men, who argued that a capitulation was inevitable. But matters were brought to a crisis by the natives, who refused to repair the fortifications, and the Europeans were unable to perform such hard labor. Great confusion reigned in the city—the clergy fled through the Puerta del Parian, where there was still a native guard. According to Zuniga, the British spent twenty thousand cannon balls and five thousand shells in the bombardment of the city.

Major Fell entered the city at the head of his troops and General Draper followed, leading his column unopposed, with two field pieces in the van, while a constant musketry fire cleared the Calle Real as they advanced. The people fled before the enemy. The gates being closed, they scrambled up the walls and got into boats or swam off.

Colonel Monson was sent by Draper to the archbishop-governor to say that he expected immediate surrender. This was disputed by the archbishop, who presented a paper purporting to be terms of capitulation. The colonel refused to take it, and demanded an unconditional surrender. Then the archbishop, a colonel of the Spanish troops and Colonel Monson went to interview the general, whose quarters were in the palace. The archbishop, offering himself as a prisoner, presented the terms of capitulation, which provided for the free exercise of their religion; security of private property; free trade to all the inhabitants of the islands, and the continuation of the powers of the supreme court to keep order among the ill-disposed. These terms were granted, but General Draper, on his part, stipulated for an indemnity of four millions of dollars, and it was agreed to pay one-half of this sum in specie and valuables and the other half in treasury bills on Madrid. The capitulation, with these modifications, was signed by Draper and the archbishop-governor. The Spanish colonel took the document to the fort to have it countersigned by the magistrates, which was at once done; the fort was delivered up to the British, and the magistrates retired to the palace to pay their respects to the conqueror.

When the British flag was seen floating from the fort of Santiago there was great cheering from the British fleet. The archbishop stated that when Draper reviewed the troops more than one thousand men were missing, including sixteen officers. Among these officers were a major, fatally wounded by an arrow on the first day of the assault, and the vice-admiral, who was drowned while coming ashore in a boat.

The natives who had been brought from the provinces to Manila were plundering and committing excesses in the city, so Draper had them all driven out. Guards were placed at the doors of the nunneries and convents to prevent outrages on the women, and then the city was given up to the victorious troops for pillage during three hours. Zuniga, however, remarks that the European troops were moderate, but that the Indian contingents were insatiable. They are said to have committed many atrocities, and, reveling in bloodshed, even murdered the inhabitants. They ransacked the suburbs of Santa Cruz and Binondo, and, acting like savage victorious tribes, they ravished women, and even went into the highways to murder and rob those who fled. The three hours expired, and the following day a similar scene was permitted. The archbishop thereupon besought the general to put a stop to it, and have compassion on the city. The general complied with this request, and restored order under pain of death for disobedience—some Chinese were in consequence hanged. General Draper himself killed one whom he found in the act of stealing, and he ordered that all church property should be restored, but only some priests' vestments were recovered.

Draper demanded the surrender of Cavite, which was agreed to by the archbishop and magistrates, but the commanding officer refused to comply. The major of that garrison was sent with a message to the commander, but on the way he talked with such freedom about the surrender to the British, that the natives quitted their posts and plundered the arsenal. The commander, rather than face humiliation, retired to a ship, and left all further responsibility to the major.

Measures were now taken to pay the agreed indemnity. Heavy contributions were levied upon the inhabitants, which, however, together with the silver from the pious establishments, church ornaments, plate, the archbishop's rings and breast-cross, only amounted to five hundred and forty-six thousand dollars. The British then proposed to accept one million at once and draw the rest from the cargo of the galleon "Philipino," if it result d that she had not been seized by the British previous to the day the capitulation was signed—but the one million was not forthcoming. The day before the capture of Manila, a royal messenger had been sent off with one hundred and eleven thousand dollars, with orders to secure it in some place in the Laguna de Bay. The archbishop now ordered its return to Manila, and issued a requisition to that effect; but the Franciscan friars were insubordinate, and armed the natives, whom they virtually ruled, and the treasure was secreted in Majayjay Convent. Thence, on receipt of the archbishop's message, it was carried across country to a place in North Pampanga, bordering on Cagayan and Pangasinan. The British, convinced that they were being duped, insisted on their claim.

Thomas Backhouse, commanding the troops stationed at Pasig, went up to the Laguna de Bay with eighty mixed troops, to intercept the bringing of the "Philipino" treasure. He attacked Tunasan, Viñan and Santa Rosa, and embarked for Pagsanjan, which was then the capital of the Lake Province. The inhabitants, after firing the convent and church, fled. Backhouse returned to Calamba, entered the Province of Batangas, overran it, and made several Austin friars prisoners. In Lipa he seized three thousand dollars, and there he established his quarters, expecting that the "Philipino" treasure would be carried that way; but on learning that it had been transported by sea to a Pampanga coast town, Backhouse withdrew to Pasig.

In the capitulation, the whole of the Archipelago was surrendered to the British, but Simon de Anda determined to appeal to arms. Draper used stratagem, and issued a proclamation commiserating the fate of the natives who paid tribute to Spaniards, and assuring them that the King of England would not exact it. The archbishop, as governor, became Draper's tool, sent messages to the Spanish families persuading them to return, and appointed an Englishman, married in the country, to be alderman of Tondo. Despite the strenuous opposition of the supreme court, the archbishop, at the instance of Draper, convened a council of native headmen and representative families, and proposed to them the cession of all the islands to the King of England. Draper clearly saw that the ruling powers in the colony, judging from their energy and effective measures, were the friars, so he treated them with great respect. The Frenchman Faller, who unsuccessfully opposed the British assault, was offered troops to go and take possession of Zamboanga and accept the government there, but he refused, as did also a Spaniard named Sandoval.

Draper returned to Europe; Major Fell was left in command of the troops, while Drake assumed the military government of the city, with Smith and Brock as council, and Brereton in charge of Cavite. Draper, on leaving, gave orders for two frigates to go in search of the "Philipino" treasure. The ships got as far as Capul Island and put into harbor. They were detained there by a ruse on the part of a half-caste pilot, and the treasure was got away in the meantime.

Simon de Anda, from his provincial retreat, proclaimed himself governor-general. He declared that the archbishop and the magistrates, as prisoners of war, were dead in the eye of the law; and that his assumption of authority was based upon old laws. None of his countrymen disputed his authority, and he established himself in Bacolor. The British council then convened a meeting of the chief inhabitants, at which Anda was declared a seditious person and deserving of capital punishment, together with the Marquis of Monte Castro, who had violated his parole d'honneur, and the provincial of the Austin friars, who had joined the rebel party. All the Austin friars were declared traitors for having broken their allegiance to the archbishop's authority. The British still pressed for the payment of the one million, while the Spaniards declared they possessed no more. The Austin friars were ordered to keep the natives peaceable if they did not wish to provoke hostilities against themselves. At length, the

British, convinced of the futility of decrees, determined to sally out with their forces; and five hundred men under Thomas Backhouse went up the Pasig River to secure a free passage for supplies to the camp. While opposite to Maybonga, Bustos, with his Cagayan troops, fired on them. The British returned the fire, and Bustos fled to Mariquina. The British passed the river, and sent an officer with a white flag of truce to summon surrender. Bustos was insolent, and threatened to hang the officer if he returned. Backhouse's troops then opened fire and placed two field pieces which completely scared the natives, who fled in such great confusion that many were drowned in the river. Thence the British pursued their enemy "as if they were a flock of goats," and reached the Bamban River, where the Sultan of Sulu resided with his family. The sultan, after a feigned resistance, fell a prisoner to the British, who fortified his dwelling, and occupied it during the whole of the operations. There were subsequent skirmishes on the Pasig River banks with the armed insurgents, who were driven as far as the Antipolo Mountains.

Meanwhile, Anda collected troops; and Bustos, as his lieutenant-general, vaunted the power of his chief through the Bulacan and Pampanga provinces. A Franciscan and an Austin friar, having led troops to Masilo, about seven miles from Manila, the British went out to dislodge them, but on their approach most of the natives feigned they were dead, and the British returned without any loss in arms or men.

The British, believing that the Austin friars were conspiring against them in connivance with those inside the city, placed these friars in confinement, and subsequently shipped away eleven of them to Europe. For the same reason, they at last determined to enter the St. Augustine Convent, and on ransacking it they found that the priests had been lying to them all the time. Six thousand dollars in coin were found hidden in the garden, and large quantities of wrought silver elsewhere. The whole premises were then searched and all the valuables were seized. A British expedition went out to Bulacan, sailing across the bay and up the Hagonoy River, where they disembarked at Malolos on the 19th of January, 1763. The troops, under Captain Eslay, of the Grenadiers, numbered six hundred men, many of whom were Chinese volunteers. As they advanced from Malolos, the natives and Spaniards fled. On the way to Bulacan, Bustos advanced to meet them, but retreated into ambush on seeing they were superior in numbers. Bulacan Convent was fortified with three small cannon. As soon as the troops were in sight of the convent, a desultory fire of case-shot made great havoc in the ranks of the Chinese forming the British vanguard. At length the British brought their field pieces into action, and pointing at the enemy's cannon, the first discharge carried off the head of their artilleryman Ybarra. The panic-stricken natives decamped; the convent was taken by assault; there was an indiscriminate fight and general slaughter. The alcalde and a Franciscan friar fell in action; one Austin friar escaped, and another was seized and killed to avenge the death of the British soldiers. The invading forces occupied the convent, and some of the troops were shortly sent back to Manila. Bustos reappeared near the Bulacan convent with eight thousand native troops, of which six hundred were cavalry, but they dared not attack the British. Bustos then maneuvered in the neighborhood and made occasional alarms. Small parties were sent out against him with so little effect that the British commander headed a body in person, and put the whole of Bustos' troops to flight like mosquitoes before a gust of wind, for Bustos feared they would be pursued into Pampanga. After clearing away the underwood, which served as a covert for the natives, the British reoccupied the convent; but Bustos returned to his position, and was a second time as disgracefully routed by the British, who then withdrew to Manila.

At the same time, it was alleged that a conspiracy was being organized among the Chinese in the Province of Pampanga with the object of assassinating Anda and his Spanish followers. The Chinese cut trenches and raised fortifications, avowing that their bellicose preparations were only to defend themselves against the possible attack of the British; while the Spaniards saw in all this a connivance with the invaders. The latter, no doubt, conjectured rightly. Anda, acting upon the views of his party, precipitated matters by appearing with fourteen Spanish soldiers and a crowd of native bowmen to commence the slaughter in the town of Guagua. The Chinese assembled there in great numbers, and Anda endeavored in vain to induce them to surrender to him. He then sent a Spaniard, named Miguel Garces, with a message, offering them pardon in the name of the King of Spain if they would lay down their arms; but they killed the emissary, and Anda therefore commenced the attack.

The result was favorable for Anda's party, and great numbers of the Chinese were slain. Many fled to the fields, where they were pursued by the troops, while those who were captured were hanged. Such was the inveterate hatred which Anda entertained for the Chinese, that he issued a general decree declaring all the Chinese traitors to the Spanish flag, and ordered them to be hanged wherever they might be found in the provinces. Thus thousands of Chinese were executed who had taken no part whatever in the events of this little war.

Admiral Cornish, having decided to return to Europe, again urged for the payment of the two millions of dollars. The archbishop was in great straits; he was willing to do anything, but his colleagues opposed him, and Cornish was at length obliged to content himself with a bill on the Madrid treasury. Anda appointed Bustos alcalde of Bulacan, and ordered him to recruit and train troops, as he still nurtured the hope of confining the British to Manila—perhaps even of driving them out of the colony.

The British in the city were compelled to adopt the most rigorous precautions against a rising of the population within the walls, and several Spanish residents were arrested for intriguing against them in concert with those outside.

Several French prisoners from Pondicherry deserted from the British; and some Spanish regular troops, who had been taken prisoners, effected their escape. The fiscal of the supreme court and a Senor Villa Corta were found conspiring. The latter was caught in the act of sending a letter to Anda, and was sentenced to be hanged and quartered—the quarters to be exhibited in public places.

The archbishop, however, obtained Villa Corta's pardon, on the condition that Anda should evacuate the Pampanga Province; and Villa Corta wrote to Anda, begging him to accede to this, but Anda absolutely refused to make any sacrifice to save his friend's life; and at the same time he wrote a disgraceful letter to the archbishop, couched in such insulting terms that the British commander burned it without letting the archbishop see it. Villa Corta was finally ransomed by the payment of three thousand dollars.

The treasure brought by the "Philipino" served Anda to organize a respectable force of recruits. Spaniards who were living there in misery, and a crowd of natives always ready for pay, enlisted. These forces, under Lieutenant-general Bustos, encamped at Malinta, about five miles from Manila. The officers lodged in a house belonging to the Austin friars, around which the troops pitched their tents—the whole being defended by redoubts and palisades raised under the direction of a French deserter, who led a company. From this place Bustos constantly caused alarm to the British troops, who once had to retreat before a picket guard sent to get the church bells of Quiapo. The British, in fact, were much molested by Bustos' Malinta troops, who forced the invaders to withdraw to Manila and reduce the extension of their outposts. This measure was followed up by a proclamation, in which the British commander alluded to Bustos' troops as "canaille and robbers," and offered a reward of five thousand dollars for Anda's head; declaring him and his party rebels and traitors to their majesties the kings of Spain and England. Anda, chafing at his impotence to combat the invading party by force of arms, gave vent to his feelings of rage and disappointment by issuing a decree, dated from Bacolor the 19th of May, 1763, of which the translated text reads as follows:

"Royal Government Tribunal of these Islands for His Catholic Majesty: Whereas the Royal Government Tribunal, Supreme Government and Captain-Generalship of His Catholic Majesty in these Islands are gravely offended at the audacity and blindness of those men, who, forgetting all humanity, have condemned as rebellious and disobedient to both their Majesties, him, who as a faithful vassal of His Catholic Majesty, and in conformity with the law, holds the Royal Tribunal, Government and Captain-Generalship; and having suffered by a reward being offered by order of the British Governor in council to whomsoever shall deliver me alive or dead; and by their having placed the arms captured in Bulacan at the foot of the gallows—seeing that instead of their punishing and reproaching such execrable proceedings, the spirit of haughtiness and pride is increasing, as shown in the Proclamation published in Manila on the 17th instant, in which the troops of His Majesty are infamously calumniated—treating them as blackguards and disaffected to their service —charging them with plotting to assassinate the English officers and soldiers, and with having fled when attacked —the whole of these accusations being false: Now therefore by these presents, be it known to all Spaniards and true Englishmen that Messrs. Drake, Smith and Brock, who signed the Proclamation referred to, must not be considered as vassals of His Britannic Majesty, but as tyrants and common enemies unworthy of human society, and therefore, I order that they be apprehended as such, and I offer ten thousand dollars for each one of them alive or dead. At the same time, I withdraw the order to treat the vassals of His Britannic Majesty with all the humanity which the rights of war will permit, as has been practiced hitherto with respect to the prisoners and deserters."

Anda had by this time received the consent of his king to occupy the position which he had usurped, and the British commander was thus enabled to communicate officially with him, if occasion required it; and Drake replied to this proclamation, recommending Anda to carry on the war with greater moderation and humanity.

On the 27th of June, 1763, the British made a sortie from the city to dislodge Bustos, who still occupied Malinta. The attacking party consisted of three hundred and fifty fusileers, fifty horsemen, a mob of Chinese, and a number of guns and ammunition. The British took up quarters on one side of the river, while Bustos remained on the other. The opposing parties exchanged fire, but neither cared nor dared to cross the waterway. The British forces retired in good order to Masilo, and remained there until they heard that Bustos had burned Malinta House and removed his camp to Meycauayan. Then the British withdrew to Manila in the evening. On the Spanish side there were two killed, five mortally wounded and two slightly wounded. The British losses were six mortally wounded and seven disabled. This was the last encounter in open warfare. Chinamen occasionally lost their lives through their love of plunder in the vicinity occupied by the British.

During these operations, the priesthood taught the ignorant natives to believe that the invading troops were infidels—and a holy war was preached.

The friars, especially those of the Augustine order,* abandoned their mission of peace for that of the sword, and the British met with a slight reverse at Masilo, where a religious fanatic of the Austin friars had put himself at the head of a small band lying in ambush.

On the 23d of July, 1763, a British frigate brought news from Europe of an armistice—and the preliminaries of peace, by virtue of which Manila was to be evacuated (Peace of Paris, 10th of February, 1763), were received by the British commander on the 27th of August following, and communicated by him to the archbishop-governor for the "commander-in-chief" of the Spanish arms. Anda stood on his dignity and protested that he should be addressed directly, and be styled captain-general. On this plea he declined to receive the communication. Drake replied by a manifesto, dated 19th of September, to the effect that the responsibility of the blood which might be spilled, in consequence of Anda's refusal to accept his notification, would rest with him. Anda published a counter manifesto, dated 28th of September, in Bacolor (Pampanga), protesting that he had not been treated with proper courtesy.

Greater latitude was allowed to the prisoners, and Villa Corta effected his escape dressed as a woman. He

---

* So tenacious was the opposition brought by the Austin friars both in Manila and the provinces that the British appear to have regarded them as their special foes.

fled to Anda—the co-conspirator who had refused to save his life—and their superficial friendship was renewed. Villa Corta was left in charge of business in Bacolor during Anda's temporary absence. Meanwhile the archbishop fell ill; and it was discussed who should be his successor in the government in the event of his death. Villa Corta argued that it fell to him as senior magistrate. The discussion came to the knowledge of Anda, and seriously aroused his jealousy. Fearing conspiracy against his ambitious projects, he left his camp at Polo, and hastened to interrogate Villa Corta, who explained that he had only made casual remarks in the course of conversation. Anda, however, was restless on the subject of the succession, and sought the opinion of all the chief priests and bishops. Various opinions existed. Some urged that the decision be left to the supreme court—others were in favor of Anda—while many abstained from expressing their views. Anda was so nervously anxious about the matter, that he even begged the opinion of the British commander, and wrote him on the subject from Bacolor on the 2d of November, 1763.

Major Fell seriously quarreled with Drake about the Frenchman Faller, whom Admiral Cornish had left under sentence of death for having written a letter to Java accusing him of being a pirate and a robber. Drake protected Faller, while Fell demanded the execution of the prisoner; and the dispute became so heated that Fell was about to slay Drake with a bayonet, but was prevented by some soldiers. Fell then went to London to complain of Drake, hence Anda's letter was addressed to Backhouse, who took Fell's place. Anda, who months since had refused to negotiate or treat with Drake, still insisted upon being styled captain-general. Backhouse replied that he was ignorant of the Spaniards' statutes or laws, but that he knew the governor was the archbishop. Anda thereupon spread the report that the British commander had forged the preliminaries of peace because he could no longer hold out in warfare. The British necessarily had to send to the provinces to purchase provisions, and Anda caused their forage parties to be attacked, so that the war really continued, in spite of the news of peace, until the 30th of January, 1764. On this day the archbishop died, sorely grieved at the situation, and weighed down with cares. He had engaged to pay four millions of dollars and surrender the islands, but could he indeed have refused any terms? The British were in possession; and these conditions were dictated at the point of the bayonet.

Immediately after the funeral of the archbishop, Anda received dispatches from the King of Spain, by way of China, confirming the news of peace to his governor at Manila. Then the British acknowledged Anda as governor, and proceeded to evacuate the city; but rival factions were not so easily set aside, and fierce quarrels ensued between the respective parties of Anda, Villa Corta and Ustariz, as to who should be governor and receive the city officially from the British. Anda, being actually in command of the troops, had the game in his hands. The conflict was happily terminated by the arrival at Marinduque of the newly appointed governor-general from Spain—Don Francisco de la Torre. A galley was sent there by Anda to bring his excellency to Luzon, and he arrived at Bacolor, where Anda resigned the government to him on the 17th of March, 1764.

La Torre sent a message to Backhouse and Brereton —the commanding officers at Manila and Cavite—stating that he was ready to take over the city in due form. La Torre thereupon took up his residence in Santa Cruz, placed a Spanish guard with sentinels from that ward as far as the Great Bridge (Puente de Barcas, now called Puente de Espana), where the British advance guard was, and friendly communication took place. Governor Drake was indignant at being ignored in all these proceedings, and ordered the Spanish governor to withdraw his guards, under threat of appealing to force. Backhouse and Brereton resented this rudeness, and ordered the troops under arms to arrest Drake, whose hostile action, due to jealousy, they declared unwarrantable. Drake, being apprised of their intentions, escaped from the city with his suite, embarked on board a frigate, and sailed off.

La Torre was said to be indisposed on the day appointed for receiving the city. Some assert that he feigned his indisposition, as he did not wish to arouse Anda's animosity, and desired to afford him an opportunity of displaying himself as a delegate at least of the highest local authority by receiving the city from the British, while he pampered his pride by allowing him to enter triumphantly into it. As the city exchanged masters, the Spanish flag was hoisted once more on the fort of Santiago amid the hurrahs of the populace and artillery salutes.

Before embarking, Brereton offered to do justice to

any claims which might be legitimately established against the British authorities. Hence a sloop loaned to Drake, valued at four thousand dollars, was paid for to the Jesuits, and the three thousand dollars paid to ransom Villa Corta's life was returned. Brereton remarking that, if the sentence against him were valid, it should have been executed at the time, but it could not be commuted by money payment. At the instance of the British authorities, a free pardon was granted and published to the Chinese, few of whom, however, confided in it, and many left with the retiring army. Brereton, with his forces, embarked for India, after dispatching a packet-boat to restore the Sultan of Sulu to his throne.

During this convulsed period, great atrocities were committed. Unfortunately the common felons were released by the English from their prisons, and used their liberty to perpetrate murders and robbery in alliance with those always naturally bent that way. So great did this evil become, so bold were the marauders, that in time they formed large parties, infested highways, attacked plantations, and the poor peasantry had to flee, leaving their cattle and all their belongings in their power. Several avenged themselves of the friars for old scores—others settled accounts with those Europeans who had tyrannized them of old. The Chinese, whether so-called Christians or pagans, declared for and aided the British.

The proceedings of the choleric Simon de Anda y Salazar were approved by his sovereign, but his impetuous disposition drove from him his best counselors, while those who were bold enough to uphold their opinions against his were accused of connivance with the British.

Communications with Europe were scant indeed in those days, but Anda could not have been altogether ignorant of the causes of the war, which terminated with the Treaty of Paris.

On his return to Spain, after the appointment of La Torre as governor-general, he succeeded in retaining the favor of the king, who conferred several honors on him, making him Councilor of Castile, etc. In the meantime Jose Raon, who replaced La Torre, had fallen into disgrace, and Anda was appointed to the governor-generalship of the islands.

There is perhaps no imperiousness so intolerant as that of an official who vaunts his authority by the reflected light of his powerful patron. Anda on his arrival avenged himself of his opposers in all directions. He imprisoned his predecessor, several judges, military officials and others; some he sent back to Spain, others he banished from the capital. Thus he brought trouble upon himself. From all sides hostile resistance increased. He quarreled with the clergy; but when his irascible temper had exhausted itself in the course of six years, he retired to a convent of the Austin friars, where he expired in 1776, much to the relief of his numerous adversaries.

Consequent on the troubled state of the colony, a serious rebellion arose in Ylogan (Cagayan Province), among the Timava natives, who flogged the commandant, and declared they would no longer pay tribute to the Spaniards. The revolt spread to Ilocos and Pangasinan, but the ringleaders were caught, and tranquillity was restored by the gallows.

A rising far more important occurred in Ilocos Sur.

The alcalde was deposed, and escaped after he had been forced to give up his staff of office. The leader of this revolt was a cunning and cute Manila native, named Diego de Silan, who persuaded the people to cease paying tribute, and declare against the Spaniards, who, he pointed out, were unable to resist the English. The city of Vigan was in great commotion. The vicar-general parleyed with the natives; and then, collecting his troops, the rebels were dispersed, while some were taken prisoners; but the bulk of the rioters rallied and attacked, and burned down part of the city. The loyal natives fled before the flames. The vicar-general's house was taken, and the arms in it were seized. All the Austin friars within a large surrounding neighborhood had to ransom themselves by money payments. Silan was then acknowledged as chief over a large territory north and south of Vigan. He appointed his lieutenants, and issued a manifesto declaring Jesus of Nazareth to be captain-general of the place, and that he was his alcalde for the promotion of the Catholic religion and dominion of the King of Spain. His manifesto was wholly that of a religious fanatic. He obliged the natives to attend mass, to confess, and to see that their children went to school. In the midst of all this pretended piety, he robbed cattle and exacted ransoms for the lives of all those who could pay them; he levied a tax of one hundred dollars on each friar. Under the pretense of keeping out the British, he placed sentinels in all directions to prevent news reaching the terrible Simon de Anda. But Anda, though fully informed by an Austin friar of what transpired, had not sufficient troops to march north. He sent a requisition to Silan to present himself within nine days, under penalty of arrest as a traitor. While this order was published, vague reports were intentionally spread that the Spaniards were coming to Ilocos in great force. Many deserted Silan, but he contrived to deceive even the clergy and others by his feigned piety. Silan sent presents to Manila for the British, acknowledging the King of England to be his legitimate sovereign. The British governor sent, in return, a vessel bearing dispatches to Silan, appointing him alcalde mayor. Elated with pride, Silan at once made this public. The natives were undeceived, for they had counted on him to deliver them from the British; now, to their dismay, they saw him the authorized magistrate of the invader. He gave orders to make all the Austin friars prisoners, saying that the British would send other clergy in their stead. The friars surrendered themselves without resistance and joined their bishop near Vigan, awaiting the pleasure of Silan. The bishop excommunicated Silan, and then he released some of the priests. The Christian natives having refused to slay the friars, a secret compact was being made, with this object, with the mountain tribes, when a half-caste named Vicos obtained the bishop's benediction to go and kill Silan; and the rebellion, which had lasted from December 14, 1762, to May 28, 1763, ended.

Not until a score of little battles had been fought were the numerous riots in the provinces quelled. The loyal troops were divided into sections, and marched north in several directions, until peace was restored by March, 1765. Zuniga says that the Spaniards lost in these riots about seventy Europeans and one hundred and forty natives, while they cost the rebels quite ten thousand men.

Space will not permit us to cite all the revolutionary protests which ensued. In the time of Legaspi the submission of the Manila and Tondo chiefs was of but local and temporary importance. Since then, and in fact since the very beginning up to the present time, the natives have only yielded to a force which they have repeatedly tried to overthrow.

CHAPTER XII

THE HISPANO-AMERICAN WAR

THE "MAINE" — THE COURT OF INQUIRY — THE PRESIDENT'S MESSAGE — DEWEY AT MANILA — HOBSON AND THE "MERRIMAC" — CERVERA'S RUN TO RUIN — THE CAPITULATION OF SANTIAGO — THE MISSION OF PEACE

WHEN General Weyler assumed command in Cuba he issued, October 21, 1896, the following proclamation:

"I order and command:

"First—All the inhabitants of the country now outside of the line of fortifications of the towns shall within the period of eight days concentrate themselves in the towns so occupied by the troops. Any individual who after the expiration of this period is found in the uninhabited parts will be considered a rebel and tried as such."

At the time when the order was issued there was living within the western province a population of four hundred thousand men, women and children. The result of the order was to sweep them from their homes and fields and confine them in open-air prisons. No food whatever was supplied to them. As a result more than half of them died.

The indignation aroused became widespread. Weyler was recalled. At the time, especially in Havana among the officials who had been his adherents and who resented his recall, there was an expressed hatred of the United

States. That hatred it is generally understood resulted, on the night of February 15, 1898, in the blowing up of the "Maine."

The dispatch of this vessel to Cuban waters was a friendly act arranged by our government and that of Spain as one of a series of visits to be paid by the ironclads of the two countries to each other's harbors. While the "Viscaya" was en route for New York the "Maine" went to Havana. The harbor there was subsequently shown to have been sown with explosives.

The findings of the Court of Inquiry, which was then held, as embodied in the report of the Foreign Relations Committee, set forth that the destruction of the "Maine" was either compassed by the official act of the Spanish authorities, or was made possible by negligence on their part so willful and gross as to be equivalent to criminal culpability.

The line of argument is as follows: It is established that the "Maine" was destroyed by the explosion of a submarine mine in position under her in a Spanish harbor, at a place where she had been moored to a buoy by the express direction and guidance of the Spanish authorities.

The report of the Spanish board of inquiry, which reported, after the most inadequate examination, that the explosion was due to the fault of the officers of the "Maine," and took place within the vessel itself, was declared to be manifestly false, and calculated to induce public opinion to prejudge the question. Taking this together with the fact of the duplicity, treachery, and cruelty of the Spanish character, the Senate concluded that the Spanish authorities must be held responsible for the crime, either as its direct authors or as contributors thereto by willful and gross negligence.

Spain offered to refer the question as to the cause of the loss of the "Maine" and their responsibility for the catastrophe to arbitration. The President made no reply.

On April 11, anterior circumstances already sufficiently recited, joined to the findings of the American Commissioners, resulted in the President sending a message to Congress, in which he said:

"The long trial has proved that the object for which Spain has waged the war cannot be attained. The fire of insurrection may flame or may smolder with varying seasons, but it has not been, and it is plain that it cannot be, extinguished by present methods. The only hope of relief and repose from a condition which can no longer be endured is the enforced pacification of Cuba.

"In the name of humanity, in the name of civilization, in behalf of endangered American interests which give us the right and the duty to speak and to act, the war in Cuba must stop.

"In view of these facts and of these considerations, I ask the Congress to authorize and empower the President to take measures to secure a full and final termination of hostilities between the government of Spain and the people of Cuba, and to secure in the island the establishment of a stable government capable of maintaining order and observing its international obligations, insuring peace and tranquillity, and the security of its citizens as well as our own, and to use the military and naval forces of the United States as may be necessary for these purposes.

"WILLIAM MCKINLEY."

On April 19 Congress passed the following:

Joint resolution for the recognition of the independence of the people of Cuba, demanding that the government of Spain relinquish its authority and government in the island of Cuba, and to withdraw its land and naval forces from Cuba and Cuban waters, and directing the President of the United States to use the land and naval forces of the United States to carry these resolutions into effect.

"*Whereas*, The abhorrent conditions which have existed for more than three years in the island of Cuba, so near our own borders, have shocked the moral sense of the people of the United States, have been a disgrace to Christian civilization, culminating, as they have, in the destruction of a United States battleship, with two hundred and sixty of its officers and crew, while on a friendly visit in the harbor of Havana, and cannot longer be endured, as has been set forth by the President of the United States in his message to Congress of April 11, 1898, upon which the action of Congress was invited; therefore be it resolved,

"First—That the people of the island of Cuba are, and of right ought to be, free and independent.

"Second—That it is the duty of the United States to demand, and the government of the United States does hereby demand, that the government of Spain at once relinquish its authority and government in the island of Cuba, and withdraw its land and naval forces from Cuba and Cuban waters.

"Third—That the President of the United States be, and he hereby is, directed and empowered to use the entire land and naval forces of the United States, and to call into the actual service of the United States the militia of the several States to such an extent as may be necessary to carry these resolutions into effect.

"Fourth—That the United States hereby disclaims any disposition or intention to exercise sovereignty, jurisdiction or control over said island, except for the pacification thereof, and asserts its determination when that is accomplished to leave the government and control of the island to its people."

The ultimatum embodied in the foregoing being rejected by Spain, diplomatic relations were severed and hostilities ensued.

On May 1, at daybreak, the Asiatic squadron, commanded by Commodore Dewey, arrived at Manila from Hong Kong. At Cavite, within the harbor, protected by four batteries, lay the Spanish fleet. It was commanded by Admiral Patricio Montojo. The squadron proceeded up the bay unmolested and made for the naval station. Two mines were exploded, but ineffectively. At five o'clock and ten minutes the Spaniards opened fire. Commodore Dewey set the signals, and his entire squadron advanced to short range. The squadron consisted of the following cruisers and gunboats: "Olympia," "Baltimore," "Boston," "Raleigh," "Concord," "Petrel," and "McCulloch."

At 5.30 the "Olympia's" 8-inch guns opened, and the squadron swung in front of the Spanish ships and forts in single file, firing their port guns. Then, wheeling, they passed back, firing their starboard guns. This maneuver was repeated five times, the entire American fleet passing all the Spanish ships and batteries at each maneuver, and each time drawing in closer and closer and delivering fire at more deadly range. During two hours and a half there was tremendous resistance by the Spaniards. They had eleven ships and five land batteries in full play, against six American warships. But the American marksmanship was faultless. Every shot seemed to count against ship or shore battery, while most of the Spanish powder was burned in vain. At 7.45 A.M. the American fleet withdrew to ascertain damages and permit the smoke to clear. It was seen then that several Spanish ships were crippled or burning, and it was found that the American vessels had suffered hardly at all. Admiral Dewey called his captains into consultation and arrangements were made for another attack. At 10.40 the attack was renewed, the "Baltimore" leading. She advanced right upon the enemy, shelling them constantly, and the other Americans followed, working their guns as rapidly as they could load and fire. The effect of this assault was terrific. Ship after ship of the Spaniards sunk or was run ashore to keep them from sinking or falling into American hands. At 12.45 P.M. the Spaniards struck their colors in token of surrender. Admiral Patricio Montojo fled to Manila, and most of the survivors fled with him. This ended the work of May 1.

On May 2, Commodore Dewey landed a force of marines at Cavite. They completed the destruction of the Spanish fleet and batteries and established a guard for the protection of the Spanish hospitals. The resistance of the forts was weak. The "Olympia" turned a few guns on the Cavite arsenal, and its magazine at once exploded, killing some and wounding many. This practically ended the fire from the batteries, the Spanish artillerists fearing to face the American gunners. "Remember the 'Maine'!" was the word continually passed between the ships, and every American officer, every "Jackie," was eager to do his utmost.

After Manila and the defeat of Admiral Montojo, the successive and concluding events of the Hispano-American war include Admiral Sampson's bombardment of San Juan; Hobson's heroic experiment with the "Merrimac"; General Shafter's campaign; the destruction of Cervera's squadron; the capitulation of Santiago; General Miles's tour in Porto Rico, and the overtures for peace. These events may be conveniently summarized as follows:

The bombardment of San Juan was the result of a reconnaissance. The Spanish fleet, under command of Admiral Cervera, which it was the purpose of the Americans to capture or destroy, subsequently sought and found shelter within the harbor of Santiago, the entrance to which Admiral Sampson then proceeded to invest. There, while waiting to engage the enemy, it was thought wise to attempt to block the harbor and so prevent a possible escape. The plan originated with Lieutenant Hobson, and its execution was left to him. On the night of June 3, with a picked crew of seven volunteers, he steamed up in the collier "Merrimac" to the harbor's entrance and sank her. From the fleet the progress of the "Merrimac" was eagerly followed.

At 3.15 the first Spanish shot was fired, coming from one of the guns on the hill to the west of the entrance. The shot was seen to splash seaward from the "Merrimac," having passed over her. The firing became general very soon afterward, being especially fierce and rapid from the batteries inside on the left of the harbor, probably from batteries on Smith Cay. The flashes and reports were apparently those of rapid-fire guns, ranging from small automatic guns to four-inch or larger. For fifteen minutes a perfect fusillade was kept up. Then the fire slackened and by 3.30 had almost ceased. There was a little desultory firing until about 3.45, when all became quiet. Daylight came at about five o'clock.

At about 5.15 A.M., a launch, which under Cadet Powell had followed the "Merrimac," in order if possible to rescue Hobson and his men, was seen steaming from west to east, near or across the mouth of the harbor. She steamed back from east to west and began skirting the coast to the west of the entrance. The battery on the hill to the left opened fire on her, but did not make good practice. The launch continued her course as far westward as a small cove and then headed for the "Texas," steaming at full speed. Several shots were fired at her from the battery on the left as she steamed out.

It was broad daylight by this time. Cadet Powell came alongside the "Texas" and reported that "No one had come out of the entrance of the harbor." His words sounded like the death knell of all who had gone in on the "Merrimac." It seemed incredible, almost impossible, any of them could have lived through the awful fire that was directed at the ship. Cadet Powell said that he had followed behind the ship at a distance of four or five hundred yards. Hobson missed the entrance of the harbor at first, having gone too far to the westward; he almost ran aground. The launch picked up the entrance and directed the "Merrimac" in. From the launch the collier was seen until she rounded the bend of the channel and until the helm had been put to port to swing her into position across the channel. There was probably no one in the fleet who did not think that all seven of the men had perished. In the afternoon, much to the surprise of every one, a tug flying a flag of truce was seen coming out of the entrance. The "Vixen," flying a tablecloth at the fore, went to meet the tug. A Spanish officer went aboard the "Vixen" from the tug and was taken aboard the flagship. Not long afterward a signal was made that Murphy of the "Iowa" was saved and was a prisoner of war. About four o'clock another signal was made from the flagship: "Collier's crew prisoners of war; two slightly wounded. All well." It can be easily imagined what relief this signal brought to all hands, who had been mourning the death of all these men. The Spanish officer said also that the prisoners were confined in Morro Castle. He said further that Admiral Cervera considered the attempt to run in and sink the "Merrimac" across the channel an act of such great bravery and desperate daring that he (the Admiral) thought it very proper that our naval officers should be notified of the safety of these men. Whatever the motive for sending out the tug with the flag of truce, the act was a most graceful one and one of most chivalrous courtesy. The Spanish officer is reported to have said: "You have made it more difficult, but we can still get out."

The daring evinced by Hobson was instantly recognized, but the importance of his achievement was not appreciated until July 3, when Cervera's desperate attempt to escape, would, in all likelihood, have been partly successful but for the fact that his vessels were obliged to leave the harbor in single file.

Let us, however, recapitulate in their order the events

which followed the sinking of the "Merrimac," news whereof was received on June 4. On June 5, a bombardment of the Morro Castle, commanding the mouth of Santiago Harbor, took place, but no serious impression seems to have been made upon the fortress at that time, although some neighboring earthworks were destroyed. Two days later, there was a more effective bombardment of the harbor fortifications by Admiral Sampson, but the Morro Castle still held out and protected the entrance to the port by its ability to deliver a plunging fire. On June 9, it was known that twelve thousand men, or about half of our regular army, together with a number of volunteer regiments, under General Shafter, had set sail from Tampa, and, on the following day, the Spaniards began preparations for a vigorous defense of Santiago against a land force by means of carefully planned intrenchments. On June 11, a body of United States marines landed at Guantanamo Bay, and, on the three ensuing days, sustained successfully determined assaults by the Spaniards. On June 15, the "Vesuvius," carrying a pneumatic gun, which discharges a tube loaded with dynamite, arrived off Santiago, and fully justified the expectations of her inventor by the efficient part which she took in the bombardment. Since June 7, the Spaniards had attempted to repair the Santiago forts, and had, to some extent, succeeded in doing so; consequently, on June 16, Admiral Sampson ordered the ships to open fire on them again, and, in this assault, is said to have discharged five hundred thousand pounds of metal. It was not until June 22, or thirteen days after his departure from Tampa, that General Shafter landed his troops at

Baiquiri, a point on the coast some miles southwest of Santiago. There was furious fighting during the three following days, and there was a grievous loss of life on the American side, infantry and dismounted cavalry having been ordered or allowed to attack intrenchments without artillery support. The necessity of heavy siege guns was at once clear to professional soldiers, but these could not be moved from the transports to the shore, because only one lighter had been brought from Tampa, and even that one had been lost. This loss could have been quickly repaired, had not General Shafter refused to take with him from Tampa the signal train that had been made ready for him, on the ground that he "only wanted men who could carry muskets." The result of this indifference to a branch of the service which constitutes the eyes, ears and voice of a modern army, was that it required two days to transmit a request from Shafter's headquarters to the point where the cable could be used. On June 29, not having, as yet, any heavy siege guns in position, and not having so surrounded the city as to prevent the re-enforcement or escape of its garrison, General Shafter telegraphed to Washington: "I can take Santiago in forty-eight hours." On July 1 and 2, General Shafter made resolute assaults upon the Spanish intrenchments and carried many of them, advancing his own lines very much nearer the city. The advantage thus gained, however, had cost him a considerable fraction of his force. The whole number of Americans killed, wounded and missing during the land operations reached ten per cent of the number with which General Shafter landed on June 22. Of these land engagements the most notable were those of Aguadores, El Caney and San Juan.

The battle of San Juan is described as follows:

The dawn of July 1 found the troops of Wheeler's division bivouacked on the eminence of El Pozo. Kent's division bivouacked near the road back of El Pozo. Grimes's battery went into position about two hundred and fifty yards west of the ruined buildings of El Pozo soon after sunrise and prepared gun pits. Grimes's battery opened fire against San Juan a little before 8 A.M. The troops of the cavalry division were scattered about on El Pozo Hill in the rear and around the battery, without order and with no view to their protection from the Spanish fire. This condition rectified itself when the Spaniards, after five or six shots by the American battery, replied with shrapnel fire at correct range and with accurately adjusted fuses, killing two men at the first shot. After some firing soon after 9 A.M. Wheeler's division was put in march toward Santiago. Crossing Aguadores stream, it turned to the right, under General Sumner, who was in command at that time owing to General Wheeler's illness. Scattering shots were fired by the Spaniards before the arrival of the first troops at the crossing, but their volley firing did not commence until the dismounted cavalry went into position, crossing open ground. Kent's division followed Wheeler's, moving across the stream, and advanced along the road in close order under a severe enfilading fire. After advancing some distance, it turned off to the left. Lieutenant Ord (killed in battle) made a reconnaissance from a large tree on the banks of the stream.

At about one o'clock, after a delay of nearly two hours waiting for the troops to reach their positions, the whole force advanced, charged, and carried the first line of intrenchments. They were afterward formed on the crest and there threw up intrenchments facing the second line at a distance of from five hundred to one thousand yards.

We pass to the memorable naval combat of July 3, which annihilated Cervera's squadron, and dealt the deathblow to Spain's hope of making head against America on the sea. There is, of course, no foundation for the report that Admiral Cervera resolved to fly, because he knew that Santiago would be immediately taken. The truth is that, on July 2, he received peremptory orders from Madrid to leave Santiago at once, no matter what might be the consequences; to engage the American fleet, and to make his way, if possible, to Havana, where he would raise the blockade. These orders he did his best to execute on the morning of July 3, having been informed by signal that Admiral Sampson's flagship, the "New York," and a large part of the American fleet, were lying at some distance toward the east, and that only the "Brooklyn," "Texas" and "Iowa" would have to be encountered if the escaping ships moved westward. There was a mistake in this computation, for the "Oregon" also took an important part in the action, and so did the little "Gloucester," a converted yacht, which did not hesitate, single-handed, to engage both of the torpedo-boat destroyers. With such information as he could procure, however, Admiral Cervera believed that his ships could outsail all of those blockading the mouth of the harbor, except the "Brooklyn," and that, if the "Brooklyn" could be disabled, some, at least, of his vessels could escape. Accordingly, orders were issued by the Spanish admiral to proceed at full speed to the westward after clearing the entrance, and to concentrate fire upon the "Brooklyn." In the attempt to carry out this programme, the four warships, "Maria Teresa," "Almirante Oquendo," "Vizcaya" and "Cristobal Colon," followed by the torpedo-boat destroyers "Pluton" and "Furor," in the order named and in single file, pushed with all steam up through the narrow passage which had been left by the sunken "Merrimac." The concerted endeavor to disable the "Brooklyn" failed, and it turned out that both the "Oregon" and "Texas" were faster than the "Cristobal Colon," which was much the swiftest of the Spanish squadron. The "Maria Teresa," the "Almirante Oquendo" and the "Vizcaya" were successively riddled and put *hors de combat* by the rapid and accurate firing of the American ships, and were beached by their officers to avoid, not so much surrender, as the danger of explosion. The "Cristobal Colon" succeeded in reaching a point about fifty miles from Santiago, when it was headed off not only by the protected cruiser "Brooklyn," but also by the ironclads "Oregon" and "Texas." From that moment, escape was seen to be impossible, so the commander beached his ship and hauled down his flag. This closing incident of the battle took place at 1.20 P.M., almost exactly four hours after the leading vessel of the escaping column, the "Maria Teresa," had passed the Morro. Meanwhile, the little "Gloucester," under Commander Richard Wainwright, had stopped both of the torpedo-boat destroyers, received their fire, and detained them until an ironclad came up.

It will be observed that the Spanish squadron did not have to contend with the whole of the American fleet, but that, on the contrary, the forces engaged were, on paper, much more nearly equal than is generally understood. The Americans had the first-class battleships "Oregon" and "Iowa," the second-class battleship "Texas," the protected cruiser "Brooklyn" and the converted yacht "Gloucester." The Spaniards, on their part, had one armored cruiser, three protected cruisers, and two torpedo-boat destroyers. It is certainly a remarkable fact, and one almost without a parallel in naval annals, if we except Dewey's achievement at Manila, that not a single one of the Spanish vessels should have managed to escape. The honor of the almost unique victory at Santiago belongs, beyond a doubt, to Commodore Schley, for, at the beginning of the action, Admiral Sampson, in his flaghip, the "New York," was out of sight, and he remained out of signal distance until almost the end.

Almost immediately after these incidents an expedition under command of General Miles proceeded to Porto Rico, where, on the southwest coast, at the little village of Guanica, a landing was effected on July 25.

Twenty-four hours later the Spanish government, through M. Jules Cambon, the French embassador at Washington, made a formal proposal for ending the war and arranging terms of peace.

CHAPTER XIII

SPANISH ART, LITERATURE, AND SPORT

I

PAINTING AND ARCHITECTURE

EARLY Spanish paintings are feeble imitations of Italian and Flemish art. They lack the simplicity of the one and the realism of the other. In color they are somber and monotonous—two qualities which chraracterize the whole Spanish school. The value of this school has been curiously overrated. Comparatively speaking of brief existence, it has produced but two great painters—Velasquez and Murillo. Their contemporaries, Zurbaran, del Mazo, Ribera, Alonso Cana, Herrera and Roelas, were men of ability, no doubt, but they were not masters.

Excellent examples of Velasquez and of Murillo are to be found to-day in the Museum of the Prado at Madrid, and in the Art Gallery of Seville. The cathedrals and churches generally contain works of the principal painters, both of the early and later times; but placed, as a rule, in "Retablos" or altar pieces, they are poorly exposed and difficult to view.

DON DIEGO VELASQUEZ DE SILVA, or simpry VELASQUEZ, the greatest painter that Spain has produced, was born at Seville, in 1599, of parents of Portuguese origin, and died at Madrid in 1660. He married in his youth the daughter of FRANCISCO PACHECO, a painter of inferior merit, but a learned writer on art, from whose advice and instruction he derived much advantage. Velasquez showed from his childhood a genius for painting. He began by copying carefully from nature, still life, and living models, forming himself upon the study of pictures by Ribera and by Italian masters of the Naturalistic school, which had been brought from Italy to Spain. The best examples of his first manner are "The Adoration of the Kings" and his famous "Borrachos," or drunkards, in the Madrid Gallery. In them the influence of Caravaggio and Ribera is very evident. In the twenty-third year of his age he came to Madrid, and, attracting the notice of influential persons, was soon taken into the service of Philip IV.—an enthusiastic lover of art, and himself a painter. He remained there for the rest of his life, and his pictures were almost exclusively painted for his royal patron and for the grandees of the Spanish court. A friendship with Rubens, who was in Madrid as embassador from the King of England, in 1628, and two visits to Italy, in 1629 and 1648, led him to modify his early manner. From the study at Venice of the masterpieces of Titian and Tintoret, he acquired a greater harmony and transparency of color, and a freer and firmer touch, without departing from that truthful representation of nature which he always sought to attain. On his second visit to Italy he chiefly studied in Rome. He again changed his style: his coloring became more what the Italians term "sfumato," or hazy; and he returned, to some extent, to his early general soberness of tone, rarely introducing bright colors into his last pictures. Velasquez's second and third manners, as well as his first, are fully represented in the Madrid Gallery, which contains no less than sixty of his pictures, or almost the whole of his genuine works. The "Borrachos" have already been mentioned as an example of his first manner. The fine portrait of the Infante Don Carlos, second son of Philip III., is another. In his second manner are the "Surrender of Breda," perhaps the finest representation and treatment of a contemporary historical event in the world; the magnificent portrait of the Count of Benavente, and the four Dwarfs. In his third, the "Meninas," and the "Hilanderas." By studying these pictures the student will soon be able to distinguish between the three manners of the painter, and to decide for himself as to the genuineness of the many pictures which pass for Velasquez's in the public and private galleries of Europe.

It was principally as a portrait-painter that Velasquez excelled. Although he wanted the imagination of Titian, and gave less dignity and refinement than that great master to his portraits, yet in a marvelous power of rendering nature, and in truthfulness of expression, he was not his inferior. In the imaginative faculties he was singularly deficient, as his "Forge of Vulcan," the "Coronation of the Virgin," and other works of that class in the Madrid Gallery, are sufficient to prove. However, the "Crucifixion," in the same collection, is a grand and solemn conception, which has excited the enthusiastic admiration of some critics. Velasquez was essentially a "naturalistic" painter. In the representation of animals, especially dogs, and of details such as armor, drapery, and objects of still-life, he is almost without a rival. His freedom of touch and power of producing truthful effects by the simplest means are truly wonderful. His aerial perspective, his light and shade, his gradations of tone and color, are all equally excellent, and have excited the admiration of Wilkie, and of the best judges of art.

The high offices which Velasquez held at court gave him but little time to paint. The number of his pictures is, therefore, comparatively small. They were principally executed for the royal palaces; those which have escaped the fires that destroyed so many great works have been removed to the Madrid Museum. The portraits which are attributed to him in many public and private collections out of Spain are, for the most part, by his pupils, or imitators and copyists. One of the most skillful of the latter was a certain Lucas, who, not many years ago, succeeded in deceiving many collectors.

Among his best scholars were: JUAN BAUTISTA DEL MAZO (d. 1667), his son-in-law. How nearly he approached his master may be seen by his admirable portrait of D. Tiburcio de Redin, and the view of Saragossa, in which the figures have even been attributed to Velasquez, in the Madrid Gallery. PAREJA, his half-caste slave, and afterward freedman (d. 1670), who imitated his master in his portraits, but not in his religious and other subjects, in which he followed the Dutch and Italian painters of the time; as in his "Calling of St. Mark," in the same gallery. CARREÑO, a member of a noble family (b. 1614; d. 1685), who succeeded Velasquez as court painter, and who is chiefly known by his portraits of the idiot king (Charles II.), his mother, Mariana of Austria, Don John of Austria (not the hero of Lepanto), and other royal and courtly persons of the period. Spanish writers on art rank him with Vandyke, to whom, however, he was greatly inferior. His coloring is generally insipid, and wanting in vigor.

BARTOLOME ESTEBAN MURILLO was born at Seville in 1616. He studied under Juan del Castillo, a very indifferent painter, but formed his style, like Velasquez, on the works of Ribera and the Italian naturalistic painters. Like that great master, too, he modified his "manner" three times, as he gained in experience and knowledge. From his boyhood he painted pictures which were sold in the market-place of his native city, and bought by dealers; chiefly, it is said, for exportation to the Spanish colonies in America. After obtaining a considerable reputation at Seville, he went to Madrid to improve himself by the study of the works of the great Italian masters in the royal collection. Their influence led him to modify his first style, called by the Spaniards *frio* (cold), in which he had imitated the brown tints, dark shadows, and conventional treatment of drapery of Ribera; but he did not abandon it altogether. It may still be traced in his second, or *calido* (warm) manner, as in the celebrated "Holy Family," called "del Pajarito," in the Madrid Gallery. The advice of Velasquez, who treated him with great kindness, and the works of Titian and Rubens, led him to adopt a warm, harmonious and transparent coloring, and a more truthful rendering of nature; at the same time his drawing became more free, if not more correct. His third manner is termed by the Spaniards *vaporoso* (misty), from a gradual and almost imperceptible fusion of tints, producing a kind of hazy effect. In it are painted, for the most part, his well-known "Miraculous Conceptions," the Virgin standing on the crescent moon attended by angels. The three manners of Murillo are neither so well defined nor so easily recognized as those of Velasquez. He never completely abandoned one of them for the other, and in his last pictures he frequently returned to the calido style. As a painter of portraits and landscapes, he was inferior to Velasquez. It was only in religious subjects, and especially in his Holy Families, that he surpassed him. His Virgins are taken from the common type of Andalusian beauty, slightly idealized; but he gives to them an expression of youthful innocence and religious sentiment which makes him the most popular of Spanish painters. The Spaniards are naturally proud of him. They believe that he unites the best qualities of the greatest masters, and surpasses them all. All other critics place him second to Velasquez, who unquestionably possessed a more original genius. Comparisons between these two great painters are, however, more than usually pointless and misleading, the two men being essentially different in feeling, taste, and manner.

Returning to Seville, after his first and only visit to Madrid, Murillo established himself there for the rest of his life, painting, with the help of scholars, many pictures for churches and convents in Spain and her colonies. In the Peninsula, his best works are now only found at Madrid and in his native city. The French invaders and the picture-dealers carried the greater number away. Among those most worthy of note at Madrid are the "St. Elizabeth of Hungary tending the Sick," and the "Patrician's Dream," now in the Academy of San Fernando, and the two "Immaculate Conceptions" in the Gallery: at Seville, "St. Thomas of Villanueva distributing Alms to the Poor," in the public Museum; the "St. Anthony of Padua" in the Cathedral; and the pictures in the Caridad. Of his well-known sunburned beggar-boys and girls there are none, that we know of, in Spain; many of those in European collections are probably by his favorite pupil, VILLAVICENCIO, in whose arms he died at Seville in 1682. There is a picture by this painter, who was of a noble family, and rather an amateur than an artist, in the Madrid Gallery, representing a group of boys at play. It has no great merit, but shows how he attempted to imitate his master in this class of subject. He was born in 1635, and died in 1700. The imitations and copies of Murillo by TOBAR (d. 1758) are so successful that they frequently pass for originals. The same may be said of some by MENESES, who died early in the 18th century.

Among the contemporaries of Murillo was IRIARTE (b. 1620; d. 1685), one of the few landscape-painters that Spain has produced. His landscapes were much esteemed by Murillo, but they are not entitled to rank with the works of any of the great masters in this branch of the art. The Madrid Gallery contains five examples of them.

The following painters may be mentioned among the best and most characteristic of the second class in the Spanish school: FRANCISCO DE ZURBARAN, born in Estremadura in 1598, died at Madrid, 1662, was essentially a religious painter, and his somber coloring and the subjects of his pictures are characteristic of Spanish bigotry and of the Inquisition. In Spain he is chiefly known by his altar-pieces for churches and convents; out of Spain by his monks and friars. A few figures of female saints prove that he was not insensible to grace of form and beauty of color. But he is usually mannered, and without dignity. A disagreeable reddish hue pervades his larger pictures. He formed himself, like his contemporaries, on the study of the Italian painters of the Naturalistic school. Philip IV. is said to have named him "Painter of the King, and King of Painters." He enjoyed the first title, but did not merit the second. His best work in Spain is, perhaps, the "Apotheosis of St. Thomas Aquinas," in the Seville Museum. It is a grand, but somewhat stiff and unpleasing composition. Zurbaran is badly represented in the Madrid Gallery. The "Christ Sleeping on the Cross" is the most popular in it. One or two of his works are to be found in the Academy of San Fernando.

ALONSO CANO (born at Granada, 1601; died there, 1667) enjoys the highest reputation in Spain after Zurbaran. He was painter, sculptor, and architect, and, moreover, carved and painted wooden figures of the Virgin and Saints, an art in which he attained great success and renown. Many examples of his skill may be seen at Granada. One of the most celebrated is the statuette of St. Francis in the sacristy of the Cathedral of Toledo. Cano was a violent, but not unkindly man, constantly engaged in quarrels and lawsuits. He ended by becoming a canon of the Cathedral of Granada, after narrowly escaping from the clutches of the Inquisition. His drawing is carefully studied, but is frequently exaggerated, and wants ease and flow; his coloring conventional and somewhat weak; but there is a delicacy of expression and refinement in his works which have earned him the praise of some critics. The Madrid Gallery contains a few of his pictures: among them a "Dead Christ"; but he is best seen at Granada.

FRANCISCO HERRERA EL VIEJO, or the elder (b. 1576; d. 1656). His principal works are at Seville and out of Spain. The Madrid Gallery contains nothing by him. Spanish writers on art attribute to him the introduction into Spain of a new style of painting, characteristic of the national genius. It was vigorous, but coarse, and has little to recommend it even to those who admire the Italian eclectic school. Like Cano, he was a man of hot temper, quarreled with his pupils, among whom was Velasquez, and was thrown into prison on a charge of coining false money. He was released by Philip IV. on account of his merits as a painter. His best work in Spain is the "Last Judgment," in the church of St. Bernardo at Seville, which is praised for its composition and the correct anatomy of the human form. Herrera painted in fresco, for which he was well fitted from his bold and rapid execution; but his works in that material have mostly perished.

FRANCISCO HERRERA EL MOZO, or the younger (b. 1622; d. 1685), son of the former, studied at Rome, where he was chiefly known for his pictures of dead animals and still life. The Italians nicknamed him "Lo Spagnuolo dei pesci," from his clever representations of fish. He was a painter of small merit; weak and affected in his drawing, color, and composition. The Madrid Gallery contains but one of his pictures —the "Triumph of St. Hermenegildo." Like his father, he painted frescoes, some of which are still preserved in the churches of Madrid. He was also an architect, and made the plans for the "Virgen del Pilar" at Saragossa.

JUAN DE LAS ROELAS, commonly known in Spain as "El Clerigo Roelas," was born at Seville about 1558, and died in 1625. He studied at Venice; hence the richness and brilliancy of color in his best works, as in the fine picture of the "Martyrdom of St. Andrew," in the Museum of Seville. In the churches of that city are some altar-pieces by him worthy of notice. He is scarcely known out of Spain, or, indeed, out of Seville, although he may be ranked among the best of the Spanish painters of the second rank. The picture in the Madrid Gallery attributed to him, if genuine, is a very inferior work.

JUAN DE VALDÉS LEAL, born at Cordova in 1630, died at Seville 1691, was a painter of considerable ability, but of a hasty and jealous temper, which he especially displayed toward Murillo, the superiority of whose work he would not acknowledge. His pictures are rare, and are best seen at Seville. The Caridad in that city contains two, representing the "Triumph of Death," which are powerful, but coarse. He was also an engraver of skill.

FRANCISCO RIZZI, the son of a Bolognese painter who had settled in Spain, was born at Madrid in 1608, and died there in 1685. He was a rapid and not unskillful painter, and was employed to decorate in fresco, in the Italian fashion, the churches and royal palaces of the capital. His well-known picture in the Madrid Gallery representing the "Auto da Fe" held in the Plaza Mayor before Charles II. and his queen, Marie Luisa of Orleans, in 1680, although awkward and formal in composition, is cleverly painted.

CLAUDIO COELLO, died 1693, was chiefly employed by the Spanish court in portrait-painting and in decorating the royal palaces for triumphs and festivities. His best known and most important picture, in the sacristy of the Escorial, is the "Santa Forma," or "Removal of the Miraculous Wafer of Gorcum," in which he has introduced portraits of Charles II. and of the officers of his court. It is crowded and unskillful in composition, but has merits which show that he had preserved the best traditions of the Spanish school of painters, of whom he was almost the last.

The history of Spanish painting closes with the seventeenth century. During the eighteenth there appeared a few feeble painters who imitated, but were even immeasurably behind, the Luca Giordanos, Tiepolos, and other Italians whom the Bourbon kings invited to Madrid to decorate the new royal palace, and to make designs for the royal manufactory of tapestries. The first who attempted to revive Spanish art was FRANCISCO GOYA (born in 1746), a vigorous but eccentric painter and etcher in aqua fortis, not wanting in genius. He studied at Rome, and returning to Spain executed frescoes, with little success, in churches at Madrid and elsewhere. He became "pintor de camara," or court painter, to the weak Charles IV. and vicious Ferdinand VII. In numerous portraits of these kings and of members of the Spanish Bourbon family he made them, perhaps with deliberate malice—for in politics he was an ardent liberal—even more hideous than they were. His large picture of Charles IV. and his family in the Madrid Gallery is the best, but by no means an attractive example of his skill, and is in parts, especially in the details of costume, not altogether unworthy of Velasquez, whom he sought to imitate. But his genius was chiefly shown in his etchings, in which, in a grotesque, and not always decent way, he lashed the vices and corruption of his country, and vented his hatred against its French invaders. The Spaniards are very proud of Goya. The author of the "Guide to the Madrid Gallery" discovers in his works a union of the best qualities of Rembrandt, Titian, Paul Veronese, Watteau, and Lancret! He was, no doubt, a powerful and original painter, and his touch is often masterly; but he was incorrect in his drawing, and his color is frequently exaggerated and unnatural. His designs for the tapestries in the royal palaces are generally weak and illdrawn; but they are interesting as representations of national manners and costume. Goya died in voluntary exile at Bordeaux in 1828, having left Spain disgusted with the political reaction which set in on the restoration of the Bourbons, and with the persecution of the best and most enlightened of his countrymen. His works have of late years been much sought after, especially in France. His etchings, consisting chiefly of political caricatures (caprichos), scenes in the bull-ring, the horrors of war, etc., are rare. A new edition has recently been published of the "Caprichos" from the worn-out plates.

Goya may be considered the founder of the modern Spanish school of painting, which has produced Fortuny, Madrazo, Palmaroli, and a number of other clever painters who have achieved a European reputation. It is not, however, in Spain, but in the private collections of London, Paris, and New York, that their principal works are to be found. Spaniards have little love or knowledge of art, and the high prices it is now the fashion to pay for Spanish pictures are beyond their means.

The history of architecture in Spain is similar to that of France and other countries of northern Europe, with, however, the essential difference that Moorish art in the Middle Ages attained in Spain as great an importance as in the East, and when combined with Christian art, a new style was formed, known by the name of Morisco or Mudejar, which is not met with out of the Spanish Peninsula, and is of great interest.

Spanish architecture may be divided, after the prehistoric period, and invasions of the Phœnicians and Carthaginians, in the following manner:

1. Roman period, until the invasions of the Goths.
2. Latin Byzantine style, fifth to end of tenth century.
3. Moorish architecture, eighth to fifteenth century.
4. Romanesque style, eleventh, twelfth, and part of thirteenth century.
5. Pointed architecture, thirteenth, fourteenth, fifteenth, and part of sixteenth century.
6. Mudejar style, thirteenth, fourteenth, fifteenth, and part of sixteenth century.
7. Renaissance or Plateresque style, Græco-Roman, and Churrigueresque.

Several of the inscriptions which have come down to us of the Roman period (see "Corpus Inscrip.," Vol. II., Emil Hübner) mention different buildings of public utility and adornment which were in course of construction in Spain. The number which still remains is very great, and may be found in almost every province; many have, however, been sadly mutilated. The finest are undoubtedly the aqueduct at Segovia (constructed of huge stones, and still used for carrying water to the town), the Bridge of Alcantara (Estremadura), with its triumphal arch in the center and temple at one end, and the walls of Lugo and Astorga. The general structure of these monuments and their ornamentation are the same as those of ancient Rome: it is well known that the Romans imposed their art on the countries which came under their dominion.

Two remarkable specimens exist of the Visigothic period: the church of San Roman de Hornija (near Toro), 646, and San Juan de Banos (near Venta de Banos), 661. Although these churches have suffered much from later additions, they still retain a great part of their construction and part of the primitive building. A great number of fragments remain in Spain of this period. They must be examined in order to judge this architecture. Some are capitals of columns in the Cathedral of Cordova and some churches at Toledo, and different friezes and fragments which have been applied to different uses at Toledo and Merida. The votive crowns found at Guarrazar, now at Cluny (Paris) and armory of Madrid, give an excellent idea of the ornamentation of the Visigoths. Several examples of architecture remain posterior to the Visigoths, and anterior to the Romanesque style of the eleventh century. The most important are the churches of Sta. Maria Naranco and St. Miguel de Lino, near Oviedo, Sta. Christina de Lena (Asturias), a very remarkable specimen of Byzantine construction, and the churches of San Pedro and San Pablo, Barcelona.

The invasion of the Arabs in 711 caused their architecture to extend itself in the Peninsula. Its adaptation to churches and other buildings of the Christians created a new style, known as Mudejar. The finest specimen of Oriental architecture in Spain is the mosque at Cordova (ninth century). Byzantine models were copied there in the same manner as at Jerusalem, Damascus, and Cairo. The small mosque at Toledo (Cristo de la Luz) is of the same period, and part of the church of Santiago de Penalva (Vierzo), the only example which is known of a Christian church built in the Moorish style.

During the eleventh and twelfth centuries this architecture underwent radical modifications in Spain, in the same manner as in the East, and a new style arose which is very different to the earlier one. No writers on this subject have explained this transformation in the East in a satisfactory manner: it is not easy to study this transition in Spain, for it coincides with the time in which the Spanish Moors were not rich or powerful enough to build large constructions, as they did in the thirteenth century, after the kings of Granada had settled there. At this period of their art the forms of capitals, which partook of a Byzantine and classical form, changed. Tiles are used to decorate the walls, which are covered with an ornamentation in relief in stucco, in which are introduced inscriptions in Cufic and African characters; the ceilings are decorated with inlaid woodwork and stalactical pendentives in stucco. This style ends with the conquest of Granada, 1492. The Alhambra is the most important example of this architecture, and following it the Alcazar of Seville.

Owing to the gradual conquests by the Christians of towns belonging to the Mohammedans, several of them continued to be inhabited by Moors, who kept their customs and religion. They were called Moriscos or Mudejares. The chief industries of the country were in their hands, and several churches and other buildings of importance were built by them. They accommodated their architecture to European or Christian necessities, and created a new style (Mudejar), a mixture of Christian and Moorish art, which is only to be found in the Spanish Peninsula. The finest specimens are of the fourteenth century. The religious constructions of this period are remarkable for their brick-work in towers and apses, and fine wooden ceilings, artesonados. Examples exist at Toledo, Seville, and Granada. The interesting synagogues built by Moriscos are at Toledo and Segovia. As specimens of civil architecture, the finest are Casa de Pilatos (Seville), Palace of Mendoza (Guadalajara), Archbishop's Palace (Alcalá), Casa de Mesa (Toledo). This style continued in vogue during the greater part of the sixteenth century, although late Gothic was everywhere predominant. A most striking example in which the three styles—Moorish, Flamboyant, and Renaissance—are combined, is to be found in a chapel of the cathedral of Sigüenza.

The Romanesque style of architecture was imported in the eleventh and twelfth centuries from France, even more directly than in other countries, owing to the immense influence exercised by a large number of prelates and priests, who came from Cluny and Cister, and the French princes and families who settled in Spain. The general features of this architecture are similar to those of France: the differences exist chiefly in the general plan of the churches rather than in their construction and ornamentation. The choirs in Spanish cathedrals are placed in the central nave, a traditional remembrance of the early basilica. In some localities, Segovia, Avila, and Valladolid, some of these churches have external cloisters, an Oriental or Italian modification, which never occurs in France or the north of Europe. Romanesque examples are very numerous in Spain. Some, such as the doorway of the Cathedral of Santiago (Galicia), and the Old Cathedral (Salamanca), are not surpassed by any similar buildings in Europe. Specimens are only found in the northern provinces, as the south was not conquered from the Moors until the thirteenth century. Interesting examples exist in Asturias, Galicia, Castile, Aragon, and Cataluna. The cloisters of Gerona and Tarragona are unrivaled. Of the many striking examples of Transition from Romanesque to Early Pointed, the finest are the old cathedral of Lerida, the cathedrals of Tarragona and Santiago, and the collegiate church of Tudela.

The specimens of Pointed style in Spain present no other variety than the choirs in the centers of the cathedrals. Although this style was imported from France early in the thirteenth century, in the same manner as in Germany, Romanesque churches continued to be built, and Pointed architecture was only finally adopted at the end of the century. The finest cathedrals in Spain of this architecture are those of Toledo, Leon, and Burgos. A great number of civil and religious buildings of this style are to be met with in Spain, in which the art-student will find constant elements of study: it underwent the same modifications in Spain as in other countries, until it reached, in the fifteenth century, its latest period, the Flamboyant style. This style lasts longer in Spain than in other countries, and acquires great importance. The cathedrals of Salamanca (la neuva) and Segovia, both built in late Gothic, were begun in the sixteenth century, when in other parts of Europe and even in Spain itself Italian Renaissance models were largely imported. Spanish cathedrals are undoubtedly, with the exception of Italy, the most interesting in Europe; for although they cannot compete in architectural details with those of France, they are vastly superior in regard to the objects they contain of ecclesiastical furniture of every kind—iron railings, carved stalls, monstrances, church-plate, vestments, pictures, and sepulchers. Toledo and Seville cathedrals are museums in their way.

Italian models were copied in Spain from the end of the

fifteenth century. The portals of Santa Cruz at Valladolid and Toledo are of this period. Gothic architecture continued, however, for several years to alternate with this style. The combination of these styles produced an important series of models known in Spain by the name of Plateresco.

The revival of the fine arts coincided in Spain with the greatest power and richness of the country. The marriage of Ferdinand and Isabella united Castile, Aragon, and the kingdom of Naples. The conquest of Granada completed the political unity of the country: the discoveries of Columbus, Cortes, and Pizarro brought riches from a new world, and the union with the House of Austria, the Flemish States, an immense power, which it enjoyed during the reign of the Emperor Charles V. Renaissance architecture is better represented in Spain than in any other country except Italy. In almost all towns of importance admirable examples of this style will be found. The finest are at Salamanca: the University, Santo Domingo, Casa de las Conchas, and Salinas, San Marcos (Leon), Casa de Ayuntamiento (Seville), Valladolid, Saragossa, Burgos, etc.

The cathedral and palace of Charles V. (Granada) may be quoted as an example of pure Græco-Roman style. Part of the Alcazar at Toledo belongs to this same period. The tendency to copy classical models increased daily. The Monastery of the Escorial may be considered the most important specimen of this school. In the seventeenth century the Borromenisco style was imported from Italy. The Pantheon at the Escorial is a good example. This architectural decay increased in Spain with great rapidity, and in no country did it reach to such an extravagant point. It lasted during the seventeenth and part of the eighteenth centuries. In Spain this style is called Churrigueresque, after the architect Churriguera. Examples will be found everywhere. The Transparente (Cathedral of Toledo), retablos of San Esteban (Salamanca), Cartuja (Granada), and façade of Hospicio (Madrid), may be considered the most remarkable.

The creation of the Academy of San Fernando, the French architects who accompanied Philip V., and the efforts of Charles III. to favor classical studies, produced the same pretentious and classical reaction as in the rest of Europe. The Palace and Convent of Salesas (Madrid) are specimens of the first movement. The Museo and Observatory of Madrid belong to the end of the last and beginning of the present century.

II

SPANISH LITERATURE

THE history of Spanish literature commences at the end of the eleventh or beginning of the twelfth century, when the dialect emerged from the corrupted Latin, and became an independent language capable of producing literary works.

The origin of the language may be traced to the writers of the sixth, seventh, to the eleventh century. They wrote in the more or less barbarous Latin of the period. The most important authors of this time were San Isidoro and his pupils, St. Eugenio, St. Ildefonso, St. Eulogio, Alvaro, Sansom, Pero Alonso, and Oliva. The writers of the Roman period, Porcio Latro, Seneca, Lucan, Martial, Pomponius Mela, Collumela, Silius Italicus, and Quintillian, though born in Spain, must be numbered among classical authors. The Spanish language is derived in a direct manner from the Latin, though it has been enriched by a great number of words belonging to the different nations which have occupied the whole or part of the Peninsula. Iberian, Punic, Greek, Visigothic, Hebrew, and Arabic words are met with in large numbers. The abundance of these last has induced some critics to infer that the origin of the language is Semitic, but its grammatical structure is undoubtedly Latin. The abundance of Oriental words does not influence its organization, or produce any further result than to add nouns to the language.

Spanish literature is generally divided into three groups —twelfth century to end of fifteenth; sixteenth to seventeenth; eighteenth to the present day.

It is highly probable that Spanish poetry began by commemorating the heroic deeds of Pelayo and other heroes who fought against the Moors; but we can trace nothing to that period. The earliest compositions which have reached us are, a "Charter of Oviedo," 1145 (the "Charter of Aviles," 1155, has been proved to be a forgery), and two poems on the Cid, the favorite hero of popular Spanish poetry, 1040–1099. The best of these poems is the one beginning: El mio Cid (vide Ticknor). Though incomplete, it constitutes a real epic poem, and if examined in detail appears to have been written at the beginning of the twelfth century. Three contemporary works have reached us: "La Vida de Santa Maria

Egipciaca," "El Libro de los tres reyes d'Orient," and "Los tres reyes magos." The first two were evidently written under a French influence; "Los tres reyes magos" was written for recital in a church.

The same intellectual development appears in Spain in the thirteenth century as in Italy and France. The universities of Palencia and Salamanca contributed toward it. The tendency of the writers of this period is to imitate classic authors. A priest, Gonzalo de Berceo, is the first poet of any importance in the thirteenth century, 1230: he wrote a large number of verses on religious subjects. His poem to the Virgin contains some poetical passages. Two poems appeared shortly afterward, "El Libro de Apollonio" and "El Libro de Alexandre," by J. Lorenzo Segura, adapted from the history of Alexandre Le Grand, by Chatillon. The poem "Fernan Gonzalez" is of the same period: it is free from foreign influence. Prose is improved at the beginning of the century by the translation from Latin of the "Fuero Juzgo," and other historical and didactical works.

Don Alonso el Sabio, 1221-1284, absorbs the scientific and literary life of Spain during his time: the most eminent of his countrymen, Spaniards, Jews and Moors, gathered round him. So many works have appeared under his name that it is incredible they should all have been written by him. Probably only the poems, "Las Querellas," written in the Castilian dialect, are his. An extensive Universal History, the first written in Europe in a vernacular language; the "Leyes de Partidas," a series of legal works; "El Saber de Astronomia," a cyclopedia of this science as it stood at that time; the "Cantigas," a poem containing upward of four hundred compositions to the Virgin, written in the Galician dialect and in the Provençal style, and several other works, have passed hitherto as proceeding from his pen.

Don Sancho el Bravo, a son of Don Alonso, wrote the "Lucidario" and "Libro de los Castigos," a moral treatise dedicated to his son. The "Libro del Tesoro" and "La Gran Conquista de Ultramar" were translated at his instigation from the Latin. The Infante, Don Juan Manuel, 1282, a nephew of Don Alonso, wrote several works on different subjects. The finest is the interesting collection of fables, "El Conde Lucanor." They are earlier than the Decamerone or Canterbury Tales.

Spanish poetry revived in the fourteenth century. The archpriest of Hita, 1330-1343, wrote thousands of verses on different subjects. Rabbi Don Santob, 1350, a Spanish Jew, dedicated to his friend, King Peter the Cruel, his principal poetical works. The best is on the "Danza de la Muerte," a favorite subject of that time. Pero Lopez de Ayala, 1372-1407, who wrote the "Rimado de Palacio," and Rodrigo Yanez, the author of the "Poema de Alonso XI.," end the series of poets of the fourteenth century. Romances of chivalry became popular in Spain in the fifteenth century: their popularity lasted until the sixteenth, when Cervantes published his "Don Quixote." "Amadis de Gaula" was the first work of importance of this kind; "Palmerin de Oliva," etc., follow it. The Coronicas belong to this period. They are semi-historical narratives, in which the leading events of each reign are described.

Provençal style was introduced into Spain early in the fifteenth century. It became very popular owing to the patronage of Don Juan II., 1407-1454. The most important courtiers imitated the king's example, and poems have reached us by Don Alvaro de Luna, Don Alonso de Cartagena and others. The Marquis of Villena and Macias belong to this period. Fernan Perez de Guzman wrote at this time his "Livros de los claros varones de Espana," and Juan de Mena, an excellent poet, his "Laberynto" and "Dialogo delos siete Pecados mortales." The last poet of the reign of Don Juan II. is the Marquis of Santillana. Several wrote late in the century: the most excellent among them being Jorge Manrique, whose "Coplas" on the death of his father are admirable. Novels begin at this time, generally copied from Italian models. The finest is "La Celestina," written in acts like a drama, one of the best works in Spanish literature.

Romances or ballads are the most original form of Spanish poetry. They constitute the popular epic poem, and are the most spontaneous productions of the Spanish language.

The revival of literature coincides in Spain with the period of its greatest power and prosperity. The early part of the sixteenth century is called "el Siglo de oro." An Italian influence is predominant. Castillejo keeps to the earlier style in his charming compositions: "Dialogo entre el autor y su pluma," and "Sermones de Amores." Boscan and Garcilaso were the first to introduce the Italian measure into Spanish verse. Some poets wrote in both these styles. Gregorio Sylvestre is among the best of them; an excellent poet, but very little known.

Garcilaso was the earliest lyrical poet, 1503-1536. His verses are pure in style, in the manner of Virgil and Horace. His life is interesting: he fought by the side of Charles V., and was killed at the assault of the fortress of Frejus (Nice). One of his contemporaries, Hurtado de Mendoza, a soldier and statesman, popularized classical studies. His best works are the "Rebellion delos Moriscos" and the well-known "Lazarillo de Tormes." The classical style is now universally adopted in Spain. Fray Luis de Leon was undoubtedly the best poet of this period. His ode on the "Ascension" and his "Poema a la Virgen" may certainly be reckoned among the best compositions in the language. Several poets of an inferior order belong to the sixteenth century. Cesina, Acuna, Figueroa, Medrano, La Torre, Mesa and Alcazar are among the best. Their works are clever in parts, but are generally unequal. This characteristic becomes a leading feature in Spanish poetry. At the end of the seventeenth century lyrics began to decay, but no author carried affectation and exaggeration to such a height as Gongora, 1561-1627: a gifted poet, full of charm in his simple compositions (vide translations by Archdeacon Churton), though most obscure in his "Soledades" and "Polifemo." This style was called in Spain culteranismo, and not even the best dramatic authors of the seventeenth century were free from its defects. The imitators of Gongora continued until the eighteenth century, although here and there a poet like Rioja tried to check the movement.

Epic poetry in Spain is inferior to the dramatic and lyrical styles. The specimens which exist are cold and devoid of inspiration. "El Monserrate," by Virues; "La Cristiada," by Hojeda; "La Vida de San Jose," by Valdivieso, and "El Bernardo," by Balbuena, may be quoted as examples. "La Araucana," by Ercilla, contains some poetical passages, but in general is hardly more than a historical narrative. "La Gatomaquia," by Lope de Vega, though a burlesque, is considered by many critics the best epic poem in the Spanish language.

Dramatic literature unites, perhaps, the highest conditions of originality and power. Its earliest productions are the liturgical representations of the Middle Ages, "Misterios" or "Autos." Although works of this kind are mentioned as early as the thirteenth century, the first which have a distinct dramatic character are the "Coplas" de Mingo Revulgo and "El Dialogo entre el Amor y un viejo." These compositions were written under the reign of Henry IV. At the latter part of the fifteenth century a series of dramatic works already existed. Juan de la Encina began the history of the Spanish drama. Lucas Fernandez was a contemporary writer, and shortly afterward Gil Vicente. Torres Naharro, 1517, published his "Propaladia," which contains eight comedies. Lope de Rueda founded the modern school, and he is imitated and improved by his followers. The drama does not attain its highest importance until Lope de Vega (1562-1635), the most prolific of Spanish poets. He tells us he had written fifteen hundred plays, without counting "Autos" and "Entremeses." Cervantes says that forty companies of actors existed at this time in Madrid alone, consisting of no less than one thousand actors. In 1636, three hundred companies of actors acted in different parts of Spain. Lope de Vega is rather unequal as a dramatic author; but "El mejor Alcalde el rey," "La Estrella de Sevilla," "La dama boba," "La moza de cantaro," entitle him to rank among the best European dramatists. Three authors share Lope's glory, Tirso, Calderon and Alarcon.

No Spanish dramatist has surpassed Tirso in his facility of treating the most varied subjects in admirable versification. His comedy of "Don Gil de las calzas verdes" is as good as his dramas of "El Rey Don Pedro en Madrid," "El condenado por desconfiado," or "El convidado de piedra." The popular type of Don Juan is taken from this drama. Alarcon is undoubtedly the most philosophical Spanish dramatist. His comedy, "Las paredes oyen," is admirable, and "La verdad sospechosa," so much admired by Corneille, as he tells us himself, when he took the plot for his "Menteur." Calderon is the most popular dramatic author. He idealizes more than his predecessors, and his genius embraces the most varied subjects. His comedies are charming; as examples, "La dama duende" and "Casa con dos puertas" are among the best. "El medico de su honra" is full of dramatic power, and nothing can be more poetical than "La Vida es sueno." (Vide MacCarthy's translations.) The best imitators of the great dramatists are Rojas and Moreto: "Garcia del Castanar" by the former, and "Desden con el Desden" of the latter, are equal to the dramas of the great masters.

The earliest Spanish novels are "Lazarillo de Tormes," by Hurtado de Mendoza, and the "Diana Enamorada," by Monte Mayor. They are followed by "El Picaro Guzman de Alfarache" and "El Escudero Marcos de Obregon," by Aleman and Espinel. A great number of novels were written in the following century, but were all eclipsed by Cervantes' "Don Quixote," which is too well known to need any comment.

Several authors in the sixteenth and seventeenth centuries cultivated different literary styles. Quevedo is the most remarkable of them. He was the quaintest and most original of humorists. He wrote a number of works of real merit, none of which has been so popular as his "Satiras" in prose and verse.

Political and moralist writers of the sixteenth and seventeenth centuries are very numerous. Of these Guevara, Sta. Teresa, Fray Luis de Granada, Gracian, Saavedra Fajardo, Mariàna, Morales, Zurita, and Solis are the most remarkable.

The end of the seventeenth century was the worst period of Spanish literature. Philip V., the first king of the House of Bourbon, 1700, did his utmost to improve the intellectual culture of the country. The Biblioteca Real was founded in 1711, and the Academias de la Lengua, Historia, and Bellas Artes in 1714; several literary reviews also appeared. The best poets of this period are Antonio de Toledo and Gerardo Lobo. The only productions, however, of any literary merit are the critical works of Flores, Masdeu, Mayans and others. During the reign of Charles III., 1759–1788, Melendez wrote some tolerable verses. He is followed by Fr. Diego Gonzalez, Cienfuegos, Nicolas de Moratin and others. The most original writers of the end of the eighteenth century are, however, undoubtedly Leandro Moratin and Ramon. The two comedies, "El Si de las ninas" and "El Cafe," by the former, are charming, and the "Sainetes," by De la Cruz, in the manner of Plautus, continue to be very popular in Spain.

Spanish literature of the present century possesses no definite character, although several writers can bear comparison with the best Spanish authors of other periods. Every school and style has been copied: Byron, Schiller, Goethe, Victor Hugo, and Dumas. The earliest author of any importance is Quintana, a correct and inspired poet. His odes on "La Imprenta," "Panteon del Escorial," and "Batalla de Trafalgar" are very good. Martinez de la Rosa, Lista, and Nicasio Gallegos form a group of able versifiers. Espronceda is a constant imitator of Byron, although his legend of "El Estudiante de Salamanca" is original, and a very fine composition. Zorrilla is the best representative of the romantic school of 1830-40: his works are sometimes unequal, and his legends are his best lyrical compositions. His finest dramas are "Don Juan Tenorio" and "El Zapatero y el Rey." The "Romances" and drama of "Don Alvaro de Luna," by the Duke of Rivas, have been very popular; but no author is so deservingly so as Breton de los Herreres, an excellent writer, who has left behind nearly one hundred comedies, some of which, "Marcela," "Muerete y veras," "El pelo de la dehesa," etc., are perfect in their way.

III

SPORT

The Bull-fight, or rather Bull Feast (Fiesta de Toros), is a modern sport. Bulls were killed in ancient amphitheaters, but the present modus operandi is modern, and, however based on Roman institutions, is indubitably a thing devised by the Moors of Spain, for those in Africa have neither the sport, the ring, nor the recollection. The principle was the exhibition of horsemanship, courage and dexterity witn the lance, for in the early bull-fight the animal was attacked by gentlemen armed only with the Rejon, a short projectile spear about four feet long. This was taken from the original Iberian spear, the Sparus of Sil. Ital. (viii. 523), the Lancea of Livy (xxxiv. 15), and is seen in the hands of the horsemen of the old Romano-Iberian coinage. To be a good rider and lancer was essential to the Spanish Caballero. This original form of bull-fight (now only given on grand occasions) is called a Fiesta Real. Such a one Philip IV. exhibited on the Plaza Mayor of Madrid before Charles I. of England; Ferdinand VII. in 1833, as the ratification of the Juramento, the swearing allegiance to Isabella II.; and Alfonso XII., on his marriages, January 23, 1878, and November 29, 1879.

These Fiestas Reales form the coronation ceremonial of Spain, and the Caballeros en Plaza represent our champions. Bulls were killed, but no beef eaten; as a banquet was never a thing of Iberia.

The final conquest of the Moors, and the subsequent cessation of the border chivalrous habits of Spaniards, and especially the accession of Philip V., proved fatal to this ancient usage of Spain. The spectacle, which had withstood the influence of Isabella the Catholic, and had beaten the Pope's Bulls, bowed before the despotism of fashion, and by becoming the game of professionals instead of that of gentlemen it was stripped of its chivalrous character, and degenerated into the vulgar butchery of low mercenary bull-fighters, just as did the rings and tournaments of chivalry into those of ruffian pugilists.

The Spanish bulls have been immemorially famous. Hercules, that renowned cattle-fancier, was lured into Spain by the lowing of the herds of Geryon, the ancestor (se dice) of the Duque de Osuna. The best bulls in Andalusia are bred by Cabrera at Utrera, in the identical pastures where Geryon's herds were pastured and "lifted" by the demigod, whence, according to Strabo (iii. 169), they were obliged, after fifty days' feeding, to be driven off from fear of bursting from fat. Some of the finest Castilian bulls, such as appear at Madrid, are bred on the Jarama, near Aranjuez.

Bull fights are extremely expensive, costing from one thousand five hundred dollars to two thousand dollars apiece; accordingly, except in the chief capitals and Andalusia, they are only got up now and then, on great church festivals and upon royal and public rejoicings. As Andalusia is the headquarters of the ring, and Seville the capital, the alma mater of the tauromachists of the Peninsula, the necessity of sending to a distance for artists and animals increases the expense. The prices of admittance, compared to the wages of labor in Spain, are high.

The profits of the bull-fight are usually destined for the support of hospitals, and, certainly, the fever and the frays subsequent to the show provide patients as well as funds. The Plaza is usually under the superintendence of a society of noblemen and gentlemen, called Maestranzas, instituted in 1562, by Philip II., in the hope of improving the breed of Spanish horses and men-at-arms.

The first thing is to secure a good place beforehand, by sending for a Boletin de Sombra, a "ticket in the shade." The prices of the seats vary according to position; the best places are on the northern side, in the shade. The transit of the sun over the Plaza, the zodiacal progress into Taurus, is certainly not the worst calculated astronomical observation in Spain: the line of shadow defined on the arena is marked by a gradation of prices. The sun of torrid, tawny Spain, on which it once never set, is not to be trifled with, and the summer season is selected because pastures are plentiful, which keep the bulls in good condition, and the days are longer. The fights take place in the afternoon, when the sun is less vertical. The different seats and prices are detailed in the bills of the play, with the names of the combatants, and the colors and breeds of the bulls.

The day before the fight the bulls destined for the spectacle are brought to a site outside the town. No amateur should fail to ride out to the pastures from whence the cattle (ganado) are selected. The encierro, the driving them from this place to the arena, is a service of danger, but is extremely picturesque and national. No artist or aficionado should omit attending it. The bulls are enticed by tame oxen, cabestros, into a road which is barricaded on each side, and then are driven full speed by the mounted conocedores into the Plaza. It is so exciting a spectacle that the poor who cannot afford to go to the bull-fight risk their lives and cloaks in order to get the front places, and the best chance of a stray poke en passant.

The next afternoon (Sunday is usually the day) all the world crowds to the Plaza de toros; nothing, when the tide is full, can exceed the gayety and sparkle of a Spanish public going, eager and dressed in their best, to the fight. All the streets or open spaces near the outside of the arena are a spectacle. The bull-fight is to Madrid what a review is to Paris, and the Derby to London. Sporting men now put on all their majo-finery; the distinguished ladies wear on these occasions white lace mantillas; a fan, abanico, is quite necessary, as it was among the Romans. The aficionados and "the gods" prefer the pit, tendido, the lower range, in order, by being nearer, that they may not lose the nice traits of tauromaquia. The Plaza has a language to itself, a dialect peculiar to the ring. The coup d'œil on entrance is unique; the classical scene bursts on the foreigner in all the glory of the south, and he is carried back to the Coliseum under Commodus. The president sits in the center box. The proceedings open with the procession of the performers, the mounted spearmen, picadores; then follow the chulos, the attendants on foot, who wear their silk cloaks, capas de durancillo, in a peculiar manner, with the arms projecting in front; and, lastly, the slayers, the espadas, and the splendid mule-team, el tiro, which is destined to carry off the slain. The profession of bull-fighter is very low-caste in Spain, although the champions are much courted by some young nobles, like the British blackguard boxers, and are the pride and darlings of all the lower classes. Those killed on the spot were formerly denied the burial rites, as dying without confession, but a priest is now in attendance with Su Magestad (the consecrated Host), ready to give always spiritual assistance to a dying combatant.

When all the bull-fighting company have advanced and passed the president, a trumpet sounds; the president throws the key of the cell of the bull to the alguacil or policeman, which he ought to catch in his feathered hat. The different performers now take their places as fielders do at a cricket match. The bull-fight is a tragedy in three acts, lasts about twenty minutes, and each consists of precisely the same routine. From six to eight bulls are usually killed during each "funcion"; occasionally another is conceded to popluar clamor, which here will take no denial.

When the door of the cell is opened, the public curiosity to see the first rush out is intense; and as none knows whether the bull will behave well or ill, all are anxious to judge of his character from the way he behaves upon first entering the ring. The animal, turned from his dark cell into glare and crowd, feels the novelty of his position; but is happily ignorant of his fate, for die he must, however skillful or brave his fight. This death does not diminish the sustained interest of the spectators as the varied chances in the progress of the acts offer infinite incidents and unexpected combinations. In the first of the three acts the picadores are the chief performers; three of them are now drawn up, one behind the other, to the right at the tablas, the barrier between the arena and spectators; each sits bolt upright on his Rosinante, with his lance in his rest, and as valiant as Don Quixote. They wear the broad-brimmed Thessalian hat; their legs are cased with iron and leather, which gives a heavy look; and the right one, which is presented to the bull, is the best protected. This greave is termed la mona—the more scientific name is gregoriana, from the inventor, Don Gregorio Gallo—just as we say a spencer, from the noble earl. The spear, garrocha, is defensive rather than offensive; the blade ought not to exceed one inch; the sheathing is, however, pushed back when the picador anticipates an awkward customer. When the bull charges, the picador, holding the lance under his right arm, pushes to the right, and turns his horse to the left; the bull, if turned, passes on to the next picador. This is called recibir, to receive the point. If a bull is turned at the first charge, he seldom comes up well again. A bold bull is sometimes cold and shy at first, but grows warmer by being punished. Those who are very active, those who paw the ground, are not much esteemed; they are hooted by the populace, and execrated as goats, little calves, cows, which is no compliment to a bull; and, however unskilled in bucolics, all Spaniards are capital judges of bulls in the ring. Such animals as show the white feather are loathed, as depriving the public of their just rights, and are treated with insult, and, moreover, soundly beaten as they pass near the tablas, by forests of sticks, la cachiporra. The stick of the elegant majo, when going to the bull-fight, is sui generis, and is called la chivata; taper, and between four and five feet long, it terminates in a lump or knob, while the top is forked, into which the thumb is inserted. This chivata is peeled, like the rods of Laban, in alternate rings, black and white or red. The lower classes content themselves with a common shillalah; one with a knob at the end is preferred, as administering a more impressive whack. While a slow bull is beaten and abused, a murderous bull, duro chocante carnicero y pegajoso, who kills horses, upsets men, and clears the plaza, becomes deservedly a universal favorite; the conquering hero is hailed with "Viva toro! viva toro! bravo toro!" Long life is wished to the poor beast by those who know he must be killed in ten minutes.

The horses destined for the plaza are of no value; this renders Spaniards, who have an eye chiefly to what a thing is worth, indifferent to their sufferings. If you remark how cruel it is to "let that poor horse struggle in death's agonies," they will say, "Ah que! na vale na" ("Oh! he is worth nothing"). When his tail quivers in the last death-struggle, the spasm is remarked as a jest, mira que cola! The torture of the horse is the blot of the bull-fight: no lover of the noble beast can witness his sufferings without disgust; the fact of these animals being worth nothing in a money point of view increases the danger to the rider; it renders them slow, difficult to manage, and very unlike those of the ancient combats, when the finest steeds were chosen, quick as lightning, turning at touch, and escaping the deadly rush: the eyes of these poor animals, who would not otherwise face the bull, are bound with a handkerchief like criminals about to be executed; thus they await blindfold the fatal rip which is to end their life of misery. If only wounded, the gash is sewed up and stopped with tow, as a leak! and life is prolonged for new agonies. When the poor brute is dead at last, his carcass is stripped as in a battle. The high-class Spaniard admits and regrets the cruelty to the horses, but justifies it as a necessity. The bull, says he, is a tame, almost a domestic animal, and would never fight at all unless first roused by the sight of blood. The wretched horse is employed for this purpose as a corpus vile; and the bull, having gored him once or twice, becomes "game."

The picadores are subject to hairbreadth escapes and severe falls: few have a sound rib left. The bull often tosses horse and rider in one run; and when the victims fall on the ground, exhausts his rage on his prostrate enemies, till lured away by the glittering cloaks of the chulos, who come to the assistance of the fallen picador. These horsemen often show marvelous skill in managing to place their horses as a rampart between them and the bull. When these deadly struggles take place, when life hangs on a thread, the amphitheater is peopled with heads. Every expression of anxiety, eagerness, fear, horror, and delight is stamped on speaking countenances. These feelings are wrought up to a pitch when the horse, maddened with wounds and terror, plunging in the death-struggle, the crimson streams of blood streaking his sweat-whitened body, flies from the infuriated bull, still pursuing, still goring: then is displayed the nerve, presence of mind, and horsemanship of the undismayed picador. It is, in truth, a piteous sight to see the poor dying horses treading out their entrails, yet saving their riders unhurt. The miserable steed, when dead, is dragged out, leaving a bloody furrow on the sand. The picador, if wounded, is carried out and forgotten—los muertos y idos, no tienen amigos (the dead and absent have no friends)—a new combatant fills the gap, the battle rages, he is not missed, fresh incidents arise, and no time is left for regret or reflection. The bull bears on his neck a ribbon, la devisa; this is the trophy which is most acceptable to the querida of a buen torero. The bull is the hero of the scene, yet, like Milton's Satan, he is foredoomed and without reprieve. Nothing can save him from the certain fate which awaits all, whether brave or cowardly. The poor creatures sometimes endeavor in vain to escape, and leap over the barrier (barrera), into the tendido, among the spectators, upsetting sentinels, water-sellers, etc., and creating a most amusing hubbub. The bull which shows this craven turn—un tunante cobarde picaro—is not deemed worthy of a noble death, by the sword. He is baited, pulled down, and stabbed in the spine. A bull that flinches from death is scouted by all Spaniards, who neither beg for their own life nor spare that of a foe.

At the signal of the president, and sound of a trumpet, the second act commences with the chulos. This word chulo signifies, in the Arabic, a lad, a clown, as at our circus. They are picked young men, who commence in these parts their tauromachian career. The duty of this light division is to draw off the bull from the picador when endangered, which they do with their colored cloaks; their address and agility are surprising, they skim over the sand like glittering humming-birds, scarcely touching the earth. They are dressed, á lo majo, in short breeches, and without gaiters, just like Figaro in the opera of the "Barbiere de Sevilla." Their hair is tied into a knot behind, mono, and inclosed in the once universal silk net, the redecilla—the identical reticulum—of which so many instances are seen on ancient Etruscan vases. No bull-fighter ever arrives at the top of his profession without first excelling as a chulo (apprentice), then he begins to be taught how to entice the bull, llamar al toro, and to learn his mode of attack, and how to parry it. The most dangerous moment is when these chulos venture out into the middle of the plaza, and are followed by the bull to the barrier, in which there is a small ledge, on which they place their foot and vault over, and a narrow slit in the boarding, through which they slip. Their escapes are marvelous; they seem really sometimes, so close is the run, to be helped over the fence by the bull's horns. Occasionally some curious suertes are exhibited by chulos and expert toreros, which do not strictly belong to the regular drama, such as the suerte de la capa, where the bull is braved with no other defense but a cloak: another, the salto tras cuerno, when the performer, as the bull lowers his head to toss him, places his foot between his horns and is lifted over him. The chulos, in the second act, are the sole performers; another exclusive part is to place small barbed darts, banderillas, which are ornamented with cut paper of different colors, on each side of the neck of the bull. The banderilleros go right up to him, holding the arrows at the shaft's end, and pointing the barbs at the bull; just when the animal stoops to toss them, they dart them into his neck and slip aside. The service appears to be more dangerous than it is, but it requires a quick eye, a light hand and foot. The barbs should be placed exactly on each side—a pretty pair, a good match—buenos pares. Sometimes these arrows are provided with crackers, which, by means of a detonating powder, explode the moment they are affixed in the neck, banderillas de fuego. The agony of the tortured animal frequently makes him bound like a kid, to the frantic delight of the people. A very clever banderillero will sometimes seat himself in a chair, wait for the bull's approach, plant the arrows in his neck, and slip away, leaving the chair to be tossed into the air. This feat is uncommon, and gains immense applause.

The last trumpet now sounds; the arena is cleared for the third act; the espada, the executioner, the man of death, stands before his victim alone, and thus concentrates in himself an interest previously frittered among the number of combatants. On entering, he addresses the president, and throws his montera, his cap, to the ground, and swears he will do his duty. In his right hand he holds a long straight Toledan blade, la spada; in his left he waves the muleta, the red flag, the engano, the lure, which ought not (so Romero laid down) to be so large as the standard of a religious brotherhood (cofradia), nor so small as a lady's pocket-handkerchief (panuelito de senorita): it should be about a yard square. The color is red, because that best irritates the bull and conceals blood. There is always a spare matador, in case of accidents, which may happen in the best regulated bull-fights; he is called media espada, or sobresaliente. The espada (el diestro, the cunning in fence in olden books) advances to the bull, in order to entice him toward him—citarlo á la suerte, á la jurisdiccion del engano—to subpœna him, to get his head into chancery, as our ring would say; he next rapidly studies his character, plays with him a little, allows him to run once or twice on the muleta, and then prepares for the coup de grace. There are several sorts of bulls—levantados, the bold and rushing; parados, the slow and sly; aplomados, the heavy and leaden. The bold are the easiest to kill; they rush, shutting their eyes, right on to the lure or flag. The worst of all are the sly bulls; when they are marrajos, cunning and not running straight, when they are revueltos, when they stop in their charge and run at the man instead of the flag, they are most dangerous. The espada who is long killing his bull, or shows the white feather, is insulted by the jeers of the impatient populace; he nevertheless remains cool and collected, in proportion as the spectators and bull are mad. There are many suertes or ways of killing the bull; the principal is la suerte de frente—the espada receives the charge on his sword. lo mato de un recibido. The volapie, or half-volley, is beautiful, but dangerous; the matador takes him by advancing, corriendoselo. A firm hand, eye, and nerve form the essence of the art; the sword enters just between the left shoulder and the blade. In nothing is the real fancy so fastidious as in the exact nicety of the placing this death-wound; when the thrust is true—buen estoque—death is instantaneous, and the bull, vomiting forth blood, drops at the feet of his conqueror, who, drawing the sword, waves it in triumph over the fallen foe. It is indeed the triumph of knowledge over brute force; all that was fire, fury, passion, and life, falls in an instant, still forever.

The team of mules now enter, glittering with flags, and tinkling with bells, whose gay decorations contrast with the stern cruelty and blood; the dead bull is carried off at a rapid gallop, which always delights the populace. The espada wipes the hot blood from his sword, and bows with admirable sangfroid to the spectators, who throw their hats into the arena, a compliment which he returns by throwing them back again.

When a bull will not run at all at the picador, or at the muleta, he is called a toro abanto, and the media luna, the half-moon, is called for; this is the cruel ancient Oriental mode of houghing the cattle (Joshua xi. 6). The instrument is the Iberian bident—a sharp steel crescent placed on a long pole. The cowardly blow is given from behind; and when the poor beast is crippled, an assistant, the cachetero, pierces the spinal marrow with his cachete—puntilla, or pointed dagger—with a traitorous stab from behind. This is the usual method of slaughtering cattle in Spain. To perform all these operations (el desjarretar) is considered beneath the dignity of the matadores or espadas; some of them, however, will kill the bull by plunging the point of their sword in the vertebræ, el descabellar—the danger gives dignity to the difficult feat. The identical process obtains in each of the fights that follow. After a short collapse, a fresh object raises a new desire, and the fierce sport is renewed through eight repetitions; and not till darkness covers the heavens do the mob retire to sacrifice the rest of the night to Bacchus and Venus, with a passing homage to the knife.

APPENDIX

CHRONOLOGICAL TABLES

NO. I

Carthaginian Domination in Spain..................238 to 200 B.C.
Roman Domination ....200 B.C. to 414 A.D.
Visigothic Domination...........................414 A.D. to 711 A.D.

Visigothic Kings

	A.D.
Ataulfo	414, D. 417
Sigerico	417
Walia	420
Teodoredo	451
Turismundo	454
Teodorico	466
Eurico	483

This king, after conquering the Suevi and other races, is considered the founder of the monarchy.

Alarico	D. 505
Gesaleico	510
Amalarico	531
Teudis	548
Teudiselo	549
Agila	554
Atanagildo	567
Liuva I	572
Leovigildo	586

After destroying the barbarians that still remained in the country, he was the first king who ruled over the whole of the Peninsula.

Recaredo I.................................. 601

Summoned the 3d Council of Toledo, renounced Arianism, and became the first Catholic king of Spain.

Liuva II	603
Witerico	610
Gundemaro	612
Sisebuto	621
Recaredo II	621
Suintila	631
Sisenando	635
Tulga	640
Chindasvinto	650
Recesvinto	672
Wamba	680
Ervigio	687
Egica	701
Witiza	709
Don Rodrigo	711

The Moors entered Spain and defeated Don Rodrigo at the battle of Guadalete, who disappeared there. The Moors occupied in the two following years almost the whole of the Peninsula, and governed under the dependence of the Caliphs of Damascus.

Moorish Rulers in Spain

Emirs dependent on the Caliphs of Damascus	711–715
Independent Caliphate established by the Ommeyah family, the capital being Cordova	755–1009
Kings of Taifas, governors of the provinces which declared themselves independent during the last Caliphate, Hischen II	1009–1090
The Almoravides from Africa established themselves in the Moorish territory of the Peninsula	1090–1157
The Almohades conquered the Almoravides	1157–1212
Kings of Granada. The Moorish domination is reduced to the kingdom of Granada	1226–1492

The rule of the Moors in Spain ends in 1492, at the conquest of Granada.

Kings of Asturias, Leon, and Castile

Pelayo (the re-conquest begins)	718, D. 737
Favila	739
Alonso I., el Catolico	757
Favila I. (fixes his Court at Oviedo)	768
Aurelio	774
Silo	783
Mauregato	788
Bermudo I., el Diacono	795
Alonso II., el Casto	843
Ramiro I	850
Ordoño I	866

APPENDIX.

Alonso III., el Magno............ 910
   Divided the kingdom of Galicia, Leon, and Asturias, among his sons, the three following kings.
Garcia............................ 913
Ordono II 923
Fruela II......................... 924
   Ordono fixed his Court at Leon, and here end the named kings of Asturias.
Alonso IV., el Monge........... 930
Ramiro II........................ 950
Ordono III....................... 955
Sancho I., el Craso.............. 967
Ramiro III....................... 982
Bermudo II....................... 999
Alonso V., el Noble.............. 1028
Bermudo III...................... 1037
   The territory of Castile, which formed a separate state, governed by *Condes*, passed to Dona Sancha and Don Fernando I., who entitled themselves Kings of Castile and Leon.
Fernando I. and Dona Sancha.. 1065
Sancho II., el Fuerte............ 1073
Alfonso VI....................... 1108
   (Conquered Toledo in 1085.)
Dona Urraca..................... 1126
Alfonso VII., el Emperador..... 1157
   At his death the kingdoms of Castile and Leon are divided among the six following kings:
Sancho III. (Castilla)........... 1158
Fernando II. (Leon)............. 1188
Alfonso VIII. (Castilla)......... 1214
Alfonso IX. (Leon).............. 1230
Enrique I. (Castilla)............. 1217
   Dona Berenguela, who abdicated the crown of Castile in favor of her son, Fernando III., who inherited also the crown of Leon from his father, Alfonso IX.
Fernando III., King of Castile and Leon........................ 1252
   He conquered Cordova, Jaen, and Seville.
Alonso X., el Sabio.............. 1284
Sancho IV., el Bravo............ 1295
Fernando IV., el Emplazado . 1312
Alonso XI........................ 1350
Pedro I., el Cruel................ 1369
Enrique II., el Bastardo... 1379
Juan I............................ 1390
Enrique III., el Doliente... 1407
Juan II........................... 1454
Enrique IV., el Impotente...... 1474
Dona Isabel, la Catolica........ 1504
Fernando V. de Aragon......... 1516
Dona Juana, la loca............ 1555
Felipe I., e Hermoso, first king of the house of Austria....... 1505

Carlos V., Emperador.......... 1558
Felipe II......................... 1598
Felipe III........................ 1621
Felipe IV........................ 1665
Carlos II......................... 1700
Felipe V. (first king of the house of Bourbon) abdicated in..... 1724
Luis I............................ 1724
Felipe V......................... 1746
Fernando VI..................... 1759
Carlos III........................ 1788
Carlos IV., abdicated........... 1808
Fernando VII... 1833
Isabel II., dethroned............ 1868
Gobierno Provisional 1871
Amadeo de Saboya...abdicated 1873
Spanish Republic............... 1874
Alfonso XII.................died 1886

Kings of Navarre.

   The inhabitants of Navarre began the re-conquest from the middle of the 8th century. Their rulers were called condes, or kings, until Sancho Abarca widened the territory; from that time they are always called kings of Navarre.
Sancho Abarca 980-994
Garcia III....................... 1000
Sancho III., el Mayor........... 1088
Garcia IV....................... 1057
Sancho IV....................... 1076
Sancho Ramirez V.............. 1092
   This king, and the two that followed, were likewise kings of Aragon.
Pedro I.......................... 1106
Alfonso, el Batallador.......... 1134
Garcia Ramirez IV.............. 1150
Sancho VI., el Sabio............ 1194
Sancho VII., el Fuerte.......... 1234
   Here begin the kings of the House of Champagne.
Teobaldo I...................... 1253
Teobaldo II...... 1270
Enrique I........................ 1273
Juana I.......................... 1304
   On her marriage with Philip le Bel, Navarre passed to the house of France.
Luis Hutin...................... 1316
Felipe le Long................... 1320
Carlos I. de Navarra, IV. de Francia..................... 1329
Juana II......................... 1343
Carlos II. d'Evreux............. 1387
Carlos III....................... 1425
Dona Blanca y Juan I.......... 1479
Francisco Febo..... 1483
Catalina......................... 1512

Fernando V. of Navarre took possession in 1512 of Navarre, and it was then incorporated with Castile.

Kings of Aragon.

Aragon belonged to the kingdom of Navarre until Sancho III. gave it to his son Ramiro.

Ramiro I.	1035, D. 1063
Sancho I.	1094
Pedro I.	1104
Alfonso I., el Batallador.	1134
Ramiro II., el Monge.	1137

Aragon and Catalnna are united.

Petronila.	1162
Alfonso II.	1196
Pedro II.	1213
Jaime I., el Conquistador.	1276
Pedro III.	1285

Sicily is united to Aragon.

Alfonso III.	1291
Jaime II.	1327
Alfonso IV.	1336
Pedro IV.	1387
Juan I.	1395
Martin.	1410
Fernando, el de Antequera.	1416
Alfonso V.	1458
Juan II.	1479

Fernando el Catolico.
Aragon passes to the crown of Castile.

Counts of Barcelona.

In the 8th and 9th centuries Cataluna belonged to Charlemagne and his successors. Wilfredo was the first independent Conde.

Wilfredo el Belloso	864–898
Borrell I.	912
Suniario.	917
Borrell II. and his brother Miron	992
Ramon Borrell.	1018
Ramon Berenguer I.	1025
Ramon Berenguer II.	1077
Berenguer and Ramon Berenguer III.	1113
Ramon Berenguer IV.	1131

Ramon Berenguer V. married Dona Petronila de Aragon, and this kingdom was incorporated with the Condado de Cataluna.

NO. II

Contemporary Sovereigns

The periods have been selected during which leading events in Spanish history have occurred.

A.D.	Spain.	England.	France.	Rome.
800	Alonso II. el Casto	Egbert	Charlemagne	Leo III.
877	Alonso III. el Magno	Alfred	Louis II.	John VII.
996	Ramiro III.	Ethelred II.	Hugh Capet	Gregory V.
1075	Sancho II.	William the Conqueror	Philip I.	Gregory VII.
1155	Alfonso VII.	Henry II.	Louis VII.	Adrian IV. Breakspeare
1245	San Fernando	Henry III.	St. Louis	Innocent IV.
1345	Alfonso XI.	Edward III.	Philip VI.	Benedict VI.
1360	Pedro el Cruel	Edward III.	John II.	Innocent VI.
1485	Isabel la Catolica	Henry VII.	Charles VIII.	Innocent VIII.
1515	Fernando de Aragon	Henry VIII.	Francis I.	Leo X.
1550	Carlos V.	Edward VI.	Henry II.	Paul III.
1560	Felipe II.	Elizabeth	Charles IX.	Pius IV.
1644	Felipe IV.	Charles I.	Louis XIV.	Innocent X.
1705	Felipe V.	Anne	Louis XIV.	Clement XI.
1760	Carlos III.	George III.	Louis XV.	Clement XIII.
1808	Fernando VII.	George III.	Napoleon I.	Pius VII.
1840	Isabel II.		Louis Philippe Napoleon III.	Gregory XVI and Pius IX.
1877	Alfonso XII.	Victoria	French Republic	Leo XIII.
1886	Cristina, queen-regent			
1886	Alfonso XIII.			

www.ingramcontent.com/pod-product-compliance
Lightning Source LLC
Chambersburg PA
CBHW031425230426
43668CB00007B/431